Praise for Cowl

"A quarter century ago, novelist/prophet Bill Kittredge argued that the West 'needed a new story' of how to live and work with the land. Rancher Richard Collins has now given us that fresh, dynamic, and thoughtful narrative, one of families and communities in cattle country celebrating and enhancing the complexity of the landscape of which they are a part. Collins is not only a fine storyteller, but there is generosity and exuberance in his writing and thinking that I hope will spread like wildfire to renew the many landscapes and cultures of the American West." —**Gary Paul Nabhan**, author of *Food from the Radical Center* and co-editor of *Stitching the West Back Together*

"As a lifelong rancher and cowboy, I was mesmerized by Richard Collins' beautifully crafted stories. What I particularly relished was Collins' deep love of the land. His passion for conserving and improving grasslands, water, wildlife—the very environment that sustains us—shines through his articulate and moving prose. He is a down-to-earth rancher and cowboy who finds great joy in his daily tasks while never losing sight of his role as steward of the land." —**H. Alan Day**, author of *The Horse Lover* and *Cowboy Up!*

"The best description of ranching in southeast Arizona that I have yet run across." —**Bill McDonald**, co-founder of the Radical Center, past president of the Malpai Borderlands Group, and fifth generation rancher

"Collins seamlessly weaves a memoir about how he learned to ranch in southeastern Arizona with astute commentaries about the challenges of doing so in a land where most of his neighbors were exurbanites and a small endangered minnow caused more problems than the drug runners trekking through his mountain pastures." —**Thomas E. Sheridan**, professor of anthropology at University of Arizona, author of *Arizona: A History*, and co-editor of *Stitching the West Back Together*

"There is something special about being able to live and work in a landscape over many years. Each year offers a greater understanding of place and your place in it. Richard Collins shines when he is describing his beloved high-desert grasslands and the people and creatures who occupy it." —**Ross Humphreys**, owner of San Rafael Ranch

"*Cowboy is a Verb* should be read by every rancher, agency member, or any folks that just love open spaces. Using local examples to illustrate his points, Richard shows the need to add a powerful, fourth 'C' to the three Cs of successful ranching. Cowboys, Cattle, and Cow Dogs—make room for Cooperation. Anyone with feelings about the west will find things they like and things they wish Richard hadn't brought up in this book—that is the surest way to know he has written the truth about a subject that he knows and cares deeply about." —**Jim Koweek**, author of *Grassland Plant ID for Everyone*

"One of the few books available that gives a well-rounded description of modern-day ranching in the Southwest . . . a very balanced picture of the challenges facing ranchers today. Your discussion of habitat and species is a perspective that should be embraced by all land management agencies in their decisions regarding the management of large landscapes. Thanks for writing such an enlightening book and giving me the opportunity to read it." —**Walter Lane**, co-owner of Headquarters West, Ltd. and fourth generation southeastern Arizona rancher

"Collins' descriptions of abundant wildlife, expansive scenic views, and especially the watershed that divides his ranch, all attest to his deep connection to the property that he has explored, inch by inch, on horseback. The efforts of a hands-on working rancher to sustain the viability of the land he so loves makes it likely that 'cowboy' truly is a verb." —**Betty Barr**, historian and author of *Hidden Treasures of Santa Cruz County*

"Richard Collins was a leader in the vitally important task of building a *radical center* among ranchers, conservationists, and federal agencies in southern Arizona. Today, as the West and the nation continues to harden into opposing factions, we need the work of radical centrists more than ever. In this thoughtful, humorous, and heartfelt memoir, Collins captures the spirit of those heady years, sharing lessons learned for all of us along the way." —**Courtney White**, author of *Grass, Soil, Hope* and co-founder of the Quivira Coalition

"I do think this book may become a classic and sit alongside other memorable books on ranching culture." —**Richard L. Knight**, retired professor of wildlife conservation, Colorado State University

Cowboy
is a
Verb

NOTES FROM A MODERN-DAY RANCHER

★

RICHARD COLLINS

Forward by George B. Ruyle, PhD

UNIVERSITY OF NEVADA PRESS *Reno & Las Vegas*

For Diane and Richard West who rode along
and Jennifer Diane in memory.

University of Nevada Press I Reno, Nevada 89557 USA
www.unpress.nevada.edu
Copyright © 2019 by University of Nevada Press
Cover art: "Riding Out into the Apache Highlands" by Matilda Essig. www.matildaessig.com
Cover design by TG Design

LIBRARY OF CONGRESS CATALOGING-IN-PUBLICATION

Names: Collins, Richard, 1941- author.
Title: Cowboy is a verb : notes from a modern-day rancher / Richard Collins.
Description: Reno : University of Nevada Press, [2019] I Includes bibliographical references. I Summary:
   "Cowboy is a Verb is like the land itself, spreading out from Mount Wrightson on the west to the
   Mustangs and Whetstones on the east, Sonoita to Patagonia then south to the Mexican border. From
   the big picture to the smallest details, these pages describe the geology, history, and interdependency of
   land, water, native and introduced plants and animals. Embedded in the land are the rancher, cowboy,
   and the local communities. At first glance this book is a rancher's autobiography, a collection of natural
   history essays, grass management, and southwestern history thrown in as required to tell the complex
   story of the modern-day lives of cowboys and ranchers that includes much more than wild horse rides
   and cow chases. But there are also plenty of stories about quirky ranch horses, cranky cow critters, cow
   dogs, and the people who use and care for them. You will get to know some great people in this book,
   including T. N. Wegner, a professor of reproductive biology who specialized in getting cows "knocked
   up." Veterinarian Jim Pickrell, a renowned jokester who never told the same joke twice, and who would
   sit up all night to save a colicky horse. There are hardworking people: Manuel Murrietta, a cowboy
   equally at home in a mountain pasture or the rodeo arena; Diane Collins who with her neighbors built
   a Local History Matters Center at the Sonoita Fairgrounds and raised money for local scholarships;
   a father/son/family partnership not unusual in this business, but always heartwarming. The battle
   over the endangered Gila topminnow in Redrock Canyon watershed is a main event, and Cowboy
   is a Verb is the story of how ranchers got together and formed the Canelo Hills Coalition to defend
   ourselves against Endangered Species Act administrators who sought to close down grazing. Instead of
   fighting in the court room, we worked with university range scientists, forest service conservationists,
   and funding agencies to improve our ranches and the health of the watershed. Using a common sense
   approach we convinced the Bureau of Reclamation not to build a useless dam across the Canyon. After
   more than a decade, the watershed recovered and flourished and so did we. Others have noted that
   cowboys have lots of "Try." In the complex world of the twenty-first century we have to do a lot more.
   I also pose the most critical question facing conservation today: Do we attempt to preserve a vanishing
   species in a marginal habitat, or should we continue to manage our watersheds for the ecological health
   of all living creatures?"-- Provided by publisher.
Identifiers: LCCN 2019027112 (print) I LCCN 2019027113 (ebook) I ISBN 9781948908238 (paperback)
   I ISBN 9781948908245 (epub)
Subjects: LCSH: Collins, Richard, 1941- I Ranching--Arizona. I Ranch life--Arizona. I Ranchers--
   Arizona--Biography. I Range management--Arizona. I Arizona--Biography.
Classification: LCC F811 .C667 2019 (print) I LCC F811 (ebook) I DDC 979.1--dc23
LC record available at https://lccn.loc.gov/2019027112
LC ebook record available at https://lccn.loc.gov/2019027113

FIRST PRINTING

Manufactured in the United States of America

Contents

List of Illustrations

Maps are by Tom Jonas. Photographs are by Diane and Richard Collins unless otherwise noted.

Maps

Photos and Graphs

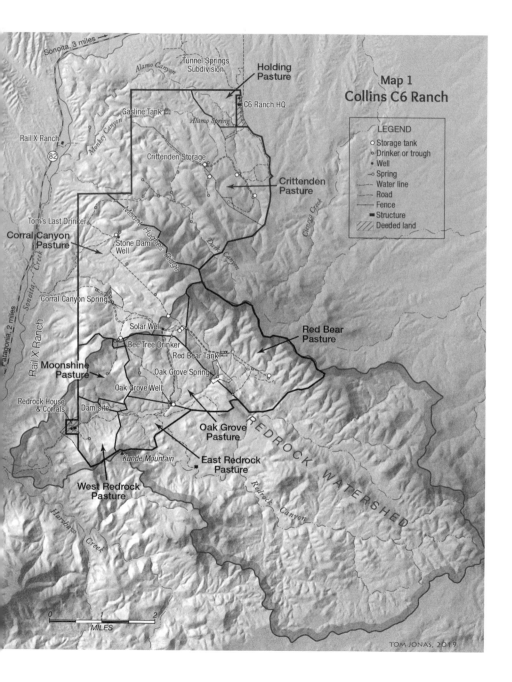

Foreword

George B. Ruyle, PhD: Marley Endowed Chair for Sustainable Rangeland Stewardship, College of Agriculture and Life Sciences, University of Arizona

"The landscape of any farm is the owner's portrait of himself."
—Aldo Leopold from *The Farmer as a Conservationist*, 1939

In 1990, after much searching, Richard Collins found his sense of place in southern Arizona's Santa Cruz County. Wading into the quagmire of public land uses, Richard put together two hardscrabble United States Forest Service grazing allotments, applied a strong and well-developed land ethic to his management practices, and twenty-five years later left them better than when he got them. *Cowboy Is a Verb: Notes from a Modern-Day Rancher* describes the complicated, demanding, and yet satisfying process he applied to the landscape, searching for some combination of ecological sensitivity and economic reality in the never-ending cycle of cattle production on semi-arid rangelands. The book does not romanticize cowboys but honors the complex and undervalued skills that it takes to husband livestock on rangelands.

While he is a credentialed scholar, Richard was never completely persuaded by science coming out of text books (although I think he still has my copy of *Range Management Principles and Practices*), rather he combined what he learned from the land and the animals every day, year after year. Ranching is a system of agricultural production that favors ecological rather than agronomic knowledge. Much of this knowledge can only come from experience and time on the land. Over time, by paying careful

attention, one can figure out what you should really pay attention to and
what to ignore. Richard exemplifies the notion that the grazing permittee
is the person on the ground, the local knowledge, and resident ecologist.

Most definitions of sustainability include the interactions among ecological, economic, and social/cultural systems. Relative to agriculture,
Wendell Berry poignantly and concisely wrote that "Sustainable agriculture depletes neither the land nor the people." I think we can extrapolate
that statement to say that "Sustainable range management depletes neither the land nor the people."

While range management involves many resources and uses, most of
us think of ranching when we think of range management. Ranching is
a large landscape endeavor and needs to be understood for how it contributes to the overall sustainability of broader ecologic, economic, and
social systems through time. Because these systems are so interconnected
the sustainability of each single ranch unit in Arizona and the Southwest
is the critical long-term challenge to maintain open space landscapes.
Every ranch counts.

The book describes ranching sustainability as a journey of continuous
improvement rather than a destination. To be sustainable requires respect
for dynamic ecological, economic, social, and cultural values, practices supported by the community and institutions that contribute to viable rural
communities while recognizing a place for urban values. This is especially
true on public land (in this case on the Coronado National Forest) where
over-zealous bureaucrats and urban-based environmental litigation groups
have often influenced the decision process relative to livestock grazing.
Cowboy Is a Verb calls them out on ideology-based rather than evidence-based
land management decisions and, in the end, the evidence perseveres.

If you want to improve a range landscape you have to know where
you are now. Throughout the book, Richard describes how he learned to
read the landscape, both in a technical sense, using ecological monitoring
protocols, but also through keen observation from the back of a horse.
It's a personal story clearly expressing a love of the land, the people, the
livestock and always the horses.

Like Bob Sharp from *Sharp's Cattle Country: Rawhide Ranching from
Both Sides of the Border* (1985), Richard developed an everlasting affection

of the open spaces of the high desert grasslands and woodlands, a "private world of beauty, freedom . . . and free-handed life on unspoiled range-land." I thank him for sharing this journey and providing the Redrock Canyon experience as a case study in grazing management in our conservation ranching course.

Canelo Hills
Eastern Santa Cruz County, Arizona

Introduction

Cowboy Is a Verb is like the land itself, spreading out from Mount Wrightson on the west to the Mustangs and Whetstones on the east, Sonoita to Patagonia then south into Sonora, Mexico. If you don't know where you are, it is hard to know who you are, to paraphrase Wendell Berry. From the big picture to the smallest details, these pages describe the geology, history, and interdependency of land, water, native and introduced plants. Animals, too, from coati mundi, white-tailed deer, bears, mountain lions to the piglike javelina that is really a relative of the dog, and even the exotic jaguar. Embedded in the land are the rancher, cowboy, and the local communities; people who live on the land next to Nature. The story is made up of many intertwining parts that work together with a natural synergy, growing and adapting to constant and accelerating change in the new millennium.

At first glance this book is a rancher's autobiography, a collection of natural history essays, grass management, and southwestern history thrown in as required to tell the complex story of the modern-day lives of cowboys and ranchers. Even so there are also plenty of stories about quirky horses, cranky cow critters and bulls, cow dogs, and the people who use and care for them. The book begins when Diane and I started to put together the C6 Ranch in 1993 from a piece of magnificent land in the Canelo Hills near Sonoita and a neglected grazing allotment on the Coronado National Forest. Over the next two decades we grew, adding another ranch and took in our son Richard West as a partner. Ranching takes place within the context of local communities and neighbors. These are described with affection, humor, and some exasperation, especially when it came to dealing with the Coronado National Forest and the Endangered Species Act.

You will get to know some great people in this book, including T. N. Wegner, a professor of reproductive biology who specialized in keeping cows happy and in a family way. Dr. Jim Pickrell, a legendary veterinarian-jokester who never told the same joke twice and who would sit up all night to save a colicky horse. Rancher Tom Hunt who was my best cow consultant and a renowned water witch. Hardworking Manuel Murrietta, a cowboy and horseman who knew what the cow or horse was going to do before they did; a father/son partnership not unusual in this business but always heartwarming; Diane Collins who with her friends and neighbors built a Local History Matters Center at the Sonoita Fairgrounds and raised money for scholarships. This is not your typical ranch life memoir. Any time you find an ex-rodeo cowboy and rancher like me crawling around on the ground examining soils and grasses with university professors and Forest Service employees, you know you are in for some unexpected rides.

The battle over the endangered Gila topminnow in the Redrock Canyon watershed is a main event, and *Cowboy Is a Verb* is the story of how a group of ranchers and cowboys got together and formed the Canelo Hills Coalition to defend ourselves against lawsuit-happy activists and the Endangered Species Act administrators who sought to close down grazing. Instead of fighting in the court room, we worked with university range scientists, forest service conservationists, and several funding agencies to improve our ranches by increasing water and fencing, changing grazing patterns, and monitoring the health of the watershed. Using a common sense approach we convinced the Bureau of Reclamation not to build a useless dam across the canyon. After more than a decade, the watershed recovered and flourished and so did we. Other writers have noted that cowboys have lots of "try." In the complex world of the twenty-first century we have to do more.

After decades of study with haystacks of data and the application of cowboy common sense, ranchers and most experts agree that grazing, properly managed, is not the enemy of wildlife and watersheds, and the real life example in *Cowboy Is a Verb* prove it. I also pose important questions facing the land conservation community today. Do we attempt to preserve all vanishing species everywhere they might be able to exist, or should we manage our watersheds for the overall ecological health?

Alamo Spring, Crittenden Pasture.

1

Alamo Spring

In 1990, after much searching, I found a long wedge of unspoiled range-land located in the southern Arizona borderlands, thirty miles north of the Mexican border and fifty-five miles southeast of Tucson, Arizona. Sonoita, the closest town, lay three miles to the north. North to south, the property ran for three-quarters of a mile alongside a back country lane that meandered southward into the mile-high, oak-juniper woodland of the Canelo Hills. The west side bordered the Coronado National Forest and overlooked Alamo Canyon, a deep arroyo that sliced through the rhyolite and limestone hills.

Near the southwestern edge of the property, the canyon surged over a granite uplift and dropped ten feet into a pocket between a jumble of boulders. During the monsoon, the pocket was deep enough to swim. Even during dry season, it still contained enough water for wildlife. The first time Diane and I rode the canyon, a troop of coati mundi scampered up the yellow lichen-covered boulders, their long tails upright and curved at the tips. As they vanished into the oak brush one turned and stared at me with its quizzical black eyes, raccoon face, and long, upturned snout.

A few yards below the pocket, a smaller tributary joined the main canyon. Together, the two streams sustained a trickle of water between low banks of rocky soil and deer grass. Deer bones scattered in the brush marked the watering hole as an ambush site for mountain lions. Cottonwoods shaded the stream, giving the canyon its Spanish name, *álamo*. On that breezy morning, their shimmering leaves sounded like people whispering without words.

The most promising building site on the property nestled in a thicket of oaks and sloped gently in the direction of Mount Wrightson thirty miles to the west across the Sonoita Creek valley. To be sure that it was the right place, Diane and I camped out under the trees for a couple of days before we put our money down. At daybreak, a thin reef of clouds parted on a full moon that loomed over the massive peak just as the sun broke over the eastern horizon behind us. The dawn glow of Mount Wrightson clenched in a haphazard collage of cliffs and trees sealed the deal. Over that entire expanse, nothing man-made interrupted the natural contours. Living in Tucson's clutter and crowds the year before had shrunk my outlook on life to that of a midge. Here on the high desert grasslands, life would not be so cramped and miserly.

Diane was not so certain. She loved her house in the suburbs, her close friends, the convenient shopping, and her work on the school board where Rich went to high school. But she also loved her horses. We had built up a band of fine broodmares and she managed their careers on the race tracks. An outgoing, energetic person, Diane charmed the best efforts out of the horse trainers and jockeys with her sunny disposition. And the ranch would be a better place to raise horses than in Tucson. When Rich graduated and loped off to college, we made the jump to Sonoita. Right away, Diane joined the Sonoita Cowbelles and also volunteered to help at the Elgin school. With her sparkling personality, she had a natural ability to produce some pleasantry and then light up the room with a sundial smile that made the remark mean a whole lot more than it would have otherwise.

Behind the house site one hundred feet south was a rounded knob, flat on top, perfectly situated for the horse barn with the breezeway facing east to the rising sun over the Mustang Mountains and west overlooking sunsets behind Mount Wrightson. Horses feel more secure when they are able to see long distances and the stunning panorama sure made it easy for me to ride out at dawn and eager to get home and watch the sunset from our back porch.

The back country lane ran due north and south, while Alamo Canyon veered northwest from the waterfall toward the main stem of Sonoita Creek. Between the canyon and the lane, the topography was level and had good soil structure for the rooting of oak and juniper, bear grass and cliff rose, as well as a cozy house site for our ranch headquarters. On the downside, a porous limestone formed the geological underpinning of the land that sequestered its water in deep, isolated pockets. We had few neighbors because domestic wells in the area were scarce and the Coronado National Forest surrounded us on two sides.

As a condition of my purchase, the seller had to drill a well that pumped at least ten gallons a minute. That task fell to Tom Hunt, a veteran cattleman who worked for the seller. Tom was into his sixties when I first met him, but he still stood tall and lanky with a straw hat shading lamb blue eyes and a face creased by a mischievous grin as if he had just heard a good joke and wanted to pass it on. He was also locally renowned as Santa Cruz County's best water witch.

Tom was also part owner with the seller, an Austrian banker of some nobility who at the time lived in Europe, and both were keen to consummate our deal. Tom's technique for dowsing a promising well site involved walking over the land with a bent coat hanger held waist high with the hook pointed straight out, level to the ground. The coat hanger (or Tom's hands) allegedly had an affinity for deep water, in addition to a mind of its own. Where the hook jumped down from Tom's gnarly fists, he tied a strip of white cloth to a nearby bush. After three weeks of triangulating back and forth to locate the strongest signals more precisely, our potential new property looked like a tattered quilt.

"I'm drilling here," Tom finally decided. He took a two-by-four stake and hammered it in the ground with a sledge. "We'll hit water below 250 feet, and pump at least twenty gallons a minute," he stated confidently.

"Let me try," I said, taking the coat hanger. I walked back and forth across the drill site with the wire in hand.

"I don't feel a damn thing, Tom," I said. "This looks like a lot of hooey to me." Tom's grin collapsed into a pained expression, like I had just insulted his best bull. "It don't work for a skeptic," he said crossly. "You got to believe." A few days later, the driller hit a strong vein of water at two hundred and fifty-seven feet. When Bailey Foster, the local well man, installed the test pump, the well yielded a steady sixty-five gallons a minute. And this in an area where dry holes nine hundred feet deep were not uncommon, and five gallons a minute was considered a blessing. Tom's water witching seemed more like a lucky draw to an inside four card straight. Even so, I've drilled several other wells since that first one and Tom Hunt witched them all just for insurance.

Bailey and Tom were two characters that I came to appreciate and rely on. The quick parts of their brains had to do with ranchcraft: the husbandry of livestock and the land and the finding and bringing forth of water. Their lives came at the expense of hands and elbows of hard work. Bailey's dad worked for the Kern County Land Company's renowned Little Boquillas Ranch on the San Pedro River. One of five children, Bailey and his siblings grew up like free range chickens as Dad was seldom home. As the one cowboy at the ranch's Wolf Camp, he was responsible for all livestock and livestock waters on several thousand acres. Bailey remembered shinning up windmills to help his Dad a time long before he turned a teenager.

Tom was born in 1924 on the IV Bar family ranch near Douglas, Arizona. His pioneer lineage included sister Dorothy Hunt Finley, cowgirl, teacher, philanthropist, and purveyor of Coors cowboy beer. Tom cowboyed in his early years, then became ranch manager, and dabbled in the real estate business. In WWII, the army turned him into a diesel mechanic, a skill that served him well on the Rail X Ranch. His boss, Count Ferdinand von Galen, collected old army vehicles, mostly of American make. Tom rose early and supervised the ranch work in the morning. In the afternoons, he pored over United States Army service manuals and tinkered on the count's toys in the Rail X's well-equipped shop.

In the evenings, he sat on the veranda sipping bourbon on the rocks, watching lizards catch bugs on the giant cottonwood trees in the yard. As the sun set, deer and wild turkeys came out of the mesquite thickets to graze on the expansive lawns irrigated by an improbable artesian spring that produced eight hundred gallons every minute, day and night.

Tom and Bailey had prodigious memories about the things that mattered to their livelihoods. Fifteen years after we moved in, a lightning bolt struck our well, frying the pump and control box, cutting off the water to our pipelines in the hottest part of the summer. Bailey showed up the next morning at dawn, wearing a greasy Foster Pump cap pulled down to his ears. He drove the well-pulling rig over the smoking hole and started pulling pipe, joint by twenty-foot joint, breaking the threaded couplers loose with pipe wrenches and big-knuckled hands while he recited the well's exact depth, pumping capacity, and depth to water.

As the years passed, the crowfoot lines etched on Bailey's wind-gnawed face deepened when he broke into a wide-mouth grin which meant he had another lame joke to share whether or not you wanted it. Bumping into Bailey for morning coffee at the Mini-Mart brought forth:

"You wanta' know what the momma cow said to her calf as the sun went down?"

"How about 'pasture bedtime?'" I groaned.

For humor, Tom had a finer sense of irony, like the trapeze artist who was afraid of heights, or the cowboy who hated cows. When branding calves, he sat on an opera chair that swiveled over the branding table and daintily dabbed a smelly fly repellent paste on the fresh brands and sev-ered scrotums, like a conductor waving his baton. The antics of certain livestock also stuck in Tom's encyclopedic memory:

"One time I had a lazy Charolais bull that hung around that prop-erty you bought up in Sonoita," he said one evening as we visited on his veranda. "Bull got into the habit of jumping the cattle guard and eating people's flowers. Well, the neighbor called me up one day as mad as a stomped-on rattlesnake."

"I'm going to shoot your damn bull," he screamed over the phone.

"If you do, he'll lay in your garden and stink," Tom replied calmly.

"Then I'll haul that son-of-a-bitch away."

"That would be cattle rustling, you'd get ten years in the clink."

"What'll I do, then?" the man yelped.

"I told him to try fixing his fence," Tom advised, chuckling at the memory.

"City folks just don't understand the open range laws."

ii

We were elated with our new nest, but some of the neighbors felt otherwise. Along with the deeded land we owned outright came the adjacent nine-thousand-acre US Forest Service grazing permit, known as the Crittenden allotment of the Coronado National Forest, Sierra Vista Ranger District. Within that allotment surrounded by US Forest Service land had been two forty-acre deeded parcels. Homesteaded by settlers a hundred years earlier, each parcel had perennial water, identified on the maps as Alamo Spring and Corral Canyon Spring. Ferdinand von Galen, the owner, could not sell the forty-acre parcels because they lacked road access. Even so, the US Forest Service wanted control of the water so they agreed to swap them for our property on the county-maintained road. The neighbors' complaint was that our property was converted from publicly owned to private, a change in ownership that erased the neighbors' right of access to, and over, it.

People in general hate sudden changes in their settled routines. The neighbors had long been accustomed to hiking and riding over the piece of land that we now owned. Even though the US Forest Service had retained public access over its north and south ends so people could reach the national forest, some neighbors had vigorously opposed the swap. False claims of fraud and favoritism spread like wildfire in the community, especially after our purchase became public knowledge. A distaff cavalry of locals rode into our building site and complained:

"You are building over our bridle path."

"Excuse me, but you ladies are trampling in my living room," Diane smiled with a narrowing of her forthright eyes which meant I am usually friendly but don't push too hard or I'll bite.

Open scream-and-shout meetings were held at the Sonoita Fire Station where residents called to task the US Forest Service officials and local politicians. After I fenced our property, the protests reached a dangerous pitch. Our fence was cut, our oak trees were decorated with toilet paper, and one neighbor threatened us with assault and battery unless we tore the fence down. I attended one meeting with the Santa Cruz Sheriff where I noted that each of my neighbor's property was similarly fenced.

After that, things settled down, but one neighbor carved a sign with Walt Whitman's verse, "Resist Much, Obey Little," and hung it on his entry gate. The sign is still there, twenty-five years later, unforgiven but perhaps propitiated. Today, older and maybe wiser, we pass each other on our morning walks down the lane and exchange greetings. The other day he asked me if the tiny, sawdust-filled holes in the woodwork of his house might be termites.

"Sounds like it to me," I answered and referred him to the bug man at the University of Arizona who later confirmed the diagnosis.

"Well, you can fumigate," I suggested. "My son had to do that when they bought that old house over on Curly Horse Ranch road."

"I don't like poisons," he replied. "The entomologist said these termites were the slow-eating kind and they'd take forty-fifty years to destroy the place. I'll be gone by then."

That's one way to look at the problem, I thought as we went our separate ways. Just give everything back to the bugs.

While Diane designed and built our home, I laid out the barn and began riding fences and checking waters on the US Forest Service grazing allotment of one hundred sixty-five cows, year-round. But rather than leap right in, poorly informed about the land's complexity and capacity, I elected not to stock it with cattle immediately. As Jack Davenport, a pioneer southern Arizona cattleman, used to say when sizing up a new piece of country: "I read what the carrying capacity is supposed to be. Now, I'll ride and see how many cows it can really carry." Jack knew damn well that vegetation, topography, climate, soils, and water would set the limits, not necessarily the numbers on the US Forest Service's paperwork, or the real estate salesman's write-up. Much later, I learned that the notion of a "fixed" carrying capacity was a contradiction in the science of rangeland ecology and the source of considerable conflict between ranchers and the caretaker agencies.

The count's neighboring Rail X Ranch owned six thousand acres of deeded land lying in the Sonoita Creek bottoms and adjacent hillsides, plus the US Forest Service grazing allotment that we had just purchased. Thirty years prior, a younger, more ambitious Tom Hunt had built a tortuous, four-mile-long pipeline that crossed the Crittenden pasture northeast to

southwest, using Mexican labor and Caterpillar-type tractor to rip open a
trench through the rocky ground. Scattered along the pipeline about a half-
mile apart, he had placed five hundred gallon "drinkers," or water troughs.
The pipeline was a multi-purpose marvel of cowboy creativity that watered
cattle, wildlife, and a retreat house Tom built at the mouth of Dark Canyon.

As Tom grew older he managed the Rail X Ranch in a fond, vague style
and grazed the US Forest Service less, neglecting the upkeep of his engineering marvel. By the time I arrived on the scene, parts of it had fallen
into disrepair. As another condition of our purchase, I required the seller
to make the pipeline functional again; pipeline fully charged with troughs
and storage tanks devoid of leaks. During the three-month contingency
period prior to closing the final deal, Tom and his crew made good on
the repairs, including replacing the float valves with solid brass fixtures.

Tom Hunt had grazed this pasture only lightly in recent years and
we took over with decent stands of perennial grasses. Even so, as a cattle
ranch, the landscape seemed better suited for goats, javelina, white-tailed
deer, big horn sheep, black bear, and mountain lion. Spanish criollo cattle,
or the long-legged, drought resistant Brahman crosses could survive and
produce calves here, but the pasture would be tough terrain and short
rations for the wide-bodied, stubby-legged Hereford and Angus.

The south side of the allotment, five thousand acres, was a sideways
piece of country that fell off the south rim of the Mount Hughes ridge and
dropped eight hundred feet into a mesquite- and ocotillo-covered valley,
five miles long and two miles wide. The ridge formed the north boundary
of the valley and fell so sharply that a slip on its rim would mean a quarter-mile roll and tumble unless one lodged against boulders. To climb
the ridge from the valley bottom would be brute labor for man or horse.
Short, steep gorges sliced down from the crest of the ridge that opened
into steep-sided bowls of grass just above the valley floor.

A barbed-wire fence divided the five thousand acres north to south.
Corral Canyon Pasture occupied the west half of the valley. Kunde Pasture
occupied the east half that I renamed Red Bear after I saw the first cin-
namon-colored bear of my life bolting up the rim on a winter morning.

Topographically, this allotment was emphatically horseback country,
best worked by a tenacious and resilient personality with a set of rock-footed

mountain horses or mules, and a pair of heavy leather chaps. A talent for finding cattle in brushy canyon country and pair of cow dogs would be a big help, too. Warner Glenn, a renowned lion hunter from Cochise County, once called the Canelo Hills the best mountain lion habitat he'd seen with its abundant javelina and white-tailed deer, not to mention the local rancher's calves and colts.

At first, I didn't meet all the qualifications to ranch this country well, but at least I knew something and was arrogant enough to believe I could learn the rest. Over the next twenty-five years, this watershed taught me a lot. Perhaps the most important lesson was an appreciation of limits. Call it humility, if you like.

Mount Hughes Ridge—Corral Canyon Pasture.

iii

Once in a moment of candor, I told my son Rich that one reason for own-
ing a cattle ranch meant that we'd have more horses to ride. To a farm
child of the twentieth century, as I was, the horse represented freedom
from the shovel, clods, and the dusty plow. I grew up on a citrus ranch
on the outskirts of Phoenix. But my hard-working father was more of an
opportunist than an orchardist. By the time I was born, he worked the race
tracks around Phoenix, calculating the odds and payouts to the bettors.
Although he never got beyond grade school, he was a whiz on figuring
the odds on a deal. On weekend jaunts to the fairgrounds, I hung around
the finish line where the horses thundered across to the roar of the crowd.
Even now, I can still hear their pounding hooves. When Dad got a little
money ahead, he'd invest in another piece of land in Maricopa County.
Our farm was one such purchase.

"Horses cost money and they don't make any," Dad said when I screwed
up the courage to ask for a horse of my own. But I persisted. After months
of quiet pleading, he agreed if I earned the money, I could buy one.

I believed him. He was my father.

For the next year, I delivered newspapers, worked on the farm and gave up the movies to save every dime. Mom opened a savings account in my name. The passbook was small and had a leather cover with Valley National Bank stamped on the front. The ledger filled up slowly as the teller wrote down my deposits in blue ink.

One day my father handed me a dozen gopher traps and a shovel, saying that it was high time I started pulling my weight around the farm. The bucked-tooth, subterranean rodents chewed on citrus tree roots, killing saplings and cutting down our crop. Also, they tunneled through the dirt irrigation ditches and we had to be alert for leaks. Our water delivery from the Salt River Project canal lasted for twenty-four hours and there was hell to pay when I fell asleep and the ditch broke. In a weak moment, Dad offered a quarter for each stiffened carcass, money that went into my horse fund. A big black dog with an unerring nose helped me excavate the burrows.

Our tractor was an underpowered Ford, two-wheel-drive, and built low to the ground with big tires in back. It looked like a giant spider creeping downhill. Four times a year we had to disc up the weeds and reshape the basins around the trees, all twenty acres of them, although it seemed to us more like a hundred. We shaped the basins with an implement called a blocker pulled behind the Ford. The blocker was an ingenious, labor-saving tool, and instrument of torture for the operator. My brother, Clarkson, outranked me by five years so he drove the tractor while I rode the blocker to trip the lever that left a dam in each furrow, forcing irrigation water around the trees. Our puny tractor had to run full throttle to pull the blocker with me sitting in the middle, only inches from the churning dirt. Dust clouds, the guttural roar of the engine, and its exhaust fumes left their marks on my lungs, ears, and dreams. Instead of more horsepower, I yearned for a horse of my own. With a horse, I could ride away from all that. Like many country-raised boys, I was drawn toward some pursuit other than the one I was born to, like the preacher's son taking to vice.

For a short while, a neighbor let us keep a small bay gelding so skinny that his front legs seemed to come out of the same hole. South of our citrus grove, a two-mile strip of undisturbed Sonoran Desert ran up to the base of South Mountain Park. When I could get away from the farm chores and my brother, I rode over that desert and into the foothills.

From atop the mountain, I could see the outlines of the city stretched out alongside the channel of the Salt River and watch the planes glide into Phoenix Sky Harbor Airport. In those days no skyscraper or television towers marred the panorama.

A wide sand wash meandered down the bajada from the hills. On its grassy banks, I learned that the Sonoran Desert was not all desolation. Gambel quail, rabbits, white-winged and mourning doves, snakes, lizards, and coyotes flourished there. I hunted them first with a Daisy BB gun; later with a single-shot .22 caliber rifle Dad gave me one Christmas. Creosote bush, saguaro, prickly pear, and cholla cacti flourished by some preordained process that rooted them with large spaces in between. Cactus wrens, woodpeckers, and curve-billed thrashers chattered in their distinctive voices. I learned to group the birds by how they made their livings and where they lived, a taxonomic habit that has stayed with me despite Peterson's Field Guides: fly catchers, carrion birds, woodpeckers, seed eaters, birds of prey like hawks and owls, I lumped them together in the same way that people were farmers, ranchers, teachers, mechanics, doctors, or dullards.

Where the sand wash bumped up against our canal bank, a messy thicket of mesquite and palo verde trees made a perfect hideout. I trimmed up the trees and built a hidden fort. Even today, a half century later, I can close my eyes and picture the exact location of each post, the hexagonal shape of the enclosure. In the summer, a tangle of amaranth, tumbleweed, Johnson grass, and Jimson weed grew up in the rich topsoil deposited by the wash. Much later, I learned O'odham youth smoked Jimson in their coming of age ceremonies. Had I known that, I would have tried smoking it, as I too was coming of age. Instead, Clarkson and I gagged on the rolled-up bark that peeled from the eucalyptus trees growing on the canal bank, mimicking our favorite western movie stars.

The desert and hills were my places of snugness, where I could escape from entrapment between a stern father and an overbearing older brother who had discovered girls and lost interest in horses and cowboys. The open desert set me free from all that. And that skinny bay horse was my ticket to freedom until he passed on.

Rural people often have two languages: one for work and home, and one for town and church. But I grew up absorbing the vernacular and contours of two distinctly different landscapes, each with unique features and value systems.

More than anything, that contrast between the orderly rows of trees, the smell of orange blossoms and wet dirt, backgrounded against the desert's casual freedoms shaped my character and personality. The farm instilled a work ethic and the value of community effort as our family struggled to make a crop each year, working as a family unit toward a common goal. The open desert spelled independence and self-determination, the chance to go at life in my own way. Out there I had free time taken from a structured childhood, time to simply run and roll, like a colt discovering how to gallop. Today, the opportunities and challenges I respond to can all be traced to those formative years and the farm-to-desert staging grounds for my ideas and aspirations. Experiencing this dichotomy at an impressionable age instilled in me an instinct for detecting links between seemingly unrelated cultures and landscapes.

Two miles down the canal bank where I caught the school bus, Doc Sinclair had a small ranch. Doc was a horse trader, a happy, gregarious man with a round belly and bald head that he kept covered with a silver belly Stetson. He had been in the United States cavalry and ranched in Texas, but moved to the Valley of the Sun for retirement and traded horses to local farmers for something to do. But mostly, he sat in a rocking chair on the back porch and chain-smoked Lucky Strike cigarettes, lighting a new one with the glowing butt of the last. Doc was full of stories and he told them through a perpetual wheeze.

Doc's tall tales always had horses in them, so real I could hear the whinny and smell their sweat. They ran the fastest; bucked the hardest; were smarter than the *Farmer's Almanac*. Doc had a positive outlook on life and his stories never mentioned a horse being the worst at anything. At every chance, I stopped by to listen to his long-winded tales and sneak a look at his horses. Once a month when Doc drove off to the horse sales in New Mexico, he hired me to feed the horses and irrigate his pastures.

Doc's favorite was a short-coupled gelding named Whirlaway, bay in color, with big dark eyes, foxy-pointed ears, and a mellow disposition. From Doc and Whirlaway, I became lessoned in the basics of ground work horsemanship: how and what to feed and how often; how to pinch the cannon bone and pick up a hoof and clean it out; how to brush and comb out the mane and tail; how to read the horse's state of mind by watching its body language, the eyes and lips and position of its ears—and never, ever, to deal with it in a fit of anger, even when it tromped on my toes.

"I wouldn't sell this horse, son," Doc said one afternoon when I got of the school bus and walked over to Doc's back porch. "Except I can't ride much anymore and he is too quick for me," as he wheezed away on his black lungs. "I want him to go to a good home, so you can have him for six hundred dollars. I'll wait for you to get the money together, and if you are short some, you can muck out my corrals to make up the difference."

I walked, ran, floated, flew the two miles home to tell my father than I found my horse and had the money. He was sitting in the old blue arm-chair in the living room listening to the radio. Dad had been spending lots of time in that chair lately, sometimes not even getting up for supper. My cute, curly-haired younger sister Kitty was the apple of his eye, but even she could not bring him out of that deep melancholy for very long.

"Dad, I've found my horse."

At first he didn't answer. I waited and asked again.

"You don't need a horse," he barked.

"But you said that if I earned the money?"

"I've changed my mind. No damn horse; you don't need one, and that's all there is to it."

"But you promised." I bawled, running out of the room, slamming the screen door behind me.

"Now I suppose you'll go and cry about it," was the last thing I remember him saying to me about anything ever.

I ran down the rows of grapefruit trees, over the canal, and into the desert. I hid in my fortress, thinking evil thoughts about my dark, heavy father. I plotted to get my money out of the bank, buy Whirlaway, and ride away to Texas and work on a ranch. Or I'd kill myself, and then he'd be sorry. Two days later I snuck into the kitchen, starving. Mother fixed a peanut butter and jelly sandwich. While I wolfed it down she sat across the table and explained that Dad changed his mind because we couldn't afford to feed a horse.

Not long afterward, Dad wasted away from cancer of the esophagus. Toward the end he couldn't eat or talk. Mother said he knew he was sick before the horse episode. That was the real reason he went back on his word.

Looking back, what hurt the most was that they didn't tell me. I think I would have understood if they had explained. That way I could have shared in the suffering and been part of the family. So I'm sorry to say that even now, the last clear memory I have of my father is that arbitrary, unexplained betrayal. And it is all mixed up with the stale smell of sickness and Dad's desperate gasping for breath at the end. . . .

My father is long since dead, and long since forgiven. My thoughts of escape, though they burned brightly at the time, quickly disappeared. Today, they only linger as testimony to how self-centered a child's perceptions can be.

We worked the farm together, Clarkson and I, until he escaped by joining the army. Sometime later, Mother sold eighty acres of land across from what became Scottsdale Municipal airport to raise money to send her children to college. The joke in our family now is that if she had kept it a few more years, we would not have needed more schooling.

Eventually I got my horse from Doc—not Whirlaway, but an eight-year-old bald-faced sorrel gelding that weighed only nine hundred pounds soaking wet. He was built like a cutting horse, moved off his hind feet as smoothly as water running down the drain, and could really run fast. The horse taught me how to rope and handle cattle in the local feedlots and cow pastures, and while working at the Cornelius Livestock Auction barn in Phoenix.

On the morning of sale days, Paul Cornelius tallied up the number of cattle and decided how much extra help he would need to hire. His regular cowboys drove bunches of cattle on horseback into the cavernous sale ring, a covered amphitheater that formed a semi-circle around a sunken corral. The buyers sat in theater chairs on one side of the amphitheater and made their bids with the lift of a finger or a nod. The auctioneer perched on the opposite side chattered away in a staccato gibberish until the bidding stopped and he cried out "SOLD."

After each bunch of cattle had been sold, a pen rider pushed them down the alleys to the designated corral where the gate boy opened and shut the gate behind them. For the first months that I worked there, I was a gate boy, shuffling on foot down the dusty alleyways to open the correct gate.

Then one day a pen rider didn't show up and Mr. Cornelius pointed to me and said: "Get on your horse."

I ran to the trailer and threw a saddle on Baldy and rode to the sale ring. After the auctioneer cried "SOLD," we delivered that first bunch to the correct pen, proud as peacocks, and trotted back to get the next bunch. The sale was a big one, and lasted into the night. The dimly lit alleyways swirled with a dust so thick I had to cover my face with a wet bandanna. A bunch of rank Hereford cows from the San Carlos Indian Reservation came roaring out of the sale ring and down the alley at top speed, running over the gate man before he could open the gate. I spurred Baldy past the runaway bunch and turned the leaders into the fence, reversing their direction. Pushing them past the gate man, we turned the bunch back on itself again and through the open gate. Trotting back to the sale ring, I noticed Mr. Cornelius watching us. From then on, Baldy and I had steady jobs.

After the sale, the pen riders and gate men often convened in a far corner of the Hilltop Bar on Washington Street to wash the dust out of our throats with a pitcher of beer. Too young to be served, I ordered iced tea. One afternoon, two ladies in high heels from the swanky hotel next to the airport came in and ordered martinis. Their scenic profiles and short skirts of stunning snugness spelled an awaited episode in life that I had only heard rumors about. Larry, an older pen rider, fancied himself a Don Juan, perhaps because of the big hat, spurs, and *ordeur de corral*. Larry pushed back from the table and started to get up to make their acquaintance, but Paul pulled him back to his seat:

"Forget it," he said in that slow drawl. "You tangling with those two ladies would be like feeding race horse oats to a burro. . . ."

I took that little bald-faced horse with me to a cow college, studied a potent mixture of history, biology, philosophy, and the animal sciences, discovered Coors beer and coeds, including one named Diane Joyce Davis. A cheerful, busy brunette, Diane was the daughter of a Wisconsin dairy farmer and thought cows and cowboys were tolerable. We've been together ever since. The second year Baldy and I made the college rodeo team.

Rodeo riders always compete for money. Each contestant pays an entry fee. The money goes into a pot that is divided among the winners. Sometimes, sponsors will drop in an added money check. The National Intercollegiate Athletic Association did not sanction rodeo as an official sport because money was involved, but we could not have cared less. In my last two years at Arizona State University, Baldy and I won regional championships and more than enough money to pay for my tuition and his oats. Later, those rodeo skills helped pay for a master of science degree at the University of Arizona.

Working in corrals and small fenced pastures, I figured out how to handle cattle in confinement. But I never had to catch wild cattle in wide open, rough country. Looking back, there have been times on our ranch when I wished I had known how, like when a couple of our Brahman heifers went feral. I admired the daring and skill of those who could and did, like Milo DeWitt, Mack Hughes, and Monk Maxwell, horsemen who cow boss and author Ed Ashurst labeled as "Real Cowboys" in the twentieth century. But I went in the low stress direction, doing everything possible to keep my ranch cattle gentle and easily caught. I am positive this made more money with less stress and fewer bruises or crippled livestock. So on our C6 Ranch, bovine bad behavior was grounds for culling and called for a trip to the sale barn. Also, at the end of the twentieth century, running a ranch had other pleasures and challenges to confront.

iv

Two miles south of our new house a conical mountain of fossil-bearing lime-stone reared up against the backdrop of Mount Hughes ridge. Riding to the summit on that first clear morning, I was stunned by the long view of seven jagged mountain ranges circling the horizons: the majestic Mount Wrightson and the Santa Ritas to the west; Santa Catalina and Rincon ranges straight north fifty miles; the Whetstones to the east; the Huachuca massif southeast on the Mexican border. Between the Huachuca and Whetstone Mountains, the curiously biscuit-shaped Mustang peaks filled in the gap (see Map 2).

The towering mountains seemed held apart by a wide, long valley that descended from rolling, tan-colored foothills. Cienega Creek meandered south to north down the valley's center, hidden from view by scattered thickets of mesquite and cottonwood. These were the southern-most remnants of the Basin and Range Province—"sky island" mountains floating above desert grassland seas. No pole lines or cell phone towers marred the view. Too far to hear the rumbling of trucks on the distant highway. In the dawn air, the vast panorama rang like a great bell in the rising sun. Surely, this was what the West looked like before it became something else.

But in the geological sweep of Deep Time, all this was a vast highland plateau laid down eons earlier by a Paleozoic ocean. Forty million years ago—that's six hundred thousand human lifetimes stacked end to end—an intense volcanic heat began to melt the continental crust to the consistency of stiff molasses. The California coast somehow became attached to the Pacific Coastal Tectonic Plate and began to drift away to the northwest. The semi-molten crust of the earth's surface began to pull apart in what geologist Robert Scarborough called a "giant, geo-taffy pull." The earth's mantle opened up on fault lines, spewing out molten rock and ash, shattering the crust into many long segments and tilting them on edge. The narrow segments sank into the taffy, while the wider slices maintained their upland heights. Over the next millions of years, the sinking valleys became interposed between the mountains; valleys and mountains running parallel to each other, southeast to northwest.

Then in a mere eye blink of Deep Time, the stretching stopped and the earth's crust cooled. The mountains and valleys stabilized. The cloudburst replaced volcanic heat as the sculptor of the watersheds, aided and abetted by wind. Rock and rock debris washed down, building up beds of sand and gravel in the valley bottoms thousands of feet thick. Grasses colonized the surface and began the inexorable, slow process of building the soil that supports all life on earth. A good part of our ranch in the Canelo Hills sat squarely on jumbled, bouldery, eroding fault lines tilting toward the west.

My horse pawed at the ancient limestone, nudging me out of my geologic trance. Every long view from up here was mighty, but what about up close? Time I had a look. In the foreground, the ranchettes of a new suburbia sprawled like ringworm infecting the clean, rolling grassland. The Santa Cruz County fairgrounds dominated the scene, with its oval horse-racing track and rodeo arena in the middle. The ranchettes ceased abruptly at the edges of the Coronado National Forest and the vast Cienega Creek preserve where the untrammeled rangeland began. Public lands and a few large, private ranches preserved the open and uncluttered space that I had fallen in love with a long time ago.

Nearby, three brush-filled canyons swept off the Mount Hughes ridge running west-northwest, each one separated from the other by narrow ridges of sharp, fossil-bearing limestone. Between each ridge, ages of water runoff had gouged through the softer rock to form the canyons the Anglo pioneers named Alamo, Little Alamo, and Monkey. But why Monkey? There were no bananas here.

The horse tiptoed down the mountain, cutting switchbacks through limestone boulders and juniper thickets. Just ahead was the heart of Tom's pipeline half hidden in a regrowth of juniper trees. The well at our house three miles to the north pumped water through a pipeline to fill a forty-thousand-gallon storage tank. The tank's elevation was twenty feet higher than any of Tom's drinking troughs. The same gravitational force that created the canyons also pushed water through the pipeline from the tank to drinkers scattered over the landscape.

I rode down Alamo Canyon and through a small wire gate into the Tunnel Springs subdivision, my next-door neighbor on the north. In the 1950s, an eastern dude with a ton of money had bought the land and divided it up into forty to sixty acre home sites that he proceeded to sell. He must have been a land conservation visionary because he created deed restrictions that allowed only one house to each parcel, locating them in places that hid the houses from view. He also installed decent roads and power lines underground. Ahead toward Mount Wrightson, I could see the green bulge that marked the cottonwoods surrounding the headwater springs of Sonoita Creek. But another big limestone hill blocked the way and diverted Alamo Canyon to the south, past Dick Reilly's rambling house situated in the canyon bottom.

Dick was at the barn feeding a pair of small, fawn-colored burros. I introduced myself as the new neighbor. Dick was the art critic for a large metropolitan newspaper chain and traveled frequently, leaving the care of the spread to his partner, an older man who seldom ventured outside the compound. Our conversation was short but courteous, as he addressed me as Mr. Collins in a high voice and asked me not to trespass, pointing out that Tunnel Springs was a gated, private property.

"Okay by me," I replied and rode on, thinking that the ex-urbanite population of Sonoita was short on friendliness.

The limestone peak pushed Alamo Canyon south into a confluence with Little Alamo and Monkey Canyons on the Rail X Ranch. Here, the underground stream gushed to the surface in an enormous artesian spring that had flowed a steady eight hundred gallons per minute for the past few thousand years. The patronal house of the Rail X Ranch perched on a hill overlooking the spring, the angular white walls of the count's castle thrusting above the green and brown pallet of the land.

Without water, the pipeline, and gravity that made it work, my ranch would be just a gorgeous pile of rocks treed with curious-looking plants, home to myriad creatures. Awed by the time scale of its creation, I have sometimes thought that should have been enough. Even so, humankind would have its way, and I was determined to occupy and use it in ways that did no harm. Was that possible? I thought so. I knew some ranchers who operated on that premise. Secretly, I vowed to leave it in better condition than when I took over.

"But what I want to know, Tom Hunt, is why in hell did you use that thin-walled plastic pipe?" I blurted out after a week of watching him repair leaks. "The thicker stuff is only ten cents a foot more."

"The boss had me on a budget," Tom brayed with his usual pussycat grin. "I got to keep any money that was left over."

V

I was vaguely aware of the contentious debate over grazing in the west, particularly on public land such as the Coronado National Forest. But I had been living out of the country for a decade and did not realize at first how bitter the conflict had become. As an Arizona native, I had seen rangeland that had been abused by overgrazing, caused by the confluence of ignorance, the weather, and greed. Even so, as the new millennium approached, some ranchers had begun to change their grazing management in ways that improved watershed and rangeland health. Those who clung to the old ways were being pushed out by lack of grass, water, and agency caretakers. Even so, the philosophical gap between ranchers and the antigrazing faction remained wide and deep.

A watershed moment for me was Richard Shelton's night course "Literature of the Southwest," at the University of Arizona. This was perhaps an incongruous subject for someone like me trained in the sciences. Professor Shelton grouped the reading selections by categories: history, memoir, biography, wanderers, dwellers, naturalists, users, and special views. The latter included Aldo Leopold and Edward Abbey. Abbey's lyrical prose was thought-provoking, mixing a possessive love of nature with anger at how other people were abusing the land. But for me, his cynicism and anarchy did not inspire, perhaps because I had no interest in blowing up dams and power lines. I couldn't see any room for people in his exclusive vision of western watersheds.

Leopold was just as hard on ranchers' and farmers' treatment of the land, but he showed a way forward based on education and cooperative effort. And he personally demonstrated that ethic by working hands-on to restore a Wisconsin farm while he taught the first-ever course in game management at the University of Wisconsin. Also, during the dust bowl years of the 1930s, he joined forces with the farmers of Coon Valley and the Soil Conservation Service to restore a deeply eroded watershed back to health and productive use.

Leopold's early place of learning had been the newly formed Apache National Forest in eastern Arizona where he was assigned as a forester in 1909, fresh out of Yale. He worked and wrote during the first half of the twentieth century as the science of ecology was in its formative stages. Today, those principles had started to seep into the culture and practice of ranching. Like Leopold and his worn-out Sand County farm, I thought I could bring this watershed back into a higher state of health. And producing food seemed a necessary and honorable profession. At middle age, I had reached the stage in life where nostalgia had become more appealing. Where I came from was more interesting and meaningful than where I'd been.

2

Fine Feathers

Despite its rugged terrain, the Canelo Hills had one essential component in its favor as a cattle ranch: an average annual rainfall of sixteen to eighteen inches. The rain came in two seasons. The monsoon started in July and lasted through September, a period of time when two thirds of the annual precipitation fell. This was growing season for most range grasses, when virtually all growth and seed production took place. The violent summer thunderstorms Mexicans call *chubascos* (and gringos call monsoons) swirled up from the Gulf of Mexico and the Sea of Cortes. Often they dumped an inch of rain in a single hour, causing the canyons to sing and filling the dirt ponds scattered over the watershed. The rangeland exploded in an intricacy of grasses and other vegetation, a fragrant outburst of almost incomprehensible botanic creativity framed in various shades of green, gold, blue, white, pink, red, and violet.

During our first summer, Diane and I rode to the top of the Mount Hughes ridge one morning to check water lines. Overhead, anvil-shaped clouds darkened ominously over the Patagonia Mountains to the south. As we reached the top, the storm suddenly turned our way, swirling up the Sonoita Creek Valley. The Santa Rita Mountains and the Canelo Hills channeled the storm's enormous energy into a towering wave of wind and dust that rolled up the valley faster than our horses could outrun. Behind the churning dust the rain came, big thudding drops that quickly grew into a snare drum roll. Dark, billowing clouds engulfed the ridge line where we stood our horses, awed by the fierce spectacle. Our shirts gave little protection and we hurried off the ridge into a Manzanita thicket where we jerked off the saddles and crouched under the blankets to ward off the hail stones. Overhead, lightning strikes provoked eerie mountain profiles out of the blackened firmament, each one followed by a deafening boom of thunder. The horses stood ground-tied, tails to the wind to wait out the storm.

Suddenly it was over. The angry clouds moved over to Mount Wrightson, trailing a thin veil of rain. Water gushed down every arroyo around us. The air sniffed of wet sage and juniper. Flying ants on gossamer wings filled the sky, king birds and phoebes snatching them in midair. Three hundred years prior when the Jesuit and Spanish conquistadors first invaded this area, they were astonished by the Tohono O'odham-Pima people dancing and drinking cactus wine to coax water out of the clouds. When the clouds finally obliged, the natives celebrated by dancing naked in the rain, while the medieval Europeans looked on, aghast at the dancers' lack of shame. But we stayed dressed. Saddling the horses, we rode happily down the ridge toward home, entranced by the natural grandeur but chilled by the twenty-degree drop in temperature.

The winter rains (*equipatas*), when they come, are gentle, slow, and widespread, originating from the Pacific Ocean sweeping off the California coasts. Often the sky is overcast for days, the drizzle sometimes changing to snow that smothers the grasses and crowns Mount Wrightson with a zucchetto papal cap. In spring, the tall, spindly cliffrose burst with cream-colored, yellow-centered flowers that saturate the damp air with an apple-blossom fragrance. Fairy duster, a small-leafed legume grazed by bovines and deer, sprout feathery-pink flowers while the canyon penstemon wake up in March and bloom bright red. Lehmann and plains love grasses, fox tail, and giant sacaton green up early around the base of the plant. And the cows follow the green.

From late spring at the end of April into early July is often exceedingly dry, a meteorological fact that has severe effects on livestock and changes the personalities of the local folks. Most of the year, people are persistently friendly, except for a few grouches still upset over our fence. When passing each other on the road, everyone waves a hearty greeting to both neighbor and stranger alike. But as the cows shrink down to shadows from lack of green feed, that wave becomes a feeble lifting of a finger off the steering wheel. One year when the rains didn't come until August, the salutations stopped altogether as we hurried to scatter protein blocks to supplement the hungry cattle. As the monsoon draws near, lightning bolts ignite range fires that race over the land; high jumping flames consume grass and brush in a hollow rush of wind.

And yet, the agaves, yuccas, and bear grass celebrate this same dry season by launching flower stalks into the breezes. On the tip of each stem, clusters of syrupy flowers attracted bats, bees, wasps, flies, and hummingbirds, as well as my gobbly cows that walk down the stalks to feast on the juicy blossoms and stems. The lesser long-nosed bat was listed as a threatened species by the US Fish and Wildlife Service, despite huge bat populations in nearby Mexico. In the Canelos, ranchers had to move their cows away from the agave plants for the benefit of bats. This was my first, first-hand introduction to the competitions arbitrated by the Endangered Species Act.

The weeks of anticipation through day-after-day of total dryness for me makes the coming of the monsoon thrilling. Its arrival feels like a reprieve from capital punishment, or recovery from cancer, or escaping bankruptcy. That first year on the ranch the monsoon broke on July 12 in mid-afternoon. I was loading protein blocks on the pack horse to spread out over the Crittenden pasture. Instead, I stripped to the waist and stood in the downpour face up and mouth open. The next morning I poured 1.6 inches from the rain gauge and hurried to write it down as if to ensure that the rain had been real.

The trees of the Canelo Hills define the rhythms of the seasons, each species leafing out or dying back out at its appointed time. The deciduous oaks drop acorns mid-summer to fall. One wet year I gathered fifty pounds around my house for my neighbor to make granola, with leftovers for my horses and the javelina to munch. During March and April the oak leaves turn to the color of tanned skin and fall to the ground. About the same time, the trees burst with waxy green foliage along with catkin tassels that make the pollen to fertilize next fall's acorns. Even in the same grove, each tree moves at its own pace. Some are covered with new green leaves while others retained the old ones, burnt-orange in color. A few have both color schemes on different parts of the same tree.

The cottonwood tree is everyone's friend because where the cottonwood takes root, water has to be close to the surface. Years ago, Tom Hunt had drilled horizontal wells into the base of Mount Hughes ridge where lone cottonwoods had rooted in the side canyons. The three old wells

I discovered in Corral Canyon and Red Bear pastures could water some wildlife now and then, and made excellent ambush sites for mountain lions.

Where the water is strong and on the surface like at the headwaters of Sonoita Creek, cottonwood thickets create a park-like setting. By early February, the buds begin to swell and the trees broadcast their white fluff. The heart-shaped leaves soon follow, pale green and dancing in the breeze. The green darkens through the summer and by autumn the leaves turn yellow, soon to lay a colorful carpet on the ground.

The sycamores grow in ones and twos in the canyon bottoms where their roots went deep between the rocks, rooted in stone. They waited until April to leaf out, as if they wanted more time to show off their angular limbs of smooth, white bark. Two massive old giants shaded Harshaw Canyon alongside the road leading to Patagonia from the San Rafael Valley. Each December, I made a special drive to see their gilded leaves, so golden that they astonished the eye, like sunlight shimmering on wind-brushed water. The gnarls and dark scars on old trunks speak of their long holding in place. No doubt these trees witnessed the cattle drives to the railroad pens in Patagonia a century before.

The reluctant mesquite leaves out last in the spring, as if fearful of the late frosts that sometimes sweep over the high desert. On my ranch, they grew only below five thousand feet elevation in Corral Canyon and Red Bear pastures. During May and June, their leguminous leaves and blossoms are often the only green forage available. One old-timer claimed that any mesquites above a mile high had been seeded by turds from the frontier cavalry horses ridden in from lower elevations. Some ranchers and government agencies curse the mesquite for taking over the rangeland, shading and starving out the grass. Much money and energy has been spent on bulldozing or poisoning mesquite trees but they always seem to survive. But mesquite beans are high in protein and make good cow feed in May and June when not much else is growing. Most ranchers who bulldoze their mesquites leave enough trees to make a bean crop.

The first fall I rode up Redrock Canyon, the mesquites looked like they had been hit by a phantom first frost. Instead, each dead twig had a perfect ring chiseled into the wood by an inch long, blunt-headed beetle. The twig girdlers had ringed the smaller stems to make a place to lay their eggs, killing the branch beyond the ring. If the gene-jockeys at the university could genetically engineer a twig girdler the size of a house cat, perhaps they would girdle the trunk and kill the whole tree.

The junipers stay green year-long. At times, they glowed with a rust-colored pollen that makes our eyes weep and noses water. A strong wind through the juniper forest raises a yellowish dust like a smoldering fire. One spring when the Dark Canyon bears came out of hibernation, they broke the limbs off one big, shaggy bark juniper at the edge of Little Alamo Canyon to get at the berries they craved. Conical piles of bear poop circled around that single tree as the bears flattened it, the resinous berries too sweet or sour for its own survival. One old-timer in Sonoita claimed that feeding juniper berries would make his hens lay gin-flavored eggs.

Every few years in midsummer, the juniper trees ring out with shrill cicada songs. After spending years below the ground feeding on tree roots, the male bugs crawl up the trunk where they break into a bug-eyed, cosmic ecstasy of screeching in hopes of attracting females. When I first heard them around the house, I clapped my hands and suddenly a minute of shocked silence ensued. Then, one cicada resumed screeching, soon followed by another and another, until the air again filled with the urgent buzz of cicada song.

Thirty species of grass carpeted my rough, irregular pastures. At first, I could only identify the most common species. In the fall when they were tall and seeded out, the vegetation seemed like a disorganized mess at first glance. But looking closer, I could see that each species had a distinctive symmetry and growth habits. On one, the seed package looked like an upside down canoe, bobbing at the end of each stem. Since grass supported our ranching enterprise, I knew that I needed to know much more. Early on, I learned the "ice cream" species by watching my cows. They grazed the blue grama and plains lovegrass first if all other things were equal. But they would go for the new green leaves no matter what the species. Lehmann lovegrass greened up in February and the cows would hit it hard first before the grama came on. That turned out to be the best way to use Lehmann because it was resistant to grazing and crowded out the native grasses unless it was knocked back. But there was much more to the management of grazing and I soon found myself on another steep learning curve.

ii

Good husbandry of both grass and cattle requires moving the herd around the ranch. And topography usually dictates the direction. Corral Canyon and Red Bear pastures had fit into the Rail X deeded land on the Sonoita Creek floodplain like a hanger on a hook. Tom Hunt had built a fine set of shipping corrals on Highway 82 between Sonoita and Patagonia, so for him moving cattle for brandling or shipping was an easy, downhill slide. But to reach my shipping corrals in the extreme northwest corner of the ranch, I had to drive the cattle from Corral Canyon over the west end of Mount Hughes ridge and up Dark Canyon, a distance of ten miles over the roughest country this side of the Grand Canyon.

At first, I tried driving cattle along Tom's old pipeline route. This was feasible only in the winter. Even then, the thousand-foot climb wore out the cows and made lapdogs out of the calves. In the summer, heat made the drive impossible. Finally, Tom Hunt and the Rail X owner graciously granted me a license to cross their land while I tried to find another way in and out.

In town, I had people living next door that I never met. In the country, "neighbor" means more than just someone who lives near. Tom had been raised in the good neighbor tradition of the West. He let me use the Rail X corrals for shipping and receiving cattle during that time. Looking back, I think that I entertained Tom with my climb up the learning curve.

Another of Tom's savvy alignments accidently smoothed my way. As the conflicts between ranchers and the grass-hugging activists heated up in the 1980s, the US Forest Service made a regular practice of reducing the number of cattle allowed on grazing allotments. The reductions often occurred when an allotment was transferred to a new owner, or during one of the regular assessments as required by environmental laws. Feeling the pressure like a counterpunching boxer, Tom invited the US Forest Service's range people to make a scientific study of the Crittenden Allotment's grazing capacity. They eventually settled on one hundred sixty-five cows, year long. Because it was their number, the local Sierra Vista Ranger District defended it from further cuts when outside pressure came to bear.

After a year, I started stocking the ranch. I had worked on ranches before, but never had to start from scratch with a new set of cattle and horses. In my conversations with Tom and other local ranchers, I had absorbed a couple of crucial lessons, usually delivered in the form of savvy sayings that encapsulated the wisdom of long experience.

"A live calf anytime of the year is better than carrying an open cow all year," Tom said. "It don't matter how good she might look."

The more progressive cattlemen put their bulls out with the cows only during the summer breeding season. I suspected that Tom left his bulls out year-round because it was easier and required less labor. In addition, he could sell his calves several different times of the year, taking advantage of fluctuating market conditions.

"The only way to get heavy calves at weaning is to get early calves," Jack Davenport chimed in. "And the only way I know of to get calves born early is to feed supplement during the winter and dry spring so the cows are in condition to take the bull and breed-back early."

On the high desert, winter can be bitterly cold, and spring is almost always dry. The cows require a protein supplement like cottonseed meal and molasses so they will have the nutritional reserves to cycle into estrus and breed-back with the bull during the dry spring. If not, the hungry cow will wait until after the summer rains to cooperate, or skip motherhood altogether that year.

"After giving birth, the cow's uterus needs about ninety days to heal up before conception with the bull," Thomas Norman Wegner declared.

T. N. should know. Armed with a PhD in reproductive physiology from the University of California at Davis, he taught the subject at the University of Arizona. Tom joked that his doctorate was in how best to get cows "Knocked Up."

Oftentimes, the theories of university professors are about as useful as a four-card flush out on the ranch. T. N. was different. He could do things. He was a horseman who shod his own horses, keen interpreter of bovine behavior and nutritional status, could pregnancy-test cows by rectal palpation, and liked to be at the rear of the herd when driving cattle.

"Riding drag is an art," T. N. said oftentimes as we worked. Contrary to John Wayne, Larry McMurtry, and other Hollywood-based cowpokes where the hero is always up front on the head-end of the herd, a successful cattle drive requires competent cowboys at the back end who knew when to push and when not to, how to maintain the proper distance from cattle, an ego that didn't require showing off their rope tricks, and a longshoreman's vocabulary.

Thomas Norman Wegner, now retired, helped so many times on the ranch that I still owe him a barn-full of hay. He rode and owned good horses, the working kind, one gelding so big that his daughters dubbed him "Sherman," after the army tank of the same name. Plus, T. N. was a journeyman welder and skilled mechanic. His pickup was twenty-five years old but it purred like a Singer sewing machine. He rebuilt it from the ground up at least twice during the time I knew him.

Sally Wegner, his spouse, was an English major and horsewoman in her own right. Sally scorned the western way, and rode the proper English style every day at home. She also had a decades-old sourdough culture and always sent a loaf of bread along with Tom when he came to help us on roundups.

Earlier, while working on desert ranches, I had developed a preference for cows with ear. "Ear" means the cow carries some Brahman blood in her pedigree. Brahman cattle are drought and insect resistant, will walk a long way to water, live longer, defend their calves from predators, have long ears, and humps on their shoulders. European breeds like Hereford and Angus originated in wet climates and have been genetically selected over hundreds of generations for milk production, fertility, and meat marbled with lots of fat. But the selection process has turned them into mobile vegetables. As a general rule, they do not enjoy mountain climbing and hustling for grass unless they happened to be born and raised in the rocks.

The second year, I bought a load of local heifer calves with one quarter Brahman blood. They had just been weaned and were as skittish as quail. To settle them down, I put them in a small pasture and drove them to water every day for two weeks. Then on a sparkling winter day, clear with a light breeze, T. N. and I drove them to the back end of Red Bear pasture. Tom Hunt said he would also help, but that only meant that he opened the gate between the Rail X and Corral Canyon pasture where he waved and wished us "Happy Trails."

A rude dirt track ran the full length of the valley and keeping the heifers lined out on the trail turned out to be a chore.

"I've got the back end covered," T. N. said. "Why don't you go up alongside the front and haze them in the right direction?" That was like trying to guide wet noodles up a wall until they got tired. A half-day later, we dropped them off at Red Bear tank, a small dirt pond, the only permanent water in the two-thousand-acre pasture.

With the cattle safely on water and in belly deep grass, we decided to scout the pasture's perimeter. The Mount Hughes ridge, a thousand feet above the valley floor, formed the north side of the pasture. Side canyons coming off the high ridge often opened up into grassy bowls. Above, the hillsides rose into lichen-stained cliffs hemmed in by thickets of juniper, oak, buckbrush, mountain mahogany, and ceanosis, the delicatessen plant for the greyhound-sized Coues whitetail deer. It was a wild and tumbled country, but as pretty as you could ask for.

At the east end, we pulled up to look into Lampshire Canyon, part of the neighboring Kunde allotment. Upwind on the lip of a hill fifty feet near, stood a thick-necked, five-point Coues whitetail deer, looking in the opposite direction. The sun gleaming off its symmetrical antlers was a thing magnificent. We stood still for the length of a held breath until the wind changed direction and the big deer sprang sideways and disappeared as quickly as an eye blink.

"Must have heard an owl fart," I said, exhaling.

"Hello there," T.N. called after him. "Why don't I see you during hunting season?"

"The big bucks can read the seasons better than the weatherman. They don't get to be big by being dull."

This was US Forest Service land, but the entrance to it was controlled by the Rail X Ranch deeded land and Tom Hunt only let a few select friends cross over. This control over hunter entry made the ranch I had bought into a game preserve, not only for whitetail deer and javelina, but also Mearns quail, another local species.

The next set of heifers came from the same ranch, except they were the first generation F-1 Hereford cows crossed on Brahman bulls, the Nalore strain from Brazil noted for their fertility and ferocity. I had a carload of these bulls on another ranch and liked the F-1 females they produced, but the bulls had to be handled with caution. Their vertical-striped heifer off- spring were colored red-on-black with white faces, dark eyelashes above almond-colored eyes, and big horns that arched upward like ice tongs.

T. N. and I took delivery at the breeder's corrals, and then branded and trailered them to the Rail X shipping corrals and unloaded. I was pressed for time that week and decided we would drive them that same day to Red Bear pasture where they could settle with last year's bunch. What I didn't know was that the breeder worked these cattle with a mob of in- experienced riders, pushing his herd at a high lope until they ricocheted off a fence. When T. N. and I started the drive through Rail X's sacaton grass bottoms, the heifers scattered like flushed partridges. We spent the rest of the day gathering them by ones and twos, only to lose them again in the horse-high tall grass.

At sundown, T. N. left for home while I trailed my horse to the Rail X headquarters to talk to Tom Hunt. Tom was sitting on the glassed-in veranda of the Rail X big house, sipping a straight bourbon on the rocks.

"How do, Tom. I'm whipped," I said, as he poured me a drink.

"You look it, too," Tom replied with a grin on his face every place there was space for it. Tom was not swacked yet, just mellow, and he gave me a good-natured lecture on how spoiled cattle, especially Brahman crosses, don't forget how they've been handled just because their own- ership changed. They expected to be chased as they had been every time they encountered a human on horseback.

Over the next week. I worked them one-by-one into a smaller trap where they had to come to water inside a corral. Every morning, I drove them to a corner of the trap and rode away after they had settled down. If they sprinted away, I circled around to hold them up, then rode off while they looked at me, confused at not being chased. Every evening, I herded them to water and fed hay as a treat. Call it bribery. After two weeks, T. N. and I drove them to Red Bear tank and left them on top of the highest hill in sight of the other cattle.

"Cows," T. N. started the lecture as we rode back to the truck, "have cloven hooves, like goats and desert bighorn sheep. They are shod for rock climbing."

"So what's the point?" I chinned back.

"Horses evolved on open plains with single hooves. They are designed for skimming over flat terrain. Those Brahman crosses can outrun our horses in the rocks every time unless we outsmart them."

The bottom-line lesson was that to work cattle efficiently, the cowboy had to be smarter than the cow; call it another lesson in humility. John Donaldson, an astute cattleman who operated the seventy-five-thousand-acre Empire Ranch in nearby Pima County, remarked that Brahman cattle were more intelligent than some of today's yearning cowboys who believed that virtuosity in the art of the cowherd required them to always whoop and holler and give chase.

Before long, the F-1 Hereford-Brahman cross heifers got scarce because they were in high demand. I found a rancher in Gila County who had to cut back his herd on orders from the US Forest Service. For the next two years, I bought his F-1 heifers and sent them to a cutting horse trainer to settle them down.

A century ago, the cutting horse had been an essential tool on the ranch. Back then, cutting the herd and sorting out individual cows was done in big, open country, instead of in corrals like today. While the outside riders held up the big bunch, the cow boss rode through the herd on the cutting horse, sorting out culls, cripples, unbranded slick-ear calves, anything that needed to be worked, or strays.

Today, cutting has developed into sporting event based on the cow's natural instinct to rejoin the herd. The cutting horse's job is to disallow that. Cattle who are "cut on" are never run or chased. Instead, the cutting horse works them gently out of the herd and then blocks them from returning. The duck and dodge of the cow and the horse's counter moves create a ballet on horseback that demonstrates the incredible athleticism of both creatures. The cows learn to honor the horse that is blocking its way back to her buddies. But once she is in the herd, she stays put. When I got my heifers back from the cutting horse trainer, they honored my horse, preferred to stay bunched up, and weighed fifty pounds heavier. They were so tame I could have driven them into our living room but they probably would have kicked a hole in the TV. When T. N. and I put them out on the ranch, we drove them to the sharp-edged limestone hills above

Dark Canyon where they stayed until we weaned their first calves. They understood that rock pile as home. Any time I was missing a full count at roundup, I could find the truants browsing there in the shin dagger agave.

When the F-1 Brahman-Hereford heifers became impossible to find, I turned to Tom Hunt for new stock. Tom liked to experiment with different breeds. Unlike many older cattlemen who stick with one breed for a lifetime, he understood the value of hybrid vigor that results from crossbreeding. Tom's basic cow herd was Red Angus purchased from reputable breeders in Wyoming and Montana. But he also tinkered with purebred Red Brahman bulls and cows, the bloodline originating from the Gyr state of India.

Near as I could tell, Tom's tinkering was uncontrolled; regardless of breed, he ran all the cows and bulls together. This "omelet" approach produced calves that could be straight Red Angus, 50:50 cross between Red Angus and Red Brahman, or straight Red Brahman. I often rode through his cattle to get to my pastures, and never once saw a Red Brahman bull breed a cow. Even so, the herd produced fifty-fifty F-1 cross calves out of proportion to the number of Red Brahman bulls. Tom claimed these bulls were shy and bred mostly at night, like another well-known species he mentioned in passing.

Tom's F-1 heifers interested me because of their moderate size, ability to travel long distances to feed and water, resistance to pinkeye, insects, and heat. Every year at fall roundup, Tom selected out the top twenty-five of the F-1 heifers for my replacements. The price was always the same; sometimes I paid a premium over market; sometimes I paid less. These were by far the best adapted cattle I ever ran in the Canelo hills; long-legged, big-footed, mountain-climbers and good foragers, moderate in temperament unless protecting their offspring. Their rangy bodies had vertical tiger stripes, black on a cherry red background, with floppy ears, long narrow faces and tails. Mixed in with Tom's Red Angus, they stood out like tall flowers in a field of short, red cabbage.

One tiger-striped old lady traveled the range with a sacred circumference around her and her calf. It was not a circle of fear, like most cattle have. Riding into her space was a quick, sure ticket to trouble. Luckily, she had no horns but her thousand pounds packed a wallop. My horses learned to recognize her on sight and shied away, but new riders got the "bumper" treatment, a source of endless amusement to the regular cowhands. Bumper could only be driven with another bunch of cows where she stayed up with the leaders. To look at, she was not pretty, but I grew inordinately fond of her, especially in the fall when she always weaned a decent calf.

In the Canelo Hills, fine feathers did not make a fine bird.

But when crossed with a straight Red or Black Angus bull the F-1 cows produced a three-quarter English breed calf, smoky black-red in color that thrived even in poor feed conditions, weaned big, and brought a good price at the sale barn. Best of all, Tom Hunt's heifers had grown up on the same kind of rocks, eating the same grasses as they would on my ranch, adapted from birth to the same environment. Plus, they were fertile and long-lived. I had several cows that produced calves every year for a dozen years and still had teeth left in their mouths.

"That's the advantage of environmental adaptation," T. N. asserted. "It is the most underrated factor in cattle production in the arid southwest."

Sometimes, newbies will buy a ranch, restock with cattle carrying the "best" genes from Nebraska, California, or Iowa, and then go to the cattleman's club bar and commence to brag on all the big calves they would

Red Brahman cow with calf.

wean that fall. When the next year rolls around, their calf crop is poor and those "best " cows have turned into a tapestry of bones—sore-footed and open, meaning they had given up on motherhood for the coming year.

All ranchers worry that their first-calf heifers will have problems giving birth; the calf too big to pass through the birth canal, or the fetus turned in the wrong direction. Luckily, bulls come with a variety of heritable characteristics, including some genetically engineered for siring calves with low birth weights. In my broken, brushy country, I didn't very often find a heifer in time to assist if she was having trouble giving birth. So all my bulls carried the low-birth-weight genes that produced small baby calves, allowing the big cross-bred heifers to handle their first bout with motherhood without my help.

Even so, the Brahman cross-bred cows came with one distasteful defect. As they grew older and had more calves, the muscle fibers in their uterine wall weakened and stretched. Sometimes, when calving time approached and they strained to pee or have the calf, their uterus pooped outside. Repairing a prolapse required that the cow be restrained while I stuffed her uterus back in and took stitches across her vulva, leaving a hole at the bottom where she could pee. After suffering through this inglorious obstetrical procedure, the ungrateful cow was usually on the prod. The most dangerous part of the operation from the cowboy surgeon's perspective was getting back on the horse or over the fence before cow got there first. Fortunately, T. N. , our cowboy fertility specialist, eliminated the prolapse problem by supplementing with selenium to strengthen the cow's smooth muscles.

iii

Cow work in the Canelo Hills required a rugged type of cow horse. My best ever was Bird. Bird was a bay roan gelding with a Roman nose, crested neck, and four solid black hooves. Tom Hunt remarked that Bird's head was so long that he could drink out of the bottom of a fifty-gallon barrel and still look you in the eye. Foaled in 1991 in South Dakota on the big Cheyenne Sioux reservation; sired by Sir Fancy Bird out of the mare, Toby Country, herself an own daughter of the renowned ranch horse stallion Roan Bar Country. By the tape, Bird measured 15.2 hands tall (62 inches), had a 27-inch forearm diameter, and weighed in at 1270 pounds. I rode him for sixteen years and he never lost a shoe, never missed a day's work, never needed a vet, stayed fat on native grass, and never became friendly. Even after we had worked together for years, Bird's dark eyes followed me suspiciously each time I entered the corral, as if remembering an old grievance. Think of Mike Tyson, the heavyweight boxer, and you will get the picture.

In 1995, we needed ranch horses. Rich was in between semesters at college so we drove to a horse auction in Vernon, Texas. The catalog listed lots of high class horses, including twenty two-year-olds from the renowned 6666 outfit that had already been started in the saddle. The night we arrived, a funnel cloud dropped out of an angry sky and wiped out the Dairy Queen down the road from our cheap motel while we cowered in the bathroom, listening to the windows rattle.

"We want geldings, black hooves, no buckers, single branded, and under four years old," I said as we sat in the grandstand the next morning to watch the horses work and make our picks.

"Why only one brand?" Rich asked.

"Two brands mean two owners and two rejections," I replied.

"We need to look at their legs, too," Rich said.

"Durn tooten. Legs, legs, and more legs. Also backs. Long-backed horses will eventually break down climbing up them Canelo Hills," I said. Later, we walked into their stalls and weeded out the ones with poor conformation and soft white hooves that might go lame on the rocks.

The horse demonstrations carried on into the late afternoon: first, the dry work of loping figure-eight circles, changing leads, stop and back-up;

followed by roping, cutting and sorting cattle. We picked out a dozen that would work, including three of the gray-colored colts from the 6666 Ranch. Bird had caught our eye with his massive, muscular build, but he had two brands on the left hip, the Flying U Bar and a Seven Four Connected, so we rated him as "Maybe." His rider, a skinny Texan with a cheek-full of Red Man, trotted him around the arena and rode into the roper's box, swinging his lariat. The steer broke hard and Bird broke harder, overtaking it in the middle of the arena. The rider picked up on the reins to rate the horse behind the steer, but Bird passed up the cow and ricocheted off the back fence. The roper turned pale and swallowed his chew.

"Maybe not," Rich said.

The sale started at ten the next morning. We drove to the sale barn through a field of oil wells nodding like gigantic grasshoppers.

"Texas looks like a good place to be rich in. All privately owned land and no US Forest Service to put up with," I said in passing as we drove into the parking lot in front of the sale barn.

"Cash, check, or money order; no credit cards, and the buyers beware," the auctioneer announced in the barn as we took our seats up in the rafters. "All guarantees are between the buyer and seller." Everyone knew that, of course, but to drive home the point, the auctioneer laid on a joke:

City man drove by the rancher's corrals and saw a horse he liked. Said: "I'll give you one thousand dollars for that good looking horse. Rancher replied: "No, he don't look so good. City man said: "Well then if that don't suit you, I'll give you one thousand five hundred dollars." Rancher said: "OK, but he don't look so good." Next week the city man came back, spitting mad: "You sold me a blind horse." Rancher replied: "I told you he don't look so good."

By mid-afternoon the sale was almost over and we hadn't bought any blind horses, or anything else. Our selections were everyone else's pick and the three gray colts we liked best went for ten thousand dollars each. The prices were way out of our range. The skinny Texan rode Bird into the sale ring as cautious and mute as turtle with his rope coiled up tight to the saddle horn. No one spoke. I couldn't go home empty-handed, so I threw up my hand.

"Dad, he's all yours," Rich said. "I'm going back to school."

At home in the corral, Bird did not look like he was intent on murder or mayhem; he just wanted to get away. On the ground, he escaped the halter by running head first into a corner of the corral, his massive hindquarters pointing ominously towards me. I stepped to one side to give him a way out and tapped his butt with the rope. He wheeled away to the next corner where we repeated the maneuver. Around we went for an hour until we were both tired. When I next raised the rope, Bird suddenly turned and faced me. Each morning we went through the same routine except that it grew shorter and shorter until one morning he faced up when I walked into his corral.

The first time we gathered cattle, Bird's natural tendency to run off got us into a pickle. We rounded a big limestone hill at a trot when a speckled cow with droopy horns jumped from behind a juniper thicket. Bird took the bit between his iron jaws and jumped after her. The cow ducked off, but we kept on going straight at a high lope. The only way around this problem, I decided, was to go through it. I grabbed the uphill rein with both hands and pulled Bird upslope. We clattered through the brush, his iron shoes striking sparks from the granite boulders. A quarter-mile later, we reached the top of the mountain where Bird finally came to a halt, lathered out, flanks heaving and right on the edge of the thumps. Stopping had to be his idea.

Over the next two years, Bird became more tractable but never tame. He spooked at the sound of the lariat rope sizzling on the saddle horn; he hated the feel of the rope touching his hindquarters when dragging a steer. That fear won us a roping and a hand-tooled breast collar one time; another time it almost killed me when dragging calves to the branding fire.

Once we got used to each other, I grew to appreciate Bird's incredible athleticism as well as his stamina. He could, I thought, develop into a high-level head horse for the team roping event. As soon as I got him over the run-away stuff, I took him to Jim and Jimmy Paul, a father-and-son team of horse trainers in Cave Creek renowned for training good cow horses.

To sit with Jim and Jimmy after the day's training sessions were over and listen to the give-and-take about what each horse needed seemed like taking lessons from the masters of an ancient practice, an unwritten curriculum passed down to father and son and perfected only through first-hand experience. The horse always has a reason for its behavior, Jim often remarked. Horsemen have the duty to work with those instincts instead of against them. For Bird, the corrections always came in small doses:

"He needs time to think it over," they said.

Consistency was the key, repeating the same moves over and over, day after day, until they were built into Bird's muscle memory, like the automatic moves of a gymnast or figure skater. Gradually, Bird absorbed the lesson that instead of outrunning the steer, he could instead rate up behind and follow it out of the arena. After that, Jimmy re-introduced him to the rope by gently swinging it as he followed the steer. The rope part took Bird a long time to get used to, but eventually he figured it out.

Team roping approximates roping on the range where the safest position to work on a sick cow is when two cowboys have roped the head and heels and stretched the critter snug between their horses. At rodeos, a horned steer is held in a chute between the header on the left side and the heeler on the right. When the steer is released, the header runs and ropes it around the horns, takes a turn around the saddle horn with the loose end of the rope. With the steer caught, the header makes a ninety degree turn to the left, pulling the cow behind him. The heeler ducks in and scoops up the hind feet with his rope and stops. The head horse pulls until the steer is stretched out between each horse and then whirls and faces the steer and the flag is dropped for time.

In rodeo competition, money is won by the team with the fastest time. But at the horse shows, the horse, not the rider, is judged on how well they perform each basic maneuver. In ninety days, Bird learned all the moves well enough to show off. So we entered the big Arizona Sun Circuit show held every winter in Scottsdale, Arizona.

I nodded for the gate and Bird broke like a rocket from the starting box, rated back behind the steer until I roped it, and then took hold of the six hundred pound critter as if it were a balloon, and turned off. Jimmy on the heels swooped in and scooped up two hind feet and stopped his horse. Coming tight with the ropes against the steer, Bird sank down on his hocks and spun around on his hind feet like a ballet dancer, so quick and smooth that the spectators gasped in amazement. After the event was over, the blue ribbon breast collar adorned Bird's saddle.

That was our one shining moment together. We retired undefeated, not because our win was a fluke, but because we had other work to do. Show horses are pampered creatures whose lives are spent lounging on wood shavings, practiced on every day by their trainers to stay sharp, ridden bareback by lovely ladies stricken with "Hippophilia." Oftentimes, their owners are cowboys or cowgirls of convenience. In Texas and Oklahoma, amenity ranchers fill up the horse show arenas—good old boys struggling to get by on a few hundred thousand dollars a month from their oil wells. In Scottsdale and the West Coast shows, the entry lists are dominated by business executives, building contractors, dentists, doctors, and real estate promoters.

Who can blame them? They aspire to partake in the rites of the ancient collaboration between horse and human and uphold the myth of the American west without the pain of saddle sores or eating dust from riding drag. The kind of work Bird and I did daily was not beneficial for the high level of competence needed in the show ring. Also, Bird was not show horse pretty with his Roman nose, long head, and big feet.

"The judges," Jimmy said, "have to separate the crowd on something, and in the big shows, lots of times it's a beauty pageant."

Bird was a blue collar worker, the kind Eric Hoffer, the longshoreman philosopher, would appreciate, and working cowboys would fight over to have in their string. The judges had been momentarily mesmerized by his strength and agility. So we went home and Bird reverted to his job as an animated tool: indispensable, respected, and well cared for. And sharp enough, although Bird made me pay one day when I got careless.

"Things that don't happen for years happen in a second," the Mexican *vaqueros* say. Drum Hadley, a borderland rancher and poet, recalled true tales of incautious horsemen in his verse. A green horse flips over backward and drives the saddle horn through the rider's belly. Or the rider gets kicked in the head when upon dismounting the spurs get tangled in his horse's tail. Or the guillotine trick where the runaway horse scrapes the rider off under a low-branched tree.

On a dry day in June, we were branding calves at the Lazy RR Ranch lease, Diane and I were joined by Manuel Murrietta, and neighbors Fred and Deborah Fellows. Deborah and Fred were renowned western artists who liked to stay close to their subject matter by helping with ranch work. There were enough museums and cultists of the American west to make a fine living with their superb painting and sculpture. Manuel, a young cowboy who had just finished the semester at Cochise College, was real handy with a rope, inside or outside of the arena.

The foothill ridges of the Santa Rita Mountains ran up to the base of Mount Wrightson like the backbones of dinosaurs. We had spent the morning scraping the cow-calf pairs off the ridges and driving them into the corrals in Stevens Canyon. The cows were a burly Beefmaster breed, a little snorty, their calves Angus-sired, and big. One-by-one, we heeled and drug each calf to the fire where Manuel and I worked them over; branding, vaccinating, and castrating the bulls.

By the time we finished, Bird and I were both in a sweat and tired. I had coiled my rope loosely over the saddle horn, the loop hanging down close to the right stirrup. Getting down, my right spur caught in the loop and pulled it over Bird's butt as I stepped off. The feel of the rope against his hide and the sizzle of nylon against the saddle horn spooked him into a panicky flight. Too late to remount, I suddenly realized that I was in for a drag, so I leaned back as the rope tightened around my ankle. Bird sped out of the corral and pulled me flat on my back around the corner in a cloud of dust just like I was one of the calves.

By the sheer luck of herd instinct, Bird made a left turn and ran up to the other horses and stopped while Manuel cut the rope. Had he turned right into the pasture, I would have been a new stanza in Drum's chapbook. As it was, the Devil just wasted another loop.

Cowboy stories are often elegies because the lives of our horses and cow dogs are short compared to ours. So our best friends are always passing on. After sixteen years, Bird developed ringbone in his feet, an arthritis-like condition. I turned him out to pasture where he lived out his final years in tall grass where he could see long distances and be with other horses.

Whenever I looked at Bird, I saw a powerful equine athlete with incredible stamina. What he saw in me, I can't say for sure, but I have ideas. "A horse always remembers the first thing the human does to it," said Ray Hunt, a renowned horseman of the old school. And the last, I should add. Behind every spoiled horse is the son-of-a-bitch that spoiled him. My only regret was that I didn't catch the one who taught Bird to fear the rope alone in a stall with the butt end of a lariat.

3

Tar Paper and Tin Shacks

Ever since moving to Sonoita, I've tried to figure how this wind-blown and slope-skewed country evolved into a place where families wanted to settle down. Yes, the landscapes are jaw-dropping with the "sky island" mountains towering over an expansive grassland. Even so, the high desert lacks water and has little shelter from the blowtorch winds, soggy summer heat, and winter's cold. Native Americans built their wickiups down in the canyons to be close to water and for protection from the weather. Later, the Mexican and Anglo pioneers built their adobe huts in the same places and for the same reasons. Today, most people still do. Only recently have a few ex-urbanites built on hilltop and ridgeline, their curious-looking castles strangely out of place.

Native Americans, the Pima-speaking Sobiapuris among them, lived down canyon for a thousand years, spacing their brush huts along the rivers and marshes where they planted the American triad crops of corn, beans, and squash. In the winter and spring, they roamed the mountains to hunt and gather wild food; mesquite beans, agave, prickly pear, deer, rabbits, rats, grasshoppers, and the like.

About the twelfth century, another group of Native Americans speaking a different language started moving down from the north. These were the Athapascans, eventually called Apache and Navajo. By the 1500s, the Apache had moved into southern and eastern Arizona and the Mexican Sierra Madre Occidental. A mountain people, they lived in small, matriarchal clans of a dozen or two individuals. Hunting and raiding their neighbors formed the basis of their economy and culture. That quickly made the Apache bitter enemies of the resident tribes. Even in the twentieth century, O'odham elders told stories of their battles and retained the Apache scalps taken in revenge.

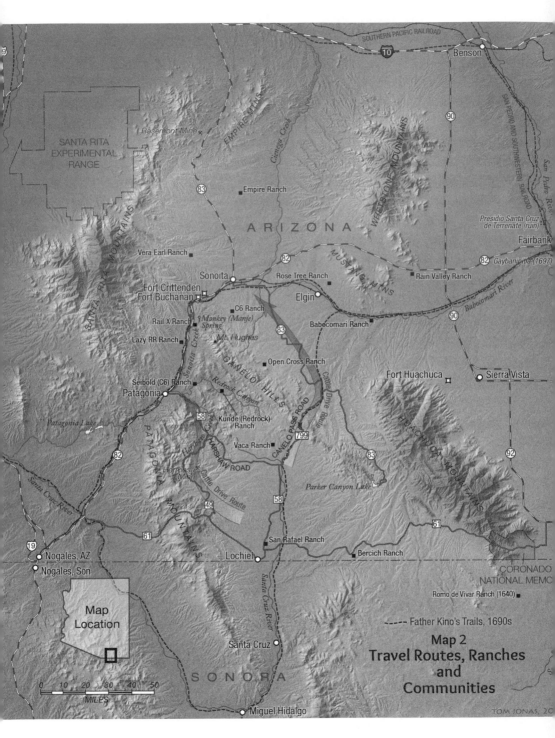

SOUTHERN PACIFIC RAILROAD

Benson

SANTA RITA
EXPERIMENTAL
RANGE

Rosemont Mine

Cienega Creek

EMPIRE MTNS.

ARIZONA

WHETSTONE MOUNTAINS

SAN PEDRO AND SOUTHWESTERN RAILROAD

San Pedro River

Presidio Santa Cruz
de Terrenate (ruin)

Empire Ranch

Fairbank

Vera Earl Ranch

Sonoita

Rose Tree Ranch

MUSTANG MTNS.

Gaybanipitea (1697)

Rain Valley Ranch

Babocomari River

SANTA RITA MOUNTAINS

Fort Crittenden
Fort Buchanan

Elgin

C6 Ranch

Rail X Ranch

Monkey (Manje)
Spring

Lazy RR Ranch

Mt. Hughes

Babocomari Ranch

Sonoita Creek

CANELO HILLS

Open Cross Ranch

Fort Huachuca

Sierra Vista

Seibold (C6) Ranch

Patagonia

Redrock Canyon

Cattle Drive Ridge

CANELO PASS ROAD

HUACHUCA MOUNTAINS

Patagonia Lake

58

Kunde (Redrock)
Ranch

PATAGONIA MOUNTAINS

Vaca Ranch

799

HARSHAW ROAD

Hermosa
Mine

Cattle Drive Route

Parker Canyon Lake

58

83

92

82

49

Santa Cruz River

61

San Rafael Ranch

Bercich Ranch

61

19

Nogales, AZ

Nogales, Son

Lochiel

CORONADO
NATIONAL MEMO

Santa Cruz River

Romo de Vivar Ranch (1640)

Map
Location

- - - - Father Kino's Trails, 1690s

Santa Cruz

Map 2
**Travel Routes, Ranches
and
Communities**

0 10 20 30 40 50
MILES

SONORA

Miguel Hidalgo

TOM JONAS, 20

Next came the Spanish conquistadores and Jesuit priests. The industrious Father Eusebio Francisco Kino arrived in the borderlands in 1687, bringing livestock, horses, and new crops to help win over the natives to the Catholic faith. By 1701, he had established five mission ranches and was running 4,200 head of cattle strung out over hundreds of square miles of what later became the states of Sonora and Arizona.

That accomplishment still astonishes anyone who operates a ranch as I did. Kino not only had to cover an enormous swath of rugged Sonoran Desert, but he had to do so using Native Americans who had never seen a cow or horse, much less ride and take care of them. It would be as if I suddenly had five big ranches to run with teenagers recruited from the inner cities of Chicago and New York. The American west's pioneer cattlemen, much celebrated in legend and song, had nothing on the energetic Jesuit.

On his travels, Kino often rode overland between two desert rivers he named the Santa Cruz and the San Pedro. On one excursion Kino rode west from the San Pedro River at Fairbank, up the Babocomari River drainage until he reached the Sonoita plain and the Sonoita Creek headwaters, and then southwest to the Santa Cruz River. In fact, many of today's travel routes follow the trails first blazed by the indefatigable padre on horseback (see map 2).

From that beginning, the culture and economy of the region have been based on ranching. Big time commercial cattle ranching moved to the Sonoita range after the 1820s Mexican war of independence from Spain. The fledgling Mexican government rewarded its elite soldiers with vast grants of land. The Elias Gonzales family from Arizpe, Sonora, became owners of the Babocomari Land Grant down the river of the same name to its junction with the San Pedro, thirty-five miles long and five miles wide, for which they paid about three hundred sixty dollars. They also held grants on the San Pedro River from about where the Mexican border is located today almost to Interstate 10. With no fencing and no one else claiming the open range, Elias Gonzales grazed thousands of cattle (some say as many as forty thousand head) over a third of a million acres, nearly five hundred square miles.

But the Apaches deemed the Mexicans and their cattle easy prey. And they did not appreciate the invasion of their sacred homelands by foreigners.

During the next decades, they hunted down the Mexican's cattle and
horses like they would any other kind of wild game. By the 1840s, they
had killed two of the Elias brothers and all of their *vaqueros*. The Mexicans
fled back to their fortified towns in northern Sonora and Chihuahua,
abandoning their northern ranching empire. The Apaches then ruled
southern Arizona until after the US Civil War, and even beyond.

After the Gadsden Purchase in 1853 made southern Arizona part of
the United States, the US Army established cavalry posts to protect the
Anglo miners and ranchers moving in to stake their claims. Locally, Fort
Buchanan (1853–1861) guarded the Sonoita Creek area until the wetlands
made the soldiers sick (probably from mosquito-transmitted malaria) and
drove them out of the Sonoita marsh the Mexicans called *ciénega*. The
army rebuilt the fort eastward a few miles closer to Sonoita and renamed it
Fort Crittenden. This time, the massive accumulation of horse dung and
attendant filth flies spread dysentery among the soldiers. After nine years,
the army abandoned Sonoita Creek for good, moving to Fort Wallen,
which later became Fort Huachuca. By 1886, the army had finally de-
feated the Apaches and forced most of the survivors onto the squalid San
Carlos Reservation.

The buildup of large-scale Anglo ranching in Southern Arizona coin-
cided with the coming of the railroads. The Southern Pacific line pushed
through Tucson and Benson in 1881, connecting southern Arizona
with Texas, the Middle West, and California. A railroad spur down the
San Pedro River linked the main line to the burgeoning copper mines
in Bisbee and Douglas. Mindful of freighting business in Nogales and
Mexico, a year or so later the railroad laid a spur from the Bisbee line at
Fairbank westward up the Babocomari drainage, following Father Kino's
horse trails over the high Sonoita plain, then southwest along Sonoita
Creek to Patagonia. With the railroad, Texas ranchers shipped in thousands of cattle into the rich Southern Arizona rangelands. The shipping
corrals on the railroad to load cattle attracted the tar paper and tin shack
settlement that eventually became Sonoita.

When automobiles first appeared, their rude dirt tracks mostly followed the railroad. The road through Sonoita officially became State
Highway 82 in 1927, and with it Sonoita town a possibility. But to reach

Tucson, traffic had to make a long detour southwest through Nogales. A shortcut northward off the highlands and down Davidson Canyon cut ninety miles off the journey. In 1929, this became State Highway 83 and Sonoita was fixed at the crossroads. Nowadays, these two highways are designated as "scenic routes."

Unlike Sonoita, Patagonia developed around the floodplain at the confluence of Sonoita Creek and Harshaw Creek, a place with human settlement for at least the past eight thousand years. Patagonia had year-round water, fertile soil, woodland for fuel and houses, and was sheltered by a ring of low hills, all the requirements needed for a frontier settlement. In the early years of Anglo ranching, the bigger outfits in the San Rafael Valley drove their cattle through Canelo Pass to the Sonoita railroad shipping pens. The smaller outfits on the west side of the valley and in the Patagonia Mountains made their drives down Harshaw Creek to Patagonia, picking up small bunches on the way.

The Patagonia and nearby Santa Rita Mountains also had considerable mining activity early on. With the railroad, Patagonia developed into a full-fledged western frontier town with homes, stores, schools, churches, livery stables, hotels, rooming houses, watering hole saloons, and brothels. Even now, across from the Patagonia Public Library on 342 Duquesne Avenue, a faded sign advertising Lopez Pool Hall hangs on a crumbling adobe building that housed a blacksmith shop restoring horse-drawn wagons from the previous century. The old Cady House Hotel became Patagonia's library, now stocked with a decent collection of southwestern history and cowboy lore.

Incorporated officially in 1898, Patagonia developed as a supply and freight hub for the mines and nearby ranches. Miners' families lived in town in tin-roofed shacks while the menfolk labored like moles down the mine shafts away from home for weeks at a time. The freight business employed muleteers, wagon masters, and chandler shops, many of them run by Mexicans, shipping ore to the smelters in Douglas and El Paso, and cattle all over the country.

The freight business died in 1962 when Patagonia shipped its last ore and the railroad was abandoned. The train depot became the Patagonia Town Hall. Giant semi-trucks took over cattle transport, fifty thousand pounds to a load. Today, the citizenry is a hybrid borderland culture made up of remnant mining and ranching families, many of them Hispanics; native southern Arizonans hunkered down in their modest homes along quiet village streets. Other more recent immigrants include New Age and aging hippies, pony-tailed veterans of the eco-wars, writers, retired academics, artists, and restoration ecologists; people who mix or don't mix with ranchers and the wealthy industrialists who prefer peace, quiet, and natural beauty to city life. But only a few have economic connections to the land. Some work out of their homes on the internet or commute to jobs in Nogales, Sierra Vista, or the University of Arizona.

Unlike Sonoita, Patagonia has rules: an elected town council; manager; sheriff; public utilities in the form of water, sewer, and garbage pick-up. The main street, Highway 83, runs past the high school where the speed limit is strictly enforced: day, night, and holidays. Speeding tickets are rumored to make up the lion's share of the town budget. The long distance produce trucks speeding from Nogales toward America's heartland also produce much of Patagonia's income.

Sometime in the 1960s, Anne C. Stradling landed in Santa Cruz County. She was a Wild Horse Annie from a wealthy back-east family who ran away to the West as a high-spirited teen. She married and wore out a couple of cowboys before settling down in Patagonia. She built the Stage Stop Hotel and the Museum of the Horse next door, filling the museum with buggies, wagons, harnesses, saddles, boots, spurs, and assorted horsey trappings. Carriage horses, preferably gray in color, were her favorites and she hooked a team to a wagon and drove down Main Street during the annual Fourth of July parade. Upon her death, she bequeathed her remaining fortune for the benefit of local youth and horse activities, for example, the royalty for Sonoita's Labor Day rodeo. In Sonoita, the queen and her attendants are selected less on looks and more on their riding skills and horse sense.

The Big Steer Bar was one of Patagonia's watering holes. Decorated with the dust-covered, decapitated head of a long-horned steer and flanked by a few old geezers who always sat at the far end of the mahogany bar. Anyone who entered got long stares as if geezers were cataloging the human race into new varieties. When the dudes from the local guest ranch dropped in, they shied away and huddled by the exit. Patagonia in recent years has attracted a colony of writers, including Jim Harrison, renowned for his novels, poetry, and prodigious capacity for food and drink. A couple of years after we took over the Seibold Ranch, a newbie bought the Big Steer and demolished it, an event that grieved the locals and found notice in one of Harrison's narratives. The new owner built a semi-elegant meeting hall in its place that was shunned by everyone but a few local "stoners," and soon closed. Jim moved to the Wagon Wheel Bar across the park to drown his grief.

The Nature Conservancy's nearby Sonoita Creek Preserve with year-round running water has become a famous bird-watching spot, even though the creek is fed by Patagonia's treated sewage. During the winter and spring, the Stage Stop Hotel fills up with birders, looking to add the Elegant Trogon and rare Gray Hawk to their life lists. On a recent day, I watched the inevitable clash of cultures on the Patagonia town square. Two local kids traipsed across the town park in front of the hotel carrying their guns and a brace of Montezuma quail for supper, while the birders, draped with high dollar Swarovski binoculars gasped in horror.

The Patagonia Mountains extending down to Mexico have been mined dating back to before Arizona statehood. But mining disappeared in the 1960s due to lower prices for metals and shrinking mineral deposits. As the miners left, artists and environmentalists moved in. Nowadays, the mines have returned, seeking governmental approval for new operations. This has created a fierce debate among Patagonia's citizenry. Families of the original settlers support renewed mining for jobs and to revive Patagonia's sagging economy.

The newcomers—conservationists, ecologists, and preservationists—as well as a few natives and ranchers, oppose mining on the grounds of rangeland destruction and watershed pollution. Historically, mines at best will make money in the short run, then leave the town and Santa Cruz County with a scarred landscape bleeding toxic residues downstream, as mining has always done. Patagonia's already abandoned mining operations still leak poisons into Harshaw Creek (not to mention at Bisbee, Arizona and Butte, Montana).

North of Sonoita in Pima County, the new Rosemont Mine is much further along in the permitting process. Rosemont will be a huge open pit operation, extracting copper from millions of tons of rock and dirt, dumping the overburden and residue into watersheds that feed into Cienega Creek and ultimately Tucson's water supply. Fiercely opposed by the majority of Pima County and Sonoita residents, Rosemont is on the cusp of governmental approval. When that happens, the lawsuits will begin. Years before, Pima County regrettably passed up the chance to buy Rosemont with the Sonoran Desert Conservation Plan bond money (more on this later).

Both mining operations are owned by foreign-based companies whose environmental histories are suspect. Opponents fear, with some reason, that these foreign companies will leave behind enormous eyesores and pollution problems for local governments to deal with. They have done so elsewhere, the opponents point out.

Ranching and mining are both in the business of extracting natural resources; grass and minerals. The difference is that mining by its very nature destroys the land, while grazing preserves the watersheds, if properly managed. Aldo Leopold observed a long time ago that land health is the land's inherent capacity for self-renewal. Ranching works to preserve that capacity in order for ranchers to survive. Mining, by its very nature, destroys it.

ii

Like the penstemon and prickly poppies that line the highways, Sonoita and Patagonia's human population comes and goes with the seasons. Some clear out for cooler places in Washington, Maine, or Montana when the temperatures creep above ninety degrees. But most of us have discovered that the summer rainy season is the most delicious time of the year and live here year-round.

Happily unincorporated, Sonoita has no elected local officials to pester the people's free spirit. Cops come infrequently from the Santa Cruz County Sheriff's office headquartered in Nogales on the Mexican border thirty-six miles to the southwest. An elected Justice of the Peace holds court in Sonoita's highway maintenance yard to settle domestic disputes and hand out fines for DUI and speeding. A US Border Patrol station houses three hundred pistoled agents but they seldom bother Sonoita residents unless they are packing weed when they pass through the checkpoint on Highway 83. Community boundaries are vague and may extend east and south to include the villages of Elgin and Canelo. The crossroads of state Highways 82 and 83 serves as Sonoita's center of gravity.

When we moved in, the crossroads had a bank, post office zip code 85637, hair dresser and barber, a half dozen cafes, a like number of realtors, and a gas station, feed store, garage, fire station, and accountant. Two or three wine-tasting bars served up local vintages, two lawyers handled the population's legal worries, and a scattering of retail shops peddled cowboy duds and Indian jewelry. The Steak-Out Saloon was and still is the local pleasure emporium featuring the best steaks in Santa Cruz County and live western music. On weekends, it fills up with aging motorcyclists from Tucson and Sierra Vista, their silver coiffures wrapped with colorful bandannas to offset black leather riding outfits.

Kitty-corner to the Steak-Out, the Mini-Mart sells groceries and snacks to complement a vast selection of beers and fancy, expensive booze. One morning when I drove to the Mini-Mart to pick up the Tucson newspaper and a fifty-cent cup of unadulterated coffee, I chanced to check the liquor stocks: Glenlivet scotch and Wild Turkey Rare Breed bourbon; Remy Martin and Dom Perignon brandies; Don Julio Anejo and Gran Patron tequilas; Gran Siele champagne, 50% Chardonnay and 50% Pinot Noir grapes (when my son announced his engagement, his cousin called up from Oregon and sent two bottles to the ranch); a wide selection of vodkas, rums, and gins, fine French and Napa Valley wines, plus locally produced vintages ranging from decent to horse-piss. I shouldn't fail to mention the deliciously venomous Sonoran mescals, including my favorite oil of joy, Agave Azul. That the well-known writer and bawdy celebrant-gourmand, Jim Harrison, and a scattering of retired millionaires spend their winters here boosts the Mini-Mart's high dollar sales. Even so, more beers pass out its doors than anything else, especially during rodeo weekends and when fishing is good on Patagonia Lake. During the annual horse races, horse show, county fair, and rodeo, only a hermit could fail to have fun at the Sonoita crossroads.

Highway 83 going north to Interstate 10 and Tucson winds treacherously down from the high Sonoita plain, a designated scenic highway of thirty-five miles. Once a month, more or less, a tipsy biker or two flies off an un-banked turn and the Medivac helicopter swoops in to pick up any survivors.

Sonoita has no at-home mail delivery. Residents pick up their mail at the local post office every day. That makes the post office a place where much important community business takes place. The parking lot fills at noon where people meet and exchange the latest gossip. The glass entry door serves as the local obituary column. When someone dies, the notice is taped on the door, usually with description of the deceased's history and survivors. Lately, I've quit reading them because often their birthdays are more recent than mine. Perhaps one day I'll go pick up the mail and find out that I too have passed on. The Patagonia post office used to fly the flag at half-mast when a pioneer died until the post office officials put a stop to that endearing local tradition.

Sonoita and Patagonia are hardly twin towns as can be seen in the 2010 census data. Sonoita's 818 people sprawl over ten square miles, or roughly eight acres per person, with about 17 percent Hispanic. Median family income was $58,571. In Patagonia, the population was 913, clustered on slightly less than one acre per person. Hispanics make up 40 percent of the population. Median family income was $31,000. One local wag when asked for the definition of the word "Patagonia" replied: "Too poor to live in Sonoita."

Even so, the income needle has tilted upward in Patagonia recently as some well-endowed newbies have moved in to take advantage of cheap seats on the bleachers of retirement. On a stroll down Patagonia's side streets one encounters mostly small to modest, open-front homes and house trailers, with a sprinkling of high walled, closed door, semi-mansions in between.

Love of the open, uncluttered landscape is shared by most folks who live in these parts. Also, most of us love horses, even though the number of ranchers who actually need them has dwindled to a dozen. These cherished, overfed, and underworked equines are mostly pets. They serve a variety of semi-essential functions; to carry their owners on jaunts over the rugged terrain; conversation pieces with fellow horse lovers about superior bloodlines; and these days, biofeedback mechanisms. Novelist and cutting horse rider Thomas McGuane observed how many horse lovers claim to have learned something important about themselves from their horses. Locally, horse whisperer psychologists make capital on the urge of horse owners to snuggle up to their trusty steeds by hosting expensive encounter sessions at the fairgrounds or private horse ranches.

The horse, once a utility item, has become a psychological aide-de-camp. Even so, the Stanford-trained historian turned cowhand Owen Ulph claimed that the horse is better understood as a congenital hysteric. Ulph got the congenital part correct. The horse has a built-in flight mechanism evolved as a prey animal on the open plains. While it is true that Sigmund Freud developed the clinical definition of hysteria while treating a frenzied human, no one ever saw a horse lying on Doctor Freud's couch. The horse comes by its excessive volatility honestly with the consequence that horses are accident prone. This makes the cowboy feel like pawing the dirt when his best horse is laid up just as the big Labor Day rodeo rolls around. Even so, the horse is not a hypocrite and is preferable company to sullen cow critters and bad-tempered people.

Throughout southern Arizona, a subculture of rodeo and roping enthusiasts thrives. Team roping was once big in Sonoita. A few years ago, it took place once a month or so at the fairgrounds with hundreds of teams and big money up for grabs. One prominent rancher sponsored a Fourth of July Rainmaker event. In 2002, I won the saddle on the good horse Stormytiptop. It rained the next week.

But the recession and soaring hay and cattle prices have put a severe crimp in the roping action. Nowadays, the event has become the occasional fundraiser for worthy causes, like an injured cowboy or family member. For a short while, mounted shooting caught on. Riders with hog-leg, frontier-type pistols strapped on their bodies or stuffed in their belts gallop through a maze of stakes, each one with a balloon tied to the top. The gunman or gunwoman who shoots the most balloons wins the prize. Their pistols fire blanks but they make so much noise that the riders have to stuff cotton in their horse's ears. That oddball fad seems to have dwindled, at least locally.

Even so, horseflesh and the tradition of equine competition remains a strong magnet. The Canelo Cowboy Church holds rodeo events one Sunday a month to bring in the faithful and anyone else who wants to have horse-based fun and donate to the plate. The pastor, Steve Lindsey, a fourth-generation rancher who hung up his spurs to become an emissary of the Almighty, built a rodeo arena first, even before the sanctuary. Kids ride sheep (mutton busting), youngsters practice roping skills, and father-daughter, father-son, wife-husband teams bond with each other, and with their horses, in the roping competition.

Sonoita had a stable of colorful characters when we first arrived. Doctor Jim Pickrell was a legendary veterinary who practiced out of his pickup truck, driving to far-flung ranches for barn calls. I first knew him in the 1970s when I studied in the University of Arizona's Animal Pathology Department in Tucson. In those days, Doc Pickrell lived in Nogales and practiced on both sides of the border. Every Thursday, he came through our laboratory door carrying a stinking carcass or tissue sample, singing his favorite borderland ditty:

My name is Poncho, I work on a rancho,
I make one dollar a day.
I go to see Suzy, She is a doozy, and
She take my dollar away.

While Dr. Ray Reed, the pathologist, cut open the corpse to look for clues to its demise, Pickrell recited all the jokes he had heard the previous week, laughing raucously at each one until he had us all rolling on the floor of the

Schantz Building. In the two years I worked there, I never heard the same yarn twice. As the years wore on, Pickrell's posture grew more and more into an "L" shape from bending over to treat his patients, displaying the crease between his buttocks. No matter, the good Doctor could be trusted to come when called to an emergency and sit up all night to save a colicky horse.

Henry Dojaquez was Sonoita's local rememberancer, a storehouse of cowboy and ranch lore. Born in 1917, Henry worked for many years on the Larrimore ranch that spanned the eastern foothills of the Santa Rita Mountains. As wide-bodied as he was short, Henry was as stout as a weathered stump, with nut brown skin color. During the Great Depression he built fence and erosion checks for the Civilian Conservation Corps on the newly formed Coronado National Forest: shelter, food, and clothing for thirty dollars a month, about the same as cowboy wages. The CCC stonemason handiwork still holds back the soil in the gullies on my Crittenden pasture after more than eighty years. He cut native grass for cattle feed during the wet years, watched the homesteaders horse-plow the thin soil, try and fail to make a crop, only to sell out to cattlemen to end their predicaments. He remembers a dairy out on Curly Horse Ranch Road that ran a few cows and home-delivered the milk in a horse drawn buggy. He met Tom Hunt when he first came out of Cochise County, tall, rail thin, and riding a good horse. Henry recalled one night at the local saloon when the still smiling Tom decked a boozed-up biker.

"I could see it coming and backed away from the bar," Henry said. "That hippie went too far bad-mouthing Tom's straw hat and ended up on the floor, out cold with one punch."

Even as he passed beyond the age of ninety-five years, Henry remained an ace poker player, called Full House Henry. The odds of drawing a full house in seven card stud poker, the game most commonly played in these parts, is thirty-seven to one. Even so, during many four-hour games, Henry would often beat those odds several times over. His ploy was to lay in wait, his face inscrutable while the others bet up the pot on three of a kind or a straight. When the hand was called and everyone showed their cards, Henry would declare "Full Boat" and lay down his cards with a flourish. As the other card sharks cursed and whined, Henry reached out his stubby fingers to rake in the cash.

Sonoita also had several stables of renowned running quarter horses, so called for their quick starts and speed over the one quarter mile distance. Art Pollard owned the famed stallion Lightning Bar that sired so many winners that he was voted into the Quarter Horse Hall of Fame. Jim Kelly, who graduated from the University of Arizona's renowned race track program, had a stable full of fast horses and owned a fractional interest in Dash for Cash for breeding to his mares. Jim named his horses after rock stars. Mars Blackman won almost four hundred thousand dollars and was the National Champion three-year-old colt of 1995. Other local breeders included Ruben Murrietta and his son Manuel, Blain and Jimmy Lewis, and Gene and Ginny Sparks, horsemen and women whose horses won on the local Arizona racing circuit.

Sonoita's Labor Day rodeo drew competitors from all over the southwest. Its large arena gave the roping cattle a big head start and required a rope horse that could really run. I competed there when I lived in the grime and crime of Phoenix while attending Arizona State University. As I crawled up Highway 83 pulling my homemade, one-horse trailer with an underpowered six-cylinder Dodge, I topped out on the pass in the Empire Mountains and was instantly captivated by the wide-open, uncluttered view. The truck had overheated so I pulled over and gazed at the open expanse of grassland encircled by high desert peaks. Exhilarated by a sudden rush of freedom, I don't remember how the rodeo came out; whether I won anything or not, but I remember that panorama as fresh today as fifty years ago. I vowed then that I would own and live on a piece of this country if I could ever scrape enough money together.

iii

Sonoita's social center has always been its fairgrounds. Ranchers Bob Bowman and Posy Piper compiled its intriguing history in the Bowman Historical Archives at the fairgrounds for all to read. At the beginning of the twentieth century, the isolated ranchers and settlers began to gather at the crossroads once a year for horse races, roping contests, pot-luck suppers, and a dance. The first rodeo arena was formed by parking cars and wagons in a big circle. Weather and cattle prices topped the local conversations. Much important business was transacted, like who was the best roper or bronc rider or who got bragging rights for the best horse, bull, or tomatoes of the year.

In 1915, the Santa Cruz County Fair and Rodeo Association drew up articles of incorporation and issued ten thousand shares of stock at one dollar each. The stockholders became the association's board of directors, who served as unpaid volunteers. Sonoita rancher Wade Purdum donated ten acres of land, provided that a fair be held annually for the

Aerial view of Sonoita Crossroads with fairgrounds in center.

next twenty years. These acts of community service and generosity guided how fairgrounds business would be conducted to this day. The fairground is owned and operated by its membership, a source of great local pride. It receives no funds from Santa Cruz County or the state, except for a pittance to help put on the kids' 4-H Fair every September.

Today, its events include: horse races held on Kentucky Derby day with live betting and simulcasting; quarter horse show first held in 1916 and now the oldest in the nation; Labor Day rodeo, voted the best little rodeo in the state with over seven hundred contestants; 4-H Fair where kids show and sell their livestock, and residents bring their best pies, vegetables, and flowers to be judged for purposes of brag; and the Ranchers' Day and Ranch Horse Competition featuring chuck wagon cooking to wind up the year's festivities.

When Diane and I first came to Sonoita, her mare, Rockys Lil Gal, was burning up the county fair race tracks all over the state. You might say the horse built our horse barn by winning nine races and a ton of money. That year we entered her in the Sonoita Quarter Horse Derby, a premier race for Arizona three-year-olds. Our trainer, Owen McDaniel, arrived with Rocky at the track early on the morning of the race. Rocky seemed unsettled by her new surroundings with all the strange horses. To calm her down, Owen led her out to the open grassy field and let her graze for an hour or two. Grazing for a horse is like meditation for a monk; it calms their nerves and clears the mind.

In the saddling paddock, Rocky stood easy-like, untroubled by the hundreds of onlookers and the seven other horses swirling around her. Owen strapped on the pancake racing saddle and led her one turn around the paddock. She pranced as if she knew that she was the center of attention. Owen legged jockey Joe Castro up on the saddle and handed them to the lead horse. Together, they danced in front of a packed grandstand to the trumpet blast of "Parade to the Post." After showing off her stuff, Rocky settled into her lead horse and rider and galloped a full circle around the track to warm up.

In the starting gate, she drew the number one post position and stood dead still while the other horses loaded alongside her. The "One Hole" was the best position provided she got a good start. We watched from the grandstand, peering through binoculars down the straightaway four hundred yards in the distance. The gates blocked our view, but we could see the horses' feet under the starting gates. Rocky never moved, while the others reared up and fidgeted. Finally, all feet were still and the gates slammed open as the starter cried "AND THEY'RE OFF." Rocky blasted out of her gate and went to the lead on the inside rail.

"COME ON ROCKY, YOU ALREADY GOT IT WON." Diane screamed. "KEEP ON COMING." I bellowed, inaudible above the shriek of the crowd. At the halfway point she was two lengths lead and leaving the field behind, all except a big bay gelding on the far outside. The bay ran with his head stretched out and muscles straining to make up what he lost at the start, every vein bulging under his sleek, shiny hide.

"KEEP GOING ROCKY, YOU CAN BEAT THE BAY." Diane screeched, as they came near and her binoculars fell to ground with a clunk. As the bay closed in, we started jumping up and down, pounding on the spectators in front of our seats.

"HOLD ALL TICKETS FOR THE PHOTO FINISH," the announcer bellowed after the two gallant creatures thundered across the finish line, nose to nose. Five minutes later the announcer cried out: "IT'S PIES ROYAL REQUEST BY A WHISKER. ROCKYS LIL GAL SECOND."

We scrambled down from the stands and hurried to the stables where Owen unsaddled the filly and put her on a mechanical horse walker to cool down. She was scarcely breathing hard as she followed the lead poles around the circle of sawdust. I had left my voice back at the finish line, and could think of nothing to say.

"I don't think she saw the other horse coming up on the outside. Otherwise she'd have hit another gear. Rocky hates to lose. I hope she's not depressed."

"It's no shame to run second to that horse," Owen said, with an element of pride echoing in his voice. Later, Pies Royal Request went on to win the most consecutive races ever by a quarter horse.

"No matter, Rocky's still the CHAMPION for us."

"Yes, I'll do it," Diane said with a sunburst smile. We were walking out our front door to the driveway where Bob Barnhill had parked. President

of the fairgrounds board of directors, Bob had just offered Diane the unpaid, volunteer job of managing the local horse show. Jeff Wright, the last
manager, had moved to Sierra Vista and the show needed new leadership.

"That takes a lot of time," I cautioned. I had been on the board for
the past year and had seen just how much work it took to pull off these
all volunteer events.

"What about the ranch and the race horses?"

"I'll get with Jeff and the bookkeeper this week," she said, shrugging
off my niggling intervention. At one time, the horse show had been the
main event, offering a venue for local ranchers and horse breeders to show
off their best stock at halter and in the performance classes of roping and
cowhorse work. But lately, the locals had either quit, moved on, or taken
their horses to the bigger shows like the Sun Circuit in Scottsdale.

A few weeks later, she started pulling her horse show committee together. In small towns, word gets around fast. At the post office and in
the saloons, people started talking up a fun event about to happen at the
fairgrounds right after the May horse races; a new, bigger, and better place
to show off your favorite cayuse.

The committee started to hold regular meetings and plan. People were
asked, rather than told, what part they wanted to help with: arena upkeep,
contestants' dinner, getting prizes donated, trail class, western pleasure,
and the special events for kids and horses on the weekend. I volunteered
to organize the roping and working cow horse events since I was already
doing them anyway.

A new group dynamic developed. Horse show tasks, once neglected or
done at the last minute, were now getting done on time. People enjoyed
each other and were having fun working together toward common goals.
Diane sought out everyone's opinion, listened, and valued their input.
And she worked harder than anyone else. When she gave progress reports
to the board of directors, people doing the work got the credit. It didn't
surprise me because I had seen her do it before on the board of trustees
at the high school where Rich graduated; as the family liaison officer for
the US embassies in El Salvador and Guatemala; as the school nurse in
a variety of venues while I labored away at the desiccated abstractions of
graduate school.

Diane also took on organizing the Sonoita Cowbelles' road clean-up crew along Highway 83. On one blustery fall morning with a threat of rain, all the volunteers showed up on time, an unusual happening given the weather and the work to be done. They dragged blue plastic bags along the roadside, loading up beer bottles, plastic bags, pieces of tires and hubcaps. Finishing up their allotted stretch, they headed to a Sonoita café for a margarita lunch and a chance to get caught up on local affairs, like how each other's kids were doing in school, who was winning at the rodeos, household doings like garden plantings and how big the fall tomatoes had grown. And always the weather; how much rain each ranch or home had gotten.

"I don't know how she does it," Chris Peterson, our neighbor, said to me later. "I never thought I'd have such fun picking up garbage in a hurricane."

Over the next decade, the Sonoita Quarter Horse Show morphed into biggest and best little show in the southwest. Riders came from all over Arizona, as well as New Mexico and California. Four full days of fun and competition for all events, from the slow-moving trail classes; to western pleasure, more a fashion show for riders and horses, to working cow horses going down the fence with a big slide. The number of horses swelled to the point that we had to build another arena and put up lights. Often, the competitions lasted until midnight.

Except on Friday nights. Diane reserved Friday for a dinner honoring the contestants and volunteers. The fairgrounds board of directors wanted to charge twenty dollars a head, but Diane and the committee held firm.

"These riders pay a lot of money to come here and enter the classes and the community volunteers do so much to help. So Friday is appreciation night. Everybody eats free."

I suggested holding a Calcutta auction that night where each contestant in their respective classes was sold to the highest bidder. The money went into a pot where the winners of the designated classes the next day got checks (after the committee skimmed off 30 percent). Friday night became "Equine Ego" night with some riders and their horses selling for hundreds of dollars, usually back to their owners. The committee cashed in on the cowboy's impulse to bet on anything including if and when the sun would come up. By Sunday evening as the last trailers exited the

Fairgrounds gate, the committee limped home exhausted to count the cash they had raised.

"We will hold a review breakfast next week to go over what worked well and what didn't. That way, next year we can improve." With that meeting, planning for the next show began a year in advance. The money made by the show went to improve the antiquated fairgrounds facilities.

"I am retiring," the old lawyer said after our Wednesday night poker game had recessed. While the others filed out the door, Bernie Solsbury pulled me aside. "I want to come over and talk to you and Diane next week about taking over the Anne Stradling Museum of the Horse down in Patagonia."

We listened to Bernie's proposal. He would transfer the assets and responsibilities of the foundation into her care, no strings attached other than to follow Anne Stradling's wish: Support local kids and their horse activities.

"Can she charge for her time?" I asked.

"Of course. You should not do this for nothing," Bernie said. "We have been charging $75 per hour."

Diane set up a board of directors with Betty Barr and Mac Donaldson as the first members. Betty and husband John Barr had retired to Sonoita from Tucson a decade ago while Mac and his father John operated the seventy-five-thousand-acre Empire ranch. Together, the committee of long-time ranchers and new families developed guidelines on what events and activities to support. When it came to the budget, Diane proposed that the foundation pay an honorarium each year. Instead, all the directors preferred to donate their time as public service to the community.

"But you are putting in hundreds of hours," I protested. "Everybody should be paid for their work."

"That money belongs to the community," Diane said. End of discussion. And the community responded in kind. Today, after two decades of supporting horse shows, rodeo queen contests, and student scholarships to veterinary schools and agriculture colleges, the original fund has doubled from new donations. Each year, Diane sends out a report to the community on the foundation's activities and gives each person and business a chance to contribute. The money dribbled in, even during the recession years. One anonymous donor sent fifteen thousand dollars.

County fairgrounds around the state used to be supported by a tax on pari-mutuel betting on horse races. The money went into a governor's fund and then doled out to each fairgrounds on a formula based on the number of people attending each fair. Also, most county governments paid the costs of maintenance and upkeep of the physical plant. But as county racing dwindled, so did the governor's fund. The shift in Arizona's demographics from a rural economy and culture to urban, suburban, and retirement centers depleted the political support for rural county fairgrounds and communities. Also, horse racing declined with the tremendous growth in Indian casino gambling that satisfied the public's urge to gamble with slot machines and card games.

The Santa Cruz County Fairgrounds had never been supported by Santa Cruz County, even though all its public schools take Friday off and come to the 4-H fair each year. As the 2008 recession deepened and state government became strapped, funds for county fairgrounds disappeared altogether. In Sonoita, Pioneer Hall needed a new roof and coolers; stall doors on the horse barns sagged and fell off the hinges; the dirt on the race track and rodeo arenas hardened from lack of maintenance. The facility was over a half century old and needed work.

Diane on Tuffy.

But the community refused to give up. Diane helped put together a new, not-for-profit foundation to benefit the fairgrounds. She and the new committee applied for tax- free status. Two years later, the IRS approved the application, and the Santa Cruz Fair and Rodeo Association Foundation, Inc., began to accept donations. Soon, the foundation's checkbook showed a substantial cash flow, all going into fairground improvements.

The day-to-day operation of the fairgrounds is governed by a board of directors elected by the community. Diane had been asked to run for the office, but she refused saying that working on events was way more fun, and avoided the board's small town politics. Most members had a pet project they wanted done, but never had they sat down as a group to make an overall assessment of needs, let alone set priorities; never until now had the money been available to do what needed to be done. Diane and her new foundation committee convened a planning meeting with the fairgrounds board of directors, facilitated by a disinterested party. Out of that process, a rough outline emerged of what to do and when.

For the people of Patagonia and Sonoita, the fairgrounds in modern times served the same social function that the Catholic mission churches filled in the southwestern borderlands two centuries ago; or that the Mormon meetinghouse filled in Utah in the 1860s. But with more fun and without the religious harangue. Families who had lived in the area for generations bonded with new arrivals to provide for the operation and upkeep of Sonoita's social center, without government help and government control. The depth of commitment to their fairgrounds on the high desert grasslands was extraordinary, a dedication to place seldom seen in these days of instant gratification and grafting onto government dole. One rancher couple who had moved to Sonoita in 1956 and lived to more than ninety years of age in the same house, working the same cattle range, bequeathed much of their estate to the fairgrounds that they had helped to build.

iv

Earth Day—April 22—marked the birth of the modern environmental movement in 1970. A national day to focus on the environment was a political act of both Democrats and Republicans that brought together groups fighting against oil spills, toxic dumps, pesticides, proliferation of freeways and loss of open space, the loss of wilderness, extinction of wildlife, and overuse and waste of natural resources, including grasslands. Nationwide rallies and public demonstrations especially by young people eventually led to the passage of the Environmental Protection Agency, the Clean Air Act, Clean Water Act, the Endangered Species Act, and other legislation that restricted and regulated the consumptive uses of natural resources. In a rural town such as Patagonia whose economy had been based on cattle and mining, an Earth Day Celebration seemed unlikely.

And yet with every generation, the West seems to re-invent itself. A new subculture had trickled into town, an eclectic group of mostly open-minded people, many retired from successful careers elsewhere. Most of them had comfortable cash flows not dependent on the local economy. Some wanted to change the town to resemble the places they had left behind; they built their castles on hilltops and complained about no garbage service and how far it was to the mega-malls. A few came with notions that ranchers were ruining the land and any grazing had to be bad. But most of them looked for the good and worked to make the community better.

In 2012, the new arrivals convened Earth Day, Patagonia style, and focused on healing the land. Looking around, they discovered Joe Quiroga and the Diamond C Ranch. The Quiroga family's roots grew deep in the borderlands dirt, extending back six generations, and to both sides of the border. As the ranch manager on the Diamond C ranch, Joe, at the age when most of Patagonia's new arrivals had retired, began a new endeavor. He looked out over the eroded landscape and decided to do something about it. With pick, digging bar, and shovel, Joe started building rock dams across the arroyos to hold back the soil and retain the rainwater runoff. Fifteen years later, I walked over the Diamond C pastures and saw hundreds of rock-solid check dams each holding a patch of topsoil behind it. Rooted in that dirt, a healthy stand of perennial grasses fed

Joe's cattle. When a famous ecologist asked why he did it, Joe replied in a gravelly voice that revealed his impatience with the question: "Because the land needed it."

The beauty of this simple intervention was that it worked, and continues to work. Also, Joe did not have to ask for anybody's permission to do it, beseech some caretaker agency for its approval, or wait for a pilot study by an "expert." From a lifetime of working and watching the land, Joe instinctively knew that holding back the soil and rainwater for as long as possible would benefit that ranch. And in so doing, Joe's work ultimately will have more impact on healing the land than most urban enviros will achieve over their lifetimes. How so? Because one of the not-so-new arrivals in Patagonia, Gary Paul Nabhan, picked up the shovel and spread Joe's good idea around.

Patagonia, just thirteen little miles southward down Highway 82 from Sonoita, is the home of Patagonia Union High School. The student body averages about seventy Hispanic and Anglo students from the ninth to the twelfth grades, many living below the so-called poverty line. Today, environmental awareness of the student body and teachers is high, thanks in large measure to an innovative program called Borderlands Earth Care Youth Corps. The brainchild of Gary Paul Nabhan and Laura Monte, each summer the program gives students jobs that pay real money while working at the intersection of watershed conservation and re-generative agriculture using Joe's simple but effective process—recognize a problem, figure out what to do, start work, and stay with it. Not new to the area, Nabhan had returned to his botanical roots near the Native Seed Search Farm he co-founded in the 1980s. Native Seed Search developed a repository for ancient and disappearing seed stocks from Native cultures all over the southwest and Mexico; a gene bank and farm for growing food plants that were in danger of extinction from the one-crop homogenization of commercial agriculture.

With boundless energy and a borderland brilliance, Nabhan left a job as director of the Center for Sustainable Environments at Northern Arizona University and moved back to home base. In moving, he exchanged the Colorado Plateau with the Hopi and Navajo for the Sonoran Desert and the Tohono O'odham, Seri, and Hispanic cultures. Unlike a stereotypical academic, Nabhan liked getting his hands dirty working out on the watershed. While ranchers like me zeroed in on cows and horses, Gary focused on all things other-than-human—plants, animals, water, and soil—plus all the "agri-cultures" rooted in a region, both indigenous and modern. Discovering sustainable ways that native and present-day Americans gather, grow, and prepare their food has been the centerpiece of his energetic career as an ethnobiologist.

The Earth Care Youth Corps' work started in June, the hottest month, with the students and their instructors planning projects that will occupy them for the next six weeks. Often, the work involved building stone dams, but projects also transplanted trees in arroyos to hold back erosion, planted a school garden, and collected rain water from rooftops to irrigate a local community food farm. The instruction followed the Outward Bound scheme of total immersion by presenting the students with a problem/opportunity, working out a solution, and then applying it. Students kept journals where they wrote down what they did each day. In afternoon discussions, they talked about their work and how it fit into the overall health of their community and the watershed. Finally, at the end of the six weeks, each student gave a stand-up talk on their project to the other students, parents, teachers, and to sponsors, including Diane and myself.

An unplanned evaluation of the project came at spring graduation where all seniors told what the years at Patagonia High had meant to them. The Earth Care students credited the program with giving them a greater awareness of the landscape and community where they lived and also a vision of how they can find jobs in, or further their education about, land conservation related issues. But the most important life lesson learned was their capacity to articulate a problem, describe what they did to solve it, and then explain how their work mattered to the landscape and local community.

Jodi Quiroga, Joe's granddaughter, worked on the Earth Care program and graduated in 2013. Today, she is a strong, sure-footed young woman who is working toward her bachelor's degree at Northern Arizona University and is destined to become a leader in the Hispanic community. Guadalupe Bueras garnered a full-ride scholarship to Arizona State University where she will study law and become a female advocate for

"Chicanos por La Causa." And on and on, kids who grew up in the rural community, many below the poverty line, are moving out to community colleges, universities, and into meaningful jobs. Hopefully, some will return home to farm and ranch.

Sonoita and Patagonia, way stations that arose out of homestead, ranching, mining, and the railroad, have become contemporary rural places where folks live free from the confines and grime of cities. Here they can see and roam over long distances unimpeded and make at least part of their living from the land. These are not the antisocial, rural western cultures as some urban, intellectual coyotes like to portray us, but a friendly, self-reliant people loyal to our families, neighbors, and the landscapes that sustains us.

4

What Goes Around

When moving cattle on the C6 ranch, I learned to take advantage of what little help the landscape allowed. Tom Hunt on the Rail X Ranch had low country and irrigated pastures down on Sonoita Creek. So for him, everything was a downhill push to better feed. After I lost access over the Rail X—more on this later—we had to push cows uphill in the opposite direction, and then south into the Redrock drainage.

When Rich, T. N., and I first gathered Red Bear pasture, we tried scraping the cows off Mount Hughes Ridge, then pushing them down to the rude dirt track that came up the middle of the valley. We camped out on the east end and picketed our horses so we could start before daybreak. But the cows had spent the night up in the stars and had no intention of coming down until they felt the urge. We spent the front end of the day climbing the steep hills and pushing down the scattered cattle one at a time until the horses wore out and our patience considerably thinned.

"There must be a better way to do this," T. N. said around the camp-fire that night, as we gnawed on steaks I had burnt over mesquite coals.

"Why don't we wait until they are ready to come down," Rich offered.

"Sounds sensible to me," I muttered. "Bird will like that too." The next day, we started at mid-morning when the cows had already started side-hill-ing down across the face of the ridge to get to water in Red Bear tank.

In the beginning, I rode alone or with one other rider, usually T. N., who knew lots more than I did about bovine behavior and bovines in general. Tom and I worked the pastures slow-like, not so strenuous as to deaden the horses with fatigue, but fast enough so that we covered the country. One of my chores was figuring out how to work the country efficiently on horseback. This put me in direct conflict with a perversely intractable critter, the range cow, and worse, the bull. Early on, I learned that to move cattle efficiently I had to be smarter and more alert than the cow, a requirement that has doomed some wannabe cowboys. The trick was to figure out what the cows might want to do on their own and lend a hand. To quote Tom Hunt: "It's a damn sight easier to move cows to where they want to go than where they don't."

So I spent many mornings just riding the country and watching. Cows are imminently creatures of habit; they seldom if ever improvise. If I had crew of cowboys, I could force the cows to swim upstream, but it was immensely more enjoyable to go with the flow, so to speak. Once, as I was putting in a dirt tank on another ranch, I asked the driver how he planned to get his big dozer into the mountainous site:

"I'll just follow the cow trails," he replied. "They never go up or down more than a ten percent grade unless they are forced to."

Cows may not be high on the animal IQ scale, but they know all they need to know. In lion and coyote country, cows tend to stay in small bunches. Usually, I'd see the same cows together all the time. If I brought a new one into the bunch, the others ganged up on her until she assumed the position at the bottom of the herd hierarchy, or fled back to home ground.

When the bunch went to water, one cow always stayed behind to babysit the calves. When the others returned, the babysitter ambled off to drink. How the herd decides who goes and who stays is a behavioral mystery known only to cows. The question cried out for scientific study. Perhaps Temple Grandin already knows the answer. Dr. Grandin is a professor of animal behavior and a best-selling author of several books explaining why animals do what they do. As an autistic person she has used her genius to see and describe the world in the same light and shapes that our horses and cows see it. Her insights have helped us humans, including ranchers, to become more humane, going with the natural flow instead of pushing against it.

After months of observation, I concluded that the cows' sullen disposition might be due to their miserable lives. My horses, when I turn them loose in the pasture will frolic about and roll in the grass, groaning with pleasure, while the cows look on enviously unable to join in the fun. The problem of nourishment takes up all their time. For most of the year, they must eat for two. If a cow doesn't eat enough to make milk her calf gets impatient and butts the milk factory—really hard. If she doesn't produce a calf every year, she goes down the road to auction where she is most likely sold for Big Macs.

Bulls are worse. You would think that bulls would be delighted to join up with their beloved cows. Not so. The cow is receptive to the bull only on special occasions, as T. N. pointed out. Most of the time, bulls are barely tolerated. So when breeding time approached each summer, my job was to put the bulls and cows together whether they wanted to or not.

Early on, my neighbor William Llorta, laid a gift on me that made the cow-bull reunion a whole lot easier. Tuerco (borderland slang for "Tough Nut") was a grizzled Australian Shepard cow dog with attitude. Tuerco had been William's stud dog on their ranch near Santa Cruz, Sonora, and sired most of their replacement dogs. Unwilling to give up his position as Top Dog, Tuerco had started picking fights with his offspring. William's gift to me gave Tuerco a new lease on life; not a career change so much as a change in scenery.

Tuerco always trotted alongside my horse on the right side, his stubby legs doing triple time to keep up. When moving cow-calf pairs, he'd move forward and nip the heels if one got pokey, and then instantly drop back out of kicking range. If a calf got tired, Tuerco grabbed its heel and squatted. The calf squealed, the cows bawled, and the herd took off at a trot. In a more extreme move, Tuerco ran sideways at a cow's rear end, biting the tail switch and swinging out of danger, like a boy swinging out over a pond on a tree rope.

On dislodging brush-hugging bulls, Tuerco-dog was an Olympic-level athlete. You would think that driving the bulls to the cows during breeding season would be easy but not during hot weather. A bull on the prod backs up into a juniper thicket, its head facing out and ready to fight my horse. Tuerco handled that problem by stealth. Circling around behind, he jumped on the bull's back and bit its ears. But as time went by, Tuerco dropped that move from his bag of tricks as the years of ranch work slowed him.

In addition to driving cattle, Tuerco's other strong suit was marking territory. He peed on our tires, flower pots, barn corners, hay bales, and anything else he took a fancy to. His supply of urine seemed inexhaustible.

When I scolded, he'd grin and trot up to be scratched. When I cussed him out in Spanish, he wriggled with pleasure at the more familiar sounds.

Once Tuerco bonded with me, he became protective. He decided right away that the Monday garbage truck was up to no good, taking away those fragrant bags stacked by the barn. Next Monday, Tuerco was hiding under the stock trailer, crouched like a cat over a gopher hole. When the driver got out to load the bags, Tuerco crept up behind and grabbed him by the heel. The next Monday, I was the garbage hauler with Tuerco perched magnificently atop the load.

Up the road from our headquarters was a goat farm. To protect their caprines from the coyotes the goat grower had installed spotlights and woven wire fences around their small paddocks. On our down days, or in the afternoon after work, Tuerco made the rounds of the neighborhood dogs, sniffing rear ends, and establishing himself as Sonoita's top dog. One day, Tuerco discovered the goats on the opposite side of a net wire fence. Every afternoon thereafter, he squatted by the fence and watched, no doubt dreaming of herding them, or something else more delicious. Perhaps the dingo side of his ancestry had started to take over. But as far as I knew, he never breeched the fence, even though the neighbor complained that he had goat chops on his mind and threatened to call the Santa Cruz County dog catcher. Even so, keeping Tuerco in my kennel seemed like judging him guilty without a trial. The coyotes had made him guilty by association.

One balmy summer evening after trotting home in a thundershower, I forgot to lock him in the kennel. My lapse had something to do with the rain, an especially delicious pot roast and potatoes that Diane had fixed and a bottle of Gato Negro wine from the Mini-Mart. When the phone rang, Diane answered.

"Oh, I am so sorry." I heard her gasp. "Yes, yes, we will see to it that Tuerco does not do that again." The neighbor had gone outside to check on the goats and Tuerco slipped through the open door and peed on her kitchen wall. It didn't help matters when I tried to explain that he only baptized places he liked.

I did not want to give Tuerco up. But even less, did I want him jailed for exercising his instincts. So I took him to Duane 'Twaits on the T-4 Ranch twenty miles west toward Nogales and nearer to the border.

"He'll be a great watch dog, once he bonds to you," I said. "You better tie him up for a few days and feed him."

A week later, I was saddled up and ready to load the horses in the trailer when Tuerco trotted up, ears chewed, and hair coat greasy like he'd been rolled by a truck.

"Tuerco." I yelped, delighted to see him again. Tuerco-dog gave me a toothy grin and anointed all my tires to show that he harbored no hard feelings over my sorry behavior.

He then trotted to the kennel where he slept for two days straight. Duane had tied him in the barn, but Tuerco chewed through his collar, whipped Duane's other dogs, marked territory, and disappeared.

Next week Duane called and needed Tuerco back. Said the illegals from across the border were running off with his place. I reluctantly said okay, but only if you take him home in your house until he bonds with you. Last time I saw the pair was at the Sonoita ranch horse competition in September. Tuerco-dog was riding in the back of Duane's pickup, happily guarding the tool boxes. No doubt he had peed on the corners to make them his. On the down-hill slide of life, Tuerco had found the ideal retirement job.

"Best guard dog I've ever had," Duane chirped.

ii

When Manuel Murrietta came to work for the C6 ranch, the work sped up. He had finished at Cochise College where he excelled on the rodeo team as their top tie-down and team roper. After graduating, he was asked back to coach.

"Everything with me is a rodeo," Manuel stated emphatically. Built like a horseman, he was slim-legged from the waist down but topped with anvil shoulders and chest from a lifetime of flanking calves and building fence. He had that heads-up, nothing-in-life-has-ever-slowed-me-down way of riding. Manuel had cut his teeth on the seventy-five-thousand-acre Empire Ranch with John and Mac Donaldson. With that much country to cover and a thousand cows or more to find, Mac and John liked to work fast with a big crew of mostly Mexican vaqueros. Manuel was a man in a hurry. In addition to working for me, he usually had two or three other jobs; riding colts, training rope horses, and managing Grandad Pyeatt's ranch on the northwest end of the Huachuca Mountains. On weekends, he worked for the rodeo contractor as a pick-up man, plucking bronc riders off bucking horses at a dead run.

I don't mean to imply that Manuel was reckless as a ranch cowboy, far from it. He moved cattle at steady pace and he was a wizard at knowing what a cow was going to do before she did, where the herd wanted to go before it made its move. Also, Manuel had an excellent memory for individual cows, especially the troublemakers. Many times, his skills kept us out of cow wrecks and allowed us to complete the job on time.

Once, I had penned a thin cow with a calf so big it had to knee down to suck. I decided I would leave the cow behind at the Oak Grove corrals and drive the calf alone to the shipping pens two miles down a brushy canyon. The calf was worth six hundred dollars and I needed the money. The calf would have none of that and it kept circling back through the brush to mother-up. When I showed up at the pens empty-handed with my shirt in shreds an hour later, I asked Manuel:

"Why didn't you tell me that was a bad idea?"

"It wasn't my place. You're the boss," Manuel grinned, as unruffled as a great horned owl perched in a shade tree. He honored the cowboy protocol of allowing me to make on-the-job mistakes as the best way to learn.

"I sign the checks alright, but that don't necessarily mean I know what I'm doing all the time," I grinned back. After that, Manuel took the lead when we worked cattle.

I've seen star rodeo performers who failed to make the grade as cowhands on the ranch, and vice-versa, but Manuel excelled in both environments. In rodeo, the cattle are confined to the arena, basically a large, smooth oval, like a dry lake. But on the ranch, cow critters have miles of space, often broken, upside down and brush-covered. Cowboy sagas arise and gain stature from the dubious excitement of chasing range cattle through thickets and over boulder slides. Often the horse plays a key role in the drama, either as an incorrigible bronc that causes the wreck or a smooth riding sucker with cow sense and a ton of "bottom," meaning that the horse has more stamina than the cows. But despite the myth, most cowhands prefer to go nice and easy-like, but that tempo does not lend itself to legend building.

Even so, cowhands brag on their favorite mounts, especially if the horse is a youngster. The brag can be an understated commentary, like: "She drug them calves okay for just a three-year-old." Or an overstatement like: "That sonovabitch is makin' the best outside horse I ever rode, bar none." Most of the time, the praise includes a gentle flip of the horse's mane or a pat on the shoulder.

"Out in the country, what goes around, comes around," is an operational imperative among ranchers and cowboys. Manuel had plenty of relatives and friends who were good hands. He had helped every rancher in the area at one time or another. On cattle ranches, neighborliness, good humor, and courtesy are the currency that cowboys trade in. Good deeds are returned in kind, one of the unspoken rules of ranch etiquette.

When we were moving the cattle out of a pasture, Manuel lined up his friends and relatives to help. In the early years before cell phones, we carried two-way radios. Manuel would ride like a forward artillery spotter to the top of a ridge in the center of the pasture and direct the eight or ten riders to cattle by radio. Lots of times, we discovered immigrant-trafficking coyotes or drug smugglers listening in on our frequencies as they trudged toward their pickup points on Highway 82.

"The Border Patrol is coming. Run for the brush!" Shouted in Spanish into the radio, this usually cleared them out of our way.

One memorable morning, Manuel and I were gathering heifers from the backside of Mount Hughes. As we drove them off the peak and down onto the trail, the cattle suddenly scattered like quail. Giving chase, we galloped through a smuggler's camp, the cook fire still burning and beans in the pot. The smugglers had posted look-outs to guide the drug mules to their meet-up site on Highway 82. We burned up the rest of the day getting the heifers back together and to the next pasture.

Often, we had to ride during fall hunting season when the eavesdroppers were deer hunters, a more dangerous situation than with Mexican backpackers because deer hunters were looking for a four-footed animal to shoot. Every year when the hunting season dates were posted, I tried to schedule our work around them, but regardless of the extra riflemen in our pastures, we still had fall roundup to do.

As a breed, cowboys are often lean on ambition, but Manuel was a notable exception. In 2003, he started producing rodeos on his own. He could make lots more money at that than day working for me. And he did. With a strong work ethic; a reputation for honest dealings; and more knowledge about cows, horses, and rodeo than a stack of encyclopedias he was soon on the road with a semi-truck load of cattle and rough stock almost every weekend.

That same year, Rich graduated from New Mexico State University. After circling around for a while he came home and started to work. We made a deal. He would work for wages for a couple of years and then we'd see about a partnership. One year later, he began building a house in Redrock Canyon so he could be close to his work; right on top of it, you might say. That turned out to be the best trade I ever made.

I thought he would make a good rancher. First, he did not like to go to town. Second, he hated to spend money. He didn't wear gloves because growing new skin was cheaper. Third, he could fix our machines, including the essential one-lung gasoline engines that drove the generators that pushed the pumps that lifted the water into our pipelines. When I tinkered on them, all I got were barked and bloody knuckles from the wrench work and a stiff right shoulder from yanking on the starter rope. But they purred after Rich worked on them. Fourth, he had an amazing intuitive feel for animal behavior, yet he was not addicted to horses and the rodeo cowboy stuff. He had tried roping competitively and gave it up as throwing good money after bad. Fifth, he was dependable, worked hard, and did not like to waste time. Tall, soft-spoken, and considerate of others, he had picked up his mother's pleasing personality.

In 2005, Rich sent me a Father's Day letter that said he was proud to say that now he ran the ranch with his father, and that we made a good team. He was surprised by the complexity of our enterprise; how one had to master many skills that did not show up on university curricula or in western movies. Even so, Rich caught on quick that specialization was for factory assembly lines workers, not ranchers or cowboys.

To be a competent cowboy or rancher on an outfit our size, you had to be able to fix everything but the break of day. "Specialization is for insects," is how one short-handed rancher Dennis Moroney described the quandary. "Jack of many trades and master of only a few," was another savvy saying that better suited my smaller set of skills.

About the letter, I was happy and humbled at the same time: proud, too. I reread it every now and then as a pick-me-up when things are not going exactly as planned.

With Rich on board, the way we worked the ranch changed. Instead of a big crew to gather pastures, he and I worked them alone. It took us longer but cost less. At branding time, or for weaning and pregnancy testing, T. N. and Brent Cole, a new neighbor, pitched in. Brent was a farm boy from Pennsylvania who had moved west to become a cowboy. He'd acquired a key prerequisite by graduating from a horse-shoeing school in Oklahoma. Tall, red bearded, and ruddy faced with a locomotive-like build, Brent was easy to be around. We became friends and roped together competitively now and then.

Even so, our collective cowboy skills could not prevent a mountain lion's natural predatory behavior. The Crittenden pasture behind our headquarters in Sonoita was rated at fifty cows and calves year round. At first, I tried cows but got a poor calf crop in return. Predators took their dues, although in the deep canyons I seldom found the kills. But the calf count at spring branding compared to the calves weaned in the fall suggested that the lions took five to ten percent.

The year that I tried cows and calves in Crittenden, I got a call one morning form Dick Reilly, my Tunnel Springs neighbor:

"Mr. Collins," he whined anxiously over the phone. "One of my donkeys has been missing for a couple of days. Can you help me find it?"

I rode up to the barn where Dick was feeding his other burro and noticed drag marks in the dirt. We followed them to a juniper thicket fifty yards away. I pulled the branches aside and a thick quilt of green and black blow flies lifted off the carcass. We gagged at the stench and let the branches back.

"Lion kill," I said. "Looks like about three days old. The cat will probably be back tonight for another feed."

"Not this close to the house." Dick yelped.

"Better lock up your other burro for a few days. The lion may be just passing through."

"She was not an ordinary burro," Dick mumbled. "She was a rare Asiatic donkey."

"Whatever; the lion didn't know the difference. You'd better call the game ranger and report the loss." Dick said he didn't want the lion killed; it was just doing what it had to do to eat. Two weeks later, Dick called again. His other burro had disappeared.

I had a little bunch of cows and calves located on Gas Line Tank just over the ridge from Dick's house. I decided I'd better move them closer to home out of harm's way, even though that had not saved Dick's donkeys. Sometimes in an emergency, a person has to try something even if he knows that it probably won't do any good.

In the 1980s, I had helped a game ranger tree and radio collar lions in the Galuiro Mountains next to the south end of the San Carlos Apache Reservation. The hunter treed the cats with hounds, darted them with tranquilizer, and then turned them loose after putting on the collars. The Game and Fish Department wanted to know how many lions were leaving the reservation (lots) and how big their territories were (thirty to fifty square miles). The coolest part of the project was that high school kids in Phoenix got to follow the lions' movements from radio telemetry data; a real-life, wildlife adventure for city-bound youth.

Back-riding the Gas Line tank country to see if I'd cleaned it out, I found fresh kill instead, a month-old, red-colored calf. From the position of the carcass, its tracks, and the drag marks in the mud, I could reconstruct the scene. A rocky bluff rimmed the west side of the tank, hidden by two huge oak trees. Striking from above, the cat had launched itself off the bluff and reached the calf in a couple of swift bounds. Striking from behind, it bit though the calf's skull, then drug the calf under the oaks on the uphill side where it ate its fill. All that remained were the head, boney legs, and few patches of red fur.

I don't usually hunt lions. For me it is a privilege to live in country wild enough to harbor lions, and bears, too. Also, I knew that if a lion is killed in this excellent habitat, another one will quickly move into its territory. But this cat had become habituated to killing livestock. Dick was out of burros, and I had a bunch of calves to protect. Also, Diane rode her bike down the dirt road every evening.

Manuel knew a lion hunter with dogs. We returned to the kill site at daybreak when the dogs could pick up the scent on the morning dew. The strike dog let out a yowl and raced into the mouth of Monkey Canyon with the other dogs hot on the trail. A few hours later, the cat treed in a giant juniper rooted on the side of a cliff. I rode across the cliff face and looked straight across to the cat not more than twenty feet away when the hunter shot. The cat slumped, still clinging to the limb with its claws. At the second shot, the cat fell into the pack of dogs whose barks and howls changed to snarls as they mauled the carcass until the hunter put them on chains.

When he sliced open the lion's paunch, a writhing mass of white-colored worms popped out between patches of red calf fur. The awful putrid stink was overwhelming. The diseased animal could no longer catch deer or javelina and had to resort to easier prey. Watching the hunter peel the hide off the creature, I felt a bit down, not guilty or shameful, because the cat had lived out its natural life. But it had to kill to live, as Dick Reilly had said.

The afternoon sun was hot and dry. We mounted and turned to leave, our sore-footed horses picking their way gingerly through the rocks, followed by the panting dogs. Already buzzards circled above the kill, nature's brooms. Tonight the coyotes will come, followed by foxes, and in the morning, blow flies and carrion beetles. Soon, bones would be all that remained. That afternoon, I reported the kill to the local game warden but the stark example of aging and mortality left me subdued.

iii

On a rough-country ranch like ours, some of the salt and protein block had to be packed in on horseback. I had an old Decker-style pack saddle but the panniers had been ripped to shreds by the brush. Rich and girl-friend Jackie Crawford took Christmas off and went to the famous Denver Livestock Show. At the trade pavilion, they found new panniers made from indestructible, space age material that fit our pack horse, Double D, like a hen on a new nest.

The trail from our headquarters crossed Alamo Canyon and climbed the long limestone ridge that led toward Gas Line Tank on the northwest end of the pasture. Bird and I trudged up the ridge leading Double D packed with three hundred pounds of salt, a load that made him dry fart like a rusty gate. The north-facing slope of the ridge was timbered with oak and big junipers. Years ago, a few big trees had been cut for fence posts or firewood. Rounding a bend, a large stump dark with age loomed on the side of the trail. The first time Bird saw that, he went ballistic and shied away, jerking the lead rope from my hand. DD did not see anything alarming and dropped his head to graze. I spurred Bird back to the stump where he snorted and arched his neck and side-stepped until I could pick up the lead rope and continue on our merry way.

Over the next decade, Bird and I rode the same trail about once a week and every time he skittered away, snorting at the stump. Then one day, the wood cutter returned and the stump was gone. The horse screeched to a halt in the middle of the trail and stared at the place where it had been. Bird knew something had changed in his world and he never forgot it. He stopped and peered at that empty space every time until the day I retired him.

In addition to salt and protein block, we horse-packed fencing material into the areas where we could not drive, like Dark Canyon and Monkey Canyon. Thickets of mountain mahogany grew on their north-facing slopes, a good browse during most of the year. But at winter's first hard frost, the plant turns deadly for cows by concentrating hydrocyanic acid in its leaves. The frost burns the grass and the only green things left are trees and shrubs so the cattle switch from grazing to browsing. Dead cattle are always found next to drinkers because water dissolves the cyanic acid from the leaves in the cow's rumen. Once inside the cow, the cyanic acid ties up the iron in the blood's hemoglobin, the red cells that make blood red and carry oxygen throughout the body. So the poisoned cow asphyxiates, even though its lungs continue to suck in air. Once symptoms start, there is no cure, even if I could get the poisoned cow to a veterinarian in time. The plant is dangerous only for a few weeks, but exactly how long, or how to know when it is safe to go back in the pasture, is guesswork.

On my maiden ride around Crittenden pasture, I found a scattering of cow bones around the last water on Tom's old pipeline; skulls, pelvis, femurs, ribs, all white as chalk and chewed by porcupines. Years earlier, Tom had his vaqueros move the cattle to that place in early December in readiness to drive them up the pipeline and down on to his irrigated pastures out of danger. But an early freeze struck and he lost the cattle to mountain mahogany before the cowboys could move them. After hearing Tom's tale, I made it a practice to clean out those canyons by December first. Even so, some cows leaked back in, and over the next twenty-five years, I lost four head that I knew of. And they were the biggest, fattest stock because those were the ones that ate the most.

One December, T. N. and I were back riding Dark Canyon to be sure we'd cleaned out all the cattle. It happened to be deer season and we both had tags. Riding the pipeline, we ran onto a pretty, roan-colored heifer at a drinker laying on her side shivering in convulsions, gasping for breath as her muscles and organs starved for oxygen. She was dying from the inside out. I rode fifty yards down the pipeline and tied my horse solid to a tree and walked back. Her dark eyes pleaded for relief as wave after wave of spasms wracked her body. My shot rang out to stop her suffering and the cow collapsed with a windy groan of death. There was nothing else to do, but I felt sick. When I opened up her rumen, it was crammed with chewed-up mountain mahogany leaves. I had her ear-tagged for a re-placement cow but instead the Dark Canyon bears had a feast just before going into hibernation. The next summer I applied for a grant to fence off the two canyons. When built, I had a safer place to move the cows to in the fall after weaning the calves, and an extra big pasture for rest and rotation. Even so, I still can see her dark, pleading eyes twenty years later.

And while I am telling stories about dangerous vegetation, I must say something about locoweed and shin dagger agave. After a wet winter, locoweed can become a problem. The plant has a single tap root and spreads out with tillers over the ground until they look like massive green dollies with tiny purple flowers. Some plants get as large as a truck tire. On my ranch, loco seemed to like limestone soils and areas around drinkers that had been heavily grazed. The poison is a neurotoxin that accumulates in the cow's nervous system. When the toxin reaches a critical level, the brain connections short-circuit and cow gets blind staggers, as if she had drunk too much mescal. Once symptoms appear, there is no cure. The only prevention is to move the cows to a pasture without loco. But some cows get addicted, like people to cocaine or heroin or weed, and have to be culled. The older cows that have been raised in the Canelos seem to know the danger and lead their calves away from the stuff.

Preventing mountain mahogany and loco poisoning made for a horseback winter and spring, a chore that I enjoyed doing, except when I found a dead or goofy cow. I know that the ultimate destination for my cows and calves is the butcher shop, but I hated to see them suffer on my watch.

The agaves, of which there are many species, have been friends of humankind for thousands of years. Roasted agave hearts was a staple food of the O'odham, Seri, and Apache people until the Anglo fast food craze took over. In Sonora, Mexicans distill agave hearts into a fiery liquor called mescal. My favorite oil of joy is made in the little Sonoran town of Bacanora. Blue agave is distilled into Tequila, a drink indigenous to the Mexican state of Jalisco, but now famous around the world. Another large agave species that grows in the southern Mexican state of Yucatan was the source of hemp fiber for ropes that propelled the sailing ships around the world and that vaqueros and cowboys used for lariats. The advent of nylon put an end to that industry during the Second World War.

My complaint is with shin dagger agave, a low-growing species with leaves about a foot tall, each leaf tipped with a long needle point. The plant throws out suckers that merge with others to form dense colonies of dagger-tipped mats that thrive on the rocky, south-facing slopes of my Red Bear and Corral Canyon pasture. In June, shin dagger sends up its flower stalks six feet tall covered with yellow, fragrant flowers that draw wasps, bees, moths, and bats that feed on the nectar and spread pollen from plant to plant. In June when any green feed is scarce, my cows will tip-toe through the mats to dine on the flower stalks, creating narrow winding trails. The trails are too narrow for a horse's hoof and the daggers are the perfect length to stab the horse's coronet bands and pasterns. At first, I tried to ride into the mats and push the cows out, but the horses refused.

While I am a modest fan of the ecologist's sacred concept of biodiversity, shin dagger agave and loco weed are two species the world could live without and never miss, in my humble opinion. There are a dozen other species of agave to feed the bats and bees, and no creature I know of requires loco to make a living. To the cowboy and rancher, shin dagger and loco seem like proof that even God gets careless now and then.

5

Living Close to Predicament

Every ranch and rancher is partially a product of its past. In my case a very long past indeed, reaching back about five hundred years. Popular histories claim that Anglo-Americans settled the West, starting with the 1804–1806 Lewis and Clark expedition that followed the Missouri and Columbia Rivers northwest, eventually reaching the Pacific Ocean. But to a western horseman, the American west really began in 1519 when the conquistador Hernán Cortes unloaded his horses near Veracruz, starting Spain's astonishingly rapid south-to-north conquest of northern New Spain that later became Mexico and the American southwest.

The Spaniards first entered southern Arizona in 1540 on a quest for the mineral wealth of the fabled Seven Cities of Cibola. Francisco Coronado and his horde, more than a thousand people in all, rode north with a thousand head of horses and other livestock. They rounded the southeast flank of the Huachuca Mountains just fifty miles from my headquarters. The conquistadors trudged northward in a fruitless search that took them all the way to Santa Fe, in present-day New Mexico, and on to Kansas and back. Along the way, they encountered tribes of pedestrian Native Americans from Apache to Zuni, whose only domesticated animals were turkeys and dogs. Awed by the Spaniard's mobility, firepower, and traveling commissary of domestic livestock, the tribes no doubt coveted their own. But Coronado apparently rode no mares and the Indians quickly hunted down and consumed the Conquistador's stray livestock.

Since that time, livestock grazing and mining have been the principal land uses of the region. The first rancher in what became southern Arizona was probably the Mexican, José Romo de Vivar, who in 1640 was running cattle a little ways south of the Huachuca Mountains, according to historian

Thomas E. Sheridan. The cows were the criollo breed, forerunners of today's Texas longhorn, and the Mexican corriente. The criollo originated in the barren Atlas Mountains of North Africa and were brought to the Iberian Peninsula when the Moors conquered Spain in the eighth century. Christopher Columbus brought them to Hispaniola on his second voyage to the New World, and Cortes sailed them across the Caribbean to Mexico in the early 1500s. A hardy, small-bodied breed, the criollo was said to be mostly horns, hide, tail, and testicles, but they flourished in Mexico and the desert southwest.

Spanish and later Mexican ranchers entered into a landscape covered by a nutritious suite of perennial grasses that had been grazed only lightly after the age of the mammals ended nine thousand years prior. Fire, whether natural or human caused, has always been a major ecological disturbance to renew and refresh the grasslands, and beat back the brush and trees.

The Native Americans lived in brush huts scattered along the watercourses where they practiced a rudimentary farming and gathered wild foods. The Spanish missionaries and stockmen established their churches and ranches near the larger native settlements. Santa Cruz, a fortified town located about thirty-five miles south of Redrock Canyon, was continuously occupied by Spanish and Mexican settlers and ranchers from Father Kino's time in the 1600s until now.

Southward from Sonoita into the San Rafael valley, early ranches also ran thousands of cattle until Apache depredations forced them to flee to the military garrison at Santa Cruz. Perhaps some of their livestock grazed parts of nearby Redrock Canyon and took shelter there during the winter; perhaps not. But it is reasonable to think so.

Go West, Americans, and grab some free land. No nation on earth ever carried through with such a powerful democratic impulse—that common people could become landed through their own labors. Starting in 1862, Homestead Laws took land from the public domain and gave it to settlers who could take up residence and eke out a living for a period of five years. In the process of doling land out to homesteaders, the landscape was reduced to arithmetic, numbered squares that added up to one hundred and sixty acres. That acreage was allegedly enough for a family to make a living from in the midwest and on the eastern Great Plans where rainfall averaged forty inches per year or more. But in the arid western states, it was one hundred sixty acres of *delusion*. The maximum acreage was increased to six hundred and forty acres by the Desert Land Act of 1877 and the Stock Raising Homestead Act of 1916. Even so, the homesteaders lived close to predicament, choring on head-down through tremendous hardship.

In southern Arizona, the first homesteaders to arrive staked their ranch claims on the best available land that had water. From the home place, they spread out and relied on unclaimed and open public lands for more graze. But even a section of good high desert grassland would run no more than twenty cows, and the small rancher had to do something else to make ends meet. Many took jobs on the bigger outfits. Others tried dry land farming to supplement their livestock. In Arizona, more than half of the homesteaders gave up because of drought and Apache raids, selling or abandoning their claims. In the Canelo Hills, the land was more likely to give the homesteader indifference or worse rather than a home.

Even so, a few gritty homesteaders with the better land hung on and even prospered. They acquired more public land under the widow's exemption or the cash option to buy land for $1.25 per acre. Also, the Stock-Raising Homestead Act increased the acreage to 640 acres of land suitable only for grazing. In nearby Elgin, Nellie Bartlett eventually became owner of one thousand acres of top grazing land on the Sonoita plain and rented grazing rights to neighboring ranchers.

The Public Land Office carved out the homesteaders' plots by standard cadastral survey, using straight lines to create multiples of forty acres. This was quick, easy, and cheap, but ignored the wrinkled shapes of western watersheds, and more importantly, their inherent aridity. John Wesley Powell, the one-armed Civil War veteran who became the head of the United States Geological Survey, pleaded with Congress to divide up the west on the basis of naturally existing watersheds. Powell testified before Congress: The minimum total acreage for a viable ranch west of the 100th Meridian is 2,640 acres, with a few acres that can be farmed to produce hay, grain, and gardens to feed the family. He also pointed out that boundaries based on topographical features have continuities of rainfall, soils, plant and animal life, similarities that make managing the land more efficient.

Today, I often wonder as I ride the country how the Redrock Canyon watershed would have looked as a single ranch under one ownership without the US Forest Service involved. The twenty thousand acres would support five hundred cows, an economic unit except that it needed more water. One ranch would mean less land fragmentation and more intact habitat for wildlife and cows. With shipping corrals at its western confluence with Harshaw Creek, the cattle drives would be mostly downhill. The grassy sacaton flood bottoms could be farmed, as Powell envisioned. Even so, this massive, rugged landscape would not easily yield to the rancher's wants and needs. Resilience, love of the land, and a large dose of gumption would be required.

Instead, Congress went the cheap, easy route of straight lines and multiples of forty acres, propelled by the perceived Jeffersonian ethic of the greatest good for the greatest number and by speculators and their lobbyists who smelled the opportunity to skirt the law's noble intentions. In many cases, the speculators bought out the homesteaders and went on to assemble empires based on grass and other natural resources. In the end, few of the small ranchers survived and their lands were snapped up by corporations and entrepreneurs.

By the early 1880s, the big ranches that came to dominate the region for decades were mostly in place. William C. Greene, called the Copper Skyrocket by his biographers, bought most of the Mexican land grants near his mines in Cananea, Sonora, as well as the ones on the San Pedro and Santa Cruz Rivers in Arizona. Other capitalists included the powerful Kern County Land and Cattle Company, the Perrin family, wealthy dairy farmers from eastern states, the newspaper magnate George Hearst, as well as cattlemen from Texas who needed new range as they ran out of grass on their homelands.

For the first decade or so, the weather was wet and the grasses virtually ungrazed. Strong summer rains followed by wet winters renewed the range and water sources, allowing ranchers to increase their herds each year. Arizona became a haven for speculators, many from Europe, seeking a quick and easy return on excess capital. Most were not ranchers and they did not settle on or work the land or their herds. Even Arizona's territorial governor got in the business of "boosterism," proclaiming: "all one has to do is to sit on the veranda of their ranch houses in splendid weather and watch their investments double with each calf crop." Open range grazing practices and homestead laws converged with greed, ignorance, and the weather to produce what historians Diana Hadley and Thomas E. Sheridan labeled: "A tragedy of the commons," a term borrowed from economist Garrett Hardin. The tragedy arose within the shared-resource landscape where individual ranchers acted independently according to their own self-interest. They ignored the "common" good or their neighbors by depleting the water and grass on which each depended. It became a situation where those with the most capital and ruthlessness prevailed for the moment and the Devil took the hindmost.

Corporate ranchers who controlled land with water expanded their herds beyond sustainable limits in order to prevent others from crowding in. Between 1883 and 1887, San Rafael Valley rancher Colin Cameron increased his herds to seventeen thousand head and ordered his cowboys to run off any competitors from the range, including those in the Redrock Canyon watershed.

The range was grossly overstocked in 1891 when the summer rains failed for three years running. Water holes, rivers, and springs dried up and cattle died of thirst and starvation. May, June, and July were the deadliest months. Cowboys could ride the range without stepping on grass, only bare dirt and bones. One survey showed that two-thirds of the cattle in southern Arizona died, perhaps as many as a million head.

When the rains did return, they came with a vengeance. The grass that previously held back the floods had been consumed by cattle. Also, woodcutting that supplied charcoal and timber for the mines had stripped the hillsides and mountains of trees and brush. Erosion down-cut the rivers and stripped the land of its topsoil. More drought followed and the investors fled back to their eastern enclaves to lick their wounds. The legitimate ranchers either moved on to better range, or dug in and held on.

The frontier grazing practices had to change to match the borderland's arid climate. Open range had to be fenced and come under private control. Wells and dirt ponds had to be built to augment the natural waters.

Most of all, the numbers of cattle had to be reduced to sustainable levels. At the turn of the nineteenth century, no one knew how much forage could be grazed off and still keep the plants and soils intact and healthy. Early ranchers who moved in during a wet cycle thought that drought was an aberration. We now know that aridity is normal and drought is a routine occurrence.

The science of range management was born in Arizona in 1902 when ranchers lobbied to establish the Santa Rita Experimental Range to look into these and other questions. In the same time frame, the fledgling US Forest Service was trying to address the tragedy of the commons in eastern Arizona and New Mexico. The research is still ongoing today as climate change, global warming, and invasive species undermine the rancher's expected norms. Much of the early work on the Santa Rita Range tried to establish proper stocking rates, or the number of cows that could be grazed and still allow the rangeland to recover and thrive. That issue is still in dispute today, largely because of the land's inherent complexity, variable rainfall, and the needs and management practices of individual ranchers.

ii

The formation of the Coronado National Forest by President Theodore Roosevelt during the early 1900s ushered in the era of private grazing allotments on southern Arizona ranches, including those in the Canelo hills. Roosevelt, an adventuresome eastern dude and wannabe rancher who liked to roam the American west on hunting trips, turned out to be a friend of the rancher and cowboy. The forest reserves were first placed in the Department of Interior where preservationists like John Muir lobbied for elimination of all grazing. Muir loathed sheep in particular, calling them "meadow maggots." But to Scottish emigrant herders, sheep were their way of life. In our time, these pioneers were memorialized in Ivan Doig's honest and beautifully written stories.

Instead, Roosevelt in 1905 transferred the reserves to the Department of Agriculture under the guidance of Gifford Pinchot, a fellow member of Roosevelt's trophy repository, the Boone and Crockett Club. Pinchot's ancestors had amassed a fortune exploiting the land and timber resources of the eastern forests. Stricken with remorse for what they had done, Gilbert's father sent the young scion to a European forestry school to learn how to rectify the damage.

Working together, Pinchot and Roosevelt declared: "The fundamental idea behind forestry is the perpetuation of forests by wise use." The "use" ethic spilled over to other natural resources including mining, minerals, and grazing, but the "perpetuation" virtue was buried by the false sense of the West's endless abundance and free land given out by the homestead laws.

The Forest Homestead Act of 1906 allowed settlers to homestead acreage inside the Coronado National Forest. Preference was given to the squatters already on the range. Within the northern parts of the San Rafael valley and the Canelo Hills, more than fifty homesteads were filed by 1924, according to historians Hadley and Sheridan. Most of the homesteaders used the deeded land as a base for small-scaled stock-raising on the surrounding US Forest Service lands. Some farmed to supplement their cattle, storing the corn and other crops in pit silos for winter feed. The San Rafael valley was already notorious for poor quality feed during the late winter and dry spring—in 1917, death losses up to 30 percent were recorded. Gradually, the larger outfits bought out many of the smaller ones, adding to their inventory of better lands with natural water and grazing privileges on the forest reserve. Hadley and Sheridan's *Land Use History of the San Rafael Valley* reported:

> During the early 20th Century, the Redrock area—part of the Sonoita Creek watershed—was dominated by Vail and Ashburn, a large outfit that ran Monkey *[sic]* Springs (later the Rail X Ranch) and Empire Ranches . . . East of them, Clyde McPhearson . . . was the largest permittee, running more than a thousand head at times.

McPhearson bought out the small operators, but allowed a few to continue farming as share-croppers, producing silage for winter supplement. Also, the adjacent Redrock Canyon had the advantages of protection from winter storms, cool season grasses, and browse. Later, this became the San Rafael allotment of 11,200 acres for grazing from November to April. Summer range of six thousand plus acres of adjacent deeded land allowed the winter range to recover during the growing season. Today, this is the Vaca Ranch that has been variously rated at four to seven hundred cows year-long, under the able management of Bob and Dusty Hudson.

The Kunde Ranch came into official existence in 1918, when the heirs of Julius Kunde filed on the northwest quarter of section 12, township 21 south, range 17 east, near the confluence of Lampshire and Redrock Canyons. Part of the 160 acres was in the level floodplain with sandy loam soil, suitable for farming. Henry Dojaquez, a relative of the Kunde family by marriage, reported that it was farmed in the early years. In fact, Henry recalls harvesting hay and other crops on several farms and ranches in the region, including the Empire and Rail X Ranches, and the western end of Redrock Canyon near its confluence with Harshaw Creek at the town of Patagonia.

The Kunde family grew old, and due to failing health could no longer manage the livestock or grazing. With no able-bodied heirs willing to step up to the chores, the Kunde ranch was sold to Chris and Larry Peterson in 1998. The US Forest Service had to hire Monk Maxwell, a wild cow catcher, to depopulate the range, including four- and five-year-old unbranded cattle. When the final head count came in, the number was in excess of the 130 cows allowed by the US Forest Service. As a condition of transferring the permit, Chris and Larry agreed to ten years of non-use; in other words, no cattle for a decade on US Forest Service land. Today, the 4,100-acre allotment is permitted for thirty-one cows, with the 160-acre deeded homestead in the center.

The Rail X Ranch encompassed the flood plain of upper Sonoita Creek, a natural marsh (ciénega) fed by *Agua de Manje*, a large artesian spring. Lieutenant Juan Mateo Manje, a Spanish soldier, discovered the spring with Father Kino in 1697 on a jaunt from the mission at Tumacacori to the San Pedro River. When the gringo ranchers took over, they were unable to pronounce the hard Spanish "J" in Manje, and renamed it Monkey Spring. Likewise, cowboys called the Chiricahua Cattle Company, a large outfit who at one time owned the Rail X Ranch, "Cherry Cows."

In the late 1920s, Vail and Ashburn sold the Empire and Rail X Ranches to the Chiricahua Cattle Company, controlled by the Boice family and assorted partnerships. The year before, Frank S. Boice and partners had lost the grazing leases on the San Carlos Indian Reservation and were forced to move. When they had gathered all their cattle, the numbers totaled over twenty-two thousand head, according to historian Peter Iverson.

The original Rail X Ranch included my Crittenden, Corral Canyon, and Red Bear pastures, plus rangeland that extended up the Harshaw Creek drainage and into the Patagonia Mountains. Around Sonoita, legend has it that the senior Mr. Boice ran a burro-mounted construction crew, developing seep springs piped to cement toughs. He regarded the job as so important that he supervised the work himself. So far, I have found four of these on my ranch, none of them with enough water now to be functional. Perhaps they worked when the weather was wetter. He also developed irrigated pastures in the Sonoita Creek floodplain using water from Monkey Spring.

The Rail X allotment and deeded land changed hands in 1935 to Jeffcott and sometime later to Walter and Helen Kolbe. Kolbe operated it as a dude ranch for eastern city slickers craving horseback vacations on a working ranch. R. A. Rich, a New York–based real estate investor, bought it from Kolbe; Rich in turn sold it to Ferdinand von Galen. Tom Hunt managed the ranch for both Rich and von Galen, and expanded the Rail

Redrock Canyon eroding the lip of San Rafael Valley.

X irrigation system. After Tom retired in 2004, von Galen subdivided or sold all but 1,600 acres of the ranch and all of Tom's cows.

Seibold's T Rail Ranch started in 1906 as a homestead to Frank Seibold in the western mouth of Redrock Canyon. Doris Seibold, his daughter, said in a recorded history that: "In those days, cattle were run communally on open range in a single herd with everyone else's. Our cattle ranged as far east as Rain Valley and south into the San Rafael Valley."

University educated, Doris Seibold became a revered teacher of English and history in Patagonia and Nogales schools. At the same time, this stalwart lady took over the ranch when her brother became ill and moved to town. When the US Forest Service was created, the Seibold allotment was permitted for one hundred cows on 3,500 acres in the lower Redrock Canyon watershed. Today, her memory resides in the Patagonia Library, and as an authenticated member of the Cowgirl Hall of Fame in Fort Worth, Texas.

Even so, old-time cattlemen today still refer to small ranchers like Seibold and Kunde as "squatters;" small freeholders who moved in with the homestead era and survived.

Although the San Rafael Ranch lies south of the Canelo Hills, the ranch's history is relevant. Once a Mexican Land Grant of seventeen thousand acres, it was owned by William C. Greene, the copper mining mogul in the early 1900s. Greene's daughter and son-in-law, Florence and Bob Sharp, inherited the ranch when Green died in 1911. Following the death of Florence Sharp in 1998, her heirs wanted to continue the ranching operation but had to sell to pay a crushing estate tax levy. They were negotiating with real estate developers when The Nature Conservancy (TNC) stepped in and bought it for eleven million dollars. TNC then placed conservation easements on the land to prevent its subdivision into home sites and limited grazing to no more than five hundred cows. Tucson business executives Ross Humphrey and Susan Lowell bought it as a cattle ranch. Today, they run a cow-calf operation with two herds, one calving in the spring and the other in the fall.

6

Rainfall, Cow Counts, and Climate Change

Patterns of rainfall in the desert southwest are notoriously fickle, even in the banana belt of the Canelo Hills. On our C6 Ranch, sometimes it wouldn't rain at all; sometimes it didn't rain in the pasture where I was scheduled to move the cows; and sometimes it rained all over the place. I once asked a hedge fund executive what he would do with a business where the major variable on production was inherently unreliable and varied as much as 50 percent in volume from one year to the next. And the owner of the business had no control over pricing the products.

Summer rain over the Santa Rita Mountain foothills.

"I'd sell it quick as soon as you have a good year," he laughed.

At our headquarters, a recent twenty-five-year annual average was 16.3 inches. To my way of thinking, the range needed at least eight-to-nine inches of summer rain to get the cattle through the fall, winter, and spring in decent condition.

Timing was critical. June 24 is San Juan's Day, celebrating Saint John the Baptist, Catholic patron saint of water, and the coming of the summer rains the Mexicans call *chubascos* and gringos misname "monsoons." Even so, I've had rain on or before June 24 only twice. If the monsoon had not started by mid-July, I figured we could be in trouble. One year when the rains did not come until July 27, I was getting suicidal. Every day, I rode the pipelines, anxiously watching the storm foundry of those southern seas where the wind might push moisture-laden air our way and bring relief.

Good winter rains helped, of course, by bringing out spring weeds and cool-season grasses, but the Canelo Hills are too chilly in the winter to grow much feed. (When I ran cattle in the hotter, dryer Altar Valley, winter wheat and the leguminous filigree were important forage plants.) Long time ranchers in our area say that they can get by with dry winters but two dry summers in a row would be hard, and three years a killer—the 1891 to 1893, 1898 to 1904, and 1950s debacles were caused by severe drought lasting for three years running.

Often, ranchers will complain about the "spotty" rains. Summer downpours are often violent and fast moving, but not widespread. Even in a good year, it may not rain enough where we needed it most. One advantage of having big pastures is that the cows can chase the rains, like wild bison or wildebeest.

Winter rains tend to be slow, gentle, and more widespread. Jim Koweek, our local nurseryman and grass monitor, claims that the oak trees rely on winter rain more than the summer, and the present die-off can be traced to a persistent wintertime drought. The other day, I was looking at old photographs from our house site taken in the 1990s and was startled by how many of the old giants had died in the last twenty-five years. Cutting firewood, I noticed that many of the trunks had been rotted out in the center by fungus. Drought lowered the oak tree's natural resistance to infection and to beetle infestation.

In 1997 and 1998, I was short on summer rain and the cows had started to resemble the framework of abandoned wickiups, especially the first calf heifers. A protein supplement helped, but cost a lot. That expense, plus lower calf weights in the fall, combined with reduced conception rates in the cow herd for the next year, would be nails in the bank account coffin. Under such circumstances, many ranchers cull the cow herd severely, saving back the most productive individuals and selling the rest. This reduces the demands on rangeland so that the grasses will be better able to grow back when rains return toward that elusive "normal."

In the meantime, the working rancher can get a part-time job driving the school bus and Mom can wait tables or pick up secretarial work in Sierra Vista. Most ranchers do enough work on wells, waters, and pipelines to qualify as plumbers. And plumbers, as everyone knows, make lots more money than "average" ranchers.

Or you can sell out the herd completely. But starting over is hard. Selling the genetics and environmental adaptations that you have spent decades building up is painful in the extreme. In another dry pair of years, 2002 to 2003, we sent half our cows and bulls to farm fields until the calves were weaned. The pasture bill ate into the profit, but the calves grew big and the cows came back to the ranch bred for the next year. Also the rangeland came back healthy when in the following two years we had over twenty inches each year and we were set up to take advantage of the good times by carrying over some heifer calves.

Why bad years seem to come in pairs remains an unexplained meteorological mystery. Some ranchers go to church and pray for rain. Reverend Steve Lindsey, pastor of the Canelo Hills Cowboy Church is also a rancher. When he got the call, he turned over the ranch to his children and took charge of asking the Almighty for rain. That seemed to work about as well as the native O'odham tradition of drinking fermented cactus juice and dancing.

Most of us just figure that it will rain again sometime. After 2003, I had a good decade except 2009 which had ten inches overall and summer rain of less than seven inches. That bad year was bracketed by eighteen inches the previous year and twenty-one the next, so we got along okay.

Even a small ranch like the C6 is made up of a conglomeration of different soil types, vegetation, elevation, and exposure to the sun, not to mention the spotty rains over the landscape. Also, total annual rainfall can vary as much as 50 percent from one year to the next. The Forest Service pegged our allotted cow count at 215 every year. But given the inherent variabilities, setting the same stocking rate each year was an exercise in informed fiction rather than a science.

"If this is global warming and climate change, bring it on," I joked with my neighbor Mac Donaldson on the Open Cross Ranch the other day after we had three good years in a row. That attitude horrifies the pessimists on climate change like my Ivy League–student grandniece who protested at the Climate Change Summits. And yet, she is right in the long term. There is no question now in the minds of climate scientists that the earth is getting dryer and warmer overall. Also, the 7 billion humans and their wasteful ways are accelerating the process. How much is a matter of much conjecture.

Climate scientists say a few regions may get wetter, so why not eastern Santa Cruz County? One can always hope. But I'd sell my beachfront property (if I had any) before the polar ice melts and sea levels rise.

City people, especially Democrats, often ask why ranchers and farmers are conservatives. The short answer is that we who live on the land are at the mercy of unpredictable weather patterns and commodity markets over which we have no control. Every year, we risk everything, so to change from what has worked in the past increases that risk. Also, the root ethic of conservatism is to pay your bills every year and don't take on unnecessary debt, something that seems to be missing in today's society.

"You have to get through this year in order to get to the next one," my farmer friend Tom Clark instructed. Tom should know. The Clark family has been raising cotton and spaghetti wheat in Marana, Arizona for a hundred years and they are still in business. The difference is that Tom Clark has irrigation water while I, as a rancher, do not.

Our changing weather patterns have to be obvious to ranchers and cowboys who take the time to reflect on the present versus the past and wonder why? In my little part of the world, the summer rains have been strong for the past decade or so. Abundant grass and weed growth has carried over to the winter and dry spring, building up more fire fodder year-by-year. At the same time, record high temperatures (a result of global warming) has dried the soils and noticeably increased our fire dangers.

In 2002, the Ryan Fire started near the southeastern edge of our ranch and burned thirty-eight thousand acres eastward over the Canelo Hills toward the military base of Fort Huachuca. That fire was eclipsed this year by the Sawmill fire ignited by a dim-witted target shooter blasting explosive targets on tinder-dry rangeland. By the end of April, it burned forty-seven thousand acres across the desert grasslands and foothills. Closer to home, an evening lightning strike in the Los Encinos subdivision consumed 1,300 acres and five homes during the night. The blaze roared toward our headquarters until a neighbor's big water truck slowed it down. We stayed up till dawn spraying water and peeing on embers until the fire burned through the power pole on the water well. Luckily, I had mowed a one-hundred-foot radius around the house and barn and trimmed up the low-hanging tree branches. The junipers burned but we managed to save most of the big oaks. Daylight revealed a scorched earth and smoking cinders. We mourned for the neighbors who lost homes and counted our blessings. Even so, the grass grew back knee-high by September, better than ever. So I bought a big water truck for insurance and continued to cast my ballots with the politicians who believe in climate change. For those who do not, they could take instructions from turkey buzzards that now arrive months earlier in Sonoita to beat the increased heat in their wintering grounds in Mexico.

ii

The question of the rancher's survival from one year to the next brings up the issue of how many cows are the "correct" number to have out on the watershed: Which brings up questions about the effects of grazing on rangeland health.

The effects that cattle have on a particular pasture are matters of timing, intensity, duration, and frequency of grazing. This sounds clear-cut in a textbook, yet in practice the complexities are many and varied. Timing is the season of use. Each year, grass plants have to replace about a third of their root system to stay healthy. This process mostly occurs during the summer growing season when the plant's leaves and stems are actively producing the nutrients required for growth by a process called photosynthesis. If leaves and stems are removed frequently during the growing season, the plant may shut down its photosynthetic factory. Repeated grazing during the growing season will weaken the tasty native grasses and they may die, or be crowded out by snakeweed, burroweed, Lehmann lovegrass, bufflegrass, whitethorn, sweet resin bush, or some other pesky plant that cows won't eat unless starved.

Intensity is how heavily plants are grazed, which is related to the number of cows per unit of land; the number per section of land or per pasture. Duration is the length of time the cows graze the pasture; number of days, weeks, or months. Frequency is the number of times a grass plant is grazed in a single growing season. All four factors are allegedly under control of the herd manager, call him or her a cowboy, if you like.

Most grass plants shut down and go dormant during the winter. If plants are grazed during the winter, the effect is less than if grazed during the summer. This is the science behind the US Forest Service's winter only grazing allotments. The plants have all spring, summer, and fall to grow stems and leaves, replace their roots, and make seed, as well as cow feed.

A larger number of cows in a pasture obviously has greater effect on grasses and soils, but this may be good for the land under certain circumstances; when plant growth is rank and stagnant, or the soil surface needs to be disturbed. On the other hand, soil compaction may be increased, and that could be hard on certain species. Some cliff rose bushes in our horse pasture have died for that reason. If the same number of cows stay in the pasture for a longer time—the duration factor—the cumulative effects of grazing will be greater.

Weather, especially amount and timing of rain, can alter the impacts of any or all of these parameters. Grazing at a set intensity during drought has greater effects on plants and soils than during an average rainfall year. In a long, severe drought there may be no regrowth at all, so the cows are eating the plants down to the dirt. Conversely, in a wet year, more cows can be run for a longer time. Winter rains during the dormant season have less effect on plant growth than do summer rains. Even so, good winter moisture gives the plants a head start when spring rolls around.

All of these factors and their interactions with each other creates a bi-ological-meteorological system of enormous complexity. Layered on top is the need of the rancher to make a profit from the production of beef. Cowboys, as the label implies, are naturally more concerned with cows than with grass because the money flows from the number of pounds of beef. That's what cowboys and cow bosses get paid to do.

Ranchers, on the other hand, are, or should be, as concerned with grass as with beef. The time scales here are important. A cow produces one calf per year, usually in the spring. On the other hand, the best forage grasses are perennial and the watershed needs to be managed for the long-term health of perennial grasses.

One method of judging when to move cows out of a pasture is when the cow's hip bones begin to stick up through its hide. She is losing weight, getting skinny, and her calf is starting to look like a hair ball coughed up by the barn cat.

Another method is looking at the amount of grass left in the pasture, and how much grass you have in reserve, all this in consideration with the time of the year, amount of rainfall, and number of cows. Making the correct calls on stocking rates and when to move the cows requires a long and detailed familiarity with the specific landscape; its grazing history; the nutritional needs of both cows and grass; plus the past, present, and predicted rainfall. That local knowledge cannot be gained by reading textbooks or pamphlets, sitting in the Cattlemen's Club bar, or behind a desk in a caretaker agency.

No single answer to the question of proper stocking rate has ever been found, despite a century of range research (See Nathan Sayre. *The Politics of Scale*). As a general principle, stocking conservatively has been shown to be an excellent policy. Out of every decade, three years will be drought, the long-term record shows. Perennial grasses will be sustained by conservative stocking and more cattle can be added when the rains return, as they always have. Humans constructed the calendar as an approximation of Nature's average weather phases. Even so, the earth moves on her own course and humans must adapt.

The carrying capacity of a grazing allotment has been the subject of disagreement between ranchers and the caretaker agency ever since the US Forest Service was created in 1905. The antecedents of this debate go back to the open range days when the number of cattle a piece of country ran was determined by how much water and feed could be monopolized and the amount of capital ranchers had at their disposal. When water ran short, death loss adjusted the stocking rate. When the downpours returned, there was little vegetation to hold back the soil. Rivers, arroyos, and watersheds were down-cut and severely eroded. The decade-long debacle starting in 1891 previously described forever changed the landscape and obliterated the original carrying capacities of southwestern ranges. The land was so quickly overwhelmed that we may never know for certain the number of cows that might have been sustained with careful management over several generations by conscientious ranch families.

In practice, the agencies first allotted ranchers the carrying capacities they were running at the time US Forest Service allotments were formed, starting in about 1916. Recently, I asked one forester why.

"It was that or get bushwhacked," he replied.

Reports from the 1920s by range evaluators in the Canelo Hills said that the forest allotments were still overgrazed and carrying capacities should be reduced further. And they were. From that beginning, US Forest Service standard practice has been to cut numbers of cattle allowed on allotments whenever they could. Often, the cuts were justified, but the Forest Service had a hard time convincing the ranchers who were struggling to survive.

Whether justified or not, that practice has been a recipe for continued conflict. In the early days, many ranchers were driven by the need to make a living from the land and didn't understand that too many cows for too long exceeded the ecological threshold of resilience for their watersheds. Also, the management abilities of the individual permittee had (and still has) a lot to do with the number of cattle a given piece of rangeland can safely carry. So the agencies did not know what else to do except cut. An exception was Aldo Leopold, a forester in the Apache National Forest in Arizona and New Mexico, who advocated for working in collaboration with ranchers to build erosion control structures and fences as early as 1922 (see Jack Stauder, *The Blue and the Green*). Many ranchers feel that the US Forest Service practice of cutting cow numbers has been their fallback position up to the end of the twentieth century all over the West.

As the old millennium came to an end, agencies and ranchers discovered that they often had similar goals for the watersheds. This has led to collaborative rancher-agency associations like the Malpai Borderlands Group and the Canelo Hills Coalition. Even so, it may be too early to say that agencies are required to cooperate with ranchers. Environmental laws, other land uses, Garden of Eden preservationists, and a few backward-looking ranchers still hold back community effort.

7.

The Seibold Ranch

Squint as hard as I could, I still could not see into tomorrow. From 1993 to 1997, everything at the C6 Ranch loped along just fine, even over the rough country—especially over the rough country. One morning I rode up to the gate between my pasture and the Rail X Ranch. Tom Hunt had hung a new sign that read in bold, black lettering:

Private Property
NO TRESPASSING
NO HUNTING
Rail X Ranch

My access over Count Ferdinand von Galen's land had been terminated. I had to find a new way into the south side of my ranch.

"Sorry about the sign," Tom said sheepishly as he gave me a key to the locks in case of an emergency. "The lawyer said it had to conform to state trespass laws."

Although at the time, it seemed downright un-neighborly, in truth I had been forewarned. In our negotiations on the purchase, the count had given me license to cross his land for five years. Now, Tom said that Ferdinand had applied for US citizenship and was moving to the Rail X as his permanent residence. What's more, he was splitting his ranch into a gated community and selling ranchette home sites. The count's attitude toward land ownership was European and he insisted on controlling all traffic over his property, as was his right. I understood that need, having dealt with open-to-the-public problems, especially the damages done by hunters and the Border Patrol.

Redrock Canyon bordered my pastures on the south, and I started looking there for a new way in (see map 1). The Seibold headquarters at the mouth of the canyon had a For Sale sign posted on its deeded land. The place had a walk-away look to it, house with a sagging roof, crumbling adobe barn, splintered board fence, and weeds in the corral. The real estate agent said that the last living Seibold, Irene, wanted to sell her US Forest Service allotment and forty acres of deeded land in the creek bottom. But there was a snag in the deal. The endangered Gila topminnow had been found in the creek and the Seibold allotment was encumbered by concerns over the effects of cows and grazing on the minnow. The US Forest Service had cut the number of cows she could run by one-half, from one hundred to fifty head.

Over the next days, I rode the Seibold Ranch, starting with a circle around the perimeter. Kunde Mountain, a lichen-stained granite outcropping loomed over the deeded land like a dirty hound's tooth. The south boundary fence crept up the escarpment and died where the mountain became so steep that it formed a natural barrier. On the southeast side, the fence tumbled down into Redrock Creek where it joined up with the neighboring Kunde allotment in a pleasant grove of willows and giant cottonwoods.

The east fence crossed the Redrock Canyon Road at a cattle guard and ran up the side of Candalerio Peak toward an abandoned mining claim. Looking out from the high saddle into Lampshire Canyon, I could make out the old Kunde homestead marked by a crumbling adobe shack. Tom

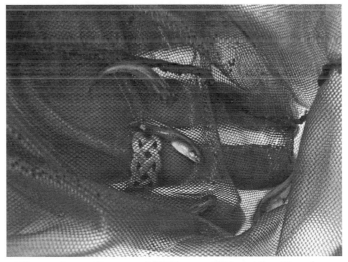

Gila topminnow. Courtesy of AZ Game and Fish and Ross Humphrey

Hunt had said that this bowl-shaped valley had been good cattle range in the old days with natural water and protected by several mountain peaks that circled the horizon.

The north fence separated the Seibold from my Red Bear and Corral Canyon pastures. Old wire dating from the 1930s sagged between rotten wooden posts. In the bottom of Oak Gove Canyon, a Boice-built drinker collected a tiny dribble of water, attracting yellow jacket wasps and bees.

The fence going west up the next steep ridge had been rebuilt after an old brush fire. A heavily-traveled game trail climbed up the ridge through ceanothus bush and fairy duster, browses much favored by whitetail deer. On top, I looked north across to Red Bear tank nested underneath the massive Mount Hughes rim. Through binoculars, I could make out a dozen of my C6 cows lounging around the pond.

To the south, the prospect opened into a broad, mesquite-covered valley that extended down to the cottonwoods growing in Redrock Creek. Riding west another half mile on what seemed like the top of the world, the ridge suddenly tumbled down into another low saddle that connected up with a jeep trail where T. N. and I had made that first heifer drive years ago. Moving cattle from Corral Canyon and Red Bear pastures into the Seibold would be mostly downhill.

So far, so good.

But the Seibold Ranch had only two waters, both in the creek bottom. Pig Camp Spring in a small tributary to the main stem of Redrock Canyon dribbled into a tiny cement catchment. It leaked water most of the year, but looked ephemeral. Oak Grove windmill, also in the canyon bottom, sat on top of a thirty-foot-deep, hand-dug well dating from the 1920s. Jimmy Lewis, who was born in the canyon and looked after Irene's cattle, told me that these waters were usually reliable, which also meant not always.

The creek bottom pastures, East and West Redrock, amounted to about thirteen hundred acres, had the better soils, and ran water in the summer monsoon and during wet winters. Compared to Mount Hughes and Dark Canyon, they looked to me like the front parlor of heaven, in spite of a little brush. The Oak Grove Canyon bottom tumbled through a split in the rocks near the old Boice water trough on Oak Grove Spring and meandered through pleasant thickets of walnut and ash until it reached a fallen-down set of corrals at the windmill.

Hidden between two massive granite mountains, the western-most Seibold pasture contained a deep, pretty ravine of slick rock and boulder slide. Jimmy Lewis called it Moonshine after a bathtub allegedly left there for making juniper berry gin. Oak and juniper covered the north-facing slopes. On top, I looked to the southwest at the town of Patagonia; in the far distance, smoke rose up in the clear dry air from the Nogales slums on the Mexican side of the border.

The sun had dropped below Mount Wrightson when I turned my tired horse southward to leave. Riding down the ravine, I passed another Boice-built water trough, this one filled by a dribble piped in from the spring box catchment. A large dragonfly, orange in color, skimmed over the surface. Four white-tail does scampered up to the oaks and disappeared over the top. Farther down the ravine, wild turkey strutted into a mesquite thicket and began to fly clumsily to their roosting sites. How such an awkward-seeming bird survives and even thrives in the midst of coyotes, bobcats, and lions remains a mystery to me.

The ravine emptied into Redrock Creek a little more than a mile from the forty deeded acres where I could build shipping corrals. But the steep hill on the road in from Patagonia would not accommodate cattle trucks so I would have to haul cattle with goose-neck trailers and pickups. The other downside was that Irene had already sold the land next to the forty acres to an architect sub-divider who planned to make big money from selling home sites. If and when that happened, the stunning seclusion and wildness I had just seen would vanish.

Even so, adding the Seibold Ranch to ours would fill two needs with one deed. First, I would have deeded land access to the south side of my ranch because her allotment and mine adjoined each other. Second, the Seibold at the lower elevation would add the critical winter country that we lacked. We negotiated a price and put the deal in escrow with an inspection period that would give me time to read up on the topminnow situation. As usual, there was a lot more that I needed to know.

Next, I studied the US Forest Service's 1991 Redrock Action Plan to see if I could meet the new requirements imposed for grazing on the

Seibold allotment. The plan seemed sensible and succinct, unusual for government documents in my experience. It covered all four ranches with grazing allotments in the canyon: Seibold, San Rafael, Kunde, and Papago (see map 3). The stated objective was to improve rangeland and riparian conditions, a laudable goal that I shared. The biggest heartburn was the reduction in the number of cows. But I was buying in after the fact and paying only for that reduced number and the deeded land.

So far, so good, again.

But for Bob Hudson, manager of the Vaca Ranch with the San Rafael allotment, it was not so good. His allotment had been cut by 40 percent which reduced his income proportionally. The justification for the reduction in cows was that his part of Redrock Canyon still had lots of topminnow and the fishery biologists wanted to reduce the effects of grazing on the creek.

"If so many minnows are still there after a century of grazing, there must be something about it they like," Bob thundered.

Bob's permit was winter only, meaning that he grazed the canyon only when most of the grasses were in the dormant stage. The rest of the year, he ran his cows on deeded land outside the watershed. The Hudson family had been on the land since 1958 when Bob's father hired on as manager. Bob returned home after college, and assumed the position when his father retired in 1987. He knew the overall landscape better than anyone.

The US Fish and Wildlife Service, the agency responsible for enforcing the Endangered Species Act, had decreed that the ranchers and US Forest Service must adhere to certain conditions in order to minimize damage to the minnow and its habitat. Getting the cows out of the creek bottom during the summer growing seasons was the most critical part. This would require new livestock waters in the upland range and I thought I had a workable plan. My new pipeline and storage tanks in Corral Canyon could do that, but we needed a more reliable water source than the four miles of fifty-year-old pipe coming from Tom Hunt's old system. A new well would do the trick, but how to pay for it?

"Are you sure you want to bite this off?" Diane mused the week before our purchase contract was set to close.

"I've read the requirements and we can meet them," I replied naively. "The alternative is to shut down and sell out, but who would want to buy with no access? The US Forest Service will give us the materials and drill the well. We will do the labor."

"You will do the labor," she corrected.

"Jeanne Wade, our district forest ranger really likes my idea," I added. "It gets her out of a bind, keeps the ranches going, and saves the minnow and habitat. From where the US Forest Service sets, it's a win-win deal," I said, pausing before laying down the most important card.

"The Seibold will up our cow count by a third. We can do better than just break even."

"I'd like that. Some black ink for a change," she cheered up. "But what if we buy and the US Forest Service decides to close the canyon to grazing anyway? Jeanne Wade might not be the decider. What about the Center for Biological Diversity and those other grass-huggers who hate cows?"

"The Endangered Species Act was not intended to put people out of business," I said, dumbly repeating what the presiding judge said in a recent unsuccessful case the center brought against continued grazing in another national forest in Arizona.

"Well, sometimes good intentions ahead of the game get disconnected from how it all plays out at the finish line." She usually gets the last word and this time she was right.

Irene Seibold had only thirty cows left to sell at closing. I passed on them because they had been born and raised in the canyon. Cows don't like sudden changes any more than people do and they would migrate back to their home territory at every chance. The US Forest Service had started to fence off the creek bottom and their sloppy work guaranteed that cows would get through. Sagging barbed wire fences are no deterrent to homeward-bound, thirsty, thick-hided critters.

One of the plan's sensible conditions was that the canyon bottoms would be grazed only during the winter, like on Bob Hudson's San Rafael allotment. This required new fences running parallel to the creek. The US Forest Service, like all federal agencies, has to bid out jobs, and accept the lowest price. A Montana snow bird put in the low bid, thinking he would winter in sunshine and make a killing. He didn't figure on caliche and rock. Abel Murrietta, Manuel's uncle, put in a higher bid, but had the last laugh when the snow bird had to rent Abel's jack hammer to get posts through the natural cement of caliche and rock. As soon as the blizzards were over back home, the Montanan left the job unfinished.

The new well required a new road to get the drill rig in. That year President Clinton had decided that national forests needed fewer roads, not more, and had set a date for the moratorium to begin. Jeanne Wade put her staff to work surveying the new route and I tagged along on horseback.

A massive oak stood just uphill from where the new road crossed between Corral Canyon pasture and the Seibold allotment. I tied Bird to a limb and showed the surveyor the well site Tom Hunt had witched a hundred yards north of the tree.

Suddenly we heard a sharp craaaack and a panicked whinny. Looking back, we saw the horse disappear into the canyon at a dead run, sparks flying off his iron shoes. About then, a bee or two circled around our heads and raced back to the hive.

"Africanized bees." I screeched. "Those were just the scouts. We'd better make a run for it."

A new swarm headed our way up the canyon. I ran in one direction and the surveyor in the opposite. Four hours later we rendezvoused back at the horse trailer where Bird stood ground-tied, his neck swollen and eyes reduced to slits. The surveyor had a dozen stings, but I had only one, luckily not enough to trigger my usual severe reaction to bee venom. Bird had run off with the antidote in my cantle bag.

The bees won that round until the US Forest Service brought in a beekeeper to move the hive. The bulldozer finished the job a week before the deadline, leaving the oak tree untouched. The bees never came back, but we dubbed the new well as "Bee Tree Drinker" on the map. New pipelines now supplied water to troughs in the high north saddles of the Seibold allotment, pulling the cows out of the Redrock Canyon bottoms.

That year, the summer rains moved in on schedule. Thunderstorms rolled up from the south every afternoon, drenching the watershed and making the canyons sing. Rain drops pounding the earth woke the spade-footed toads. Every night they bellowed out love songs and deposited their slimy eggs that quickly turned into pollywogs. The canyon ran red and muddy in the afternoons all the way past the Seibold's now abandoned house and on to its confluence with Harshaw Creek on the outskirts of Patagonia. Without any cows grazing in the bottoms, the grass and weeds spurted up to knee high to my horse.

The Montanan's fence, once finished, divided the Seibold range into canyon bottoms and uplands. My plan was to combine all cows into one herd and move it on a schedule to graze the uplands pastures during the spring and summer. At the end of October, the cows with calves at their sides would come down into the canyon bottoms through corrals at Oak Grove windmill. Here, the calves would be vaccinated and readied for weaning and sale on the first week in December. During their time in East and West Redrock pastures, I thought each calf should gain a couple of pounds per day. After weaning, the cows would go back into the Seibold pastures to heal up. In January, I would do pregnancy testing, cull the open cows, and take the herd back to the uplands, picking up the bulls along the way (see map 1).

Laura White, the Sierra Vista District range conservationist, agreed with my plan in principle, but worried about having the entire herd in Redrock Canyon at the same time. Jeanne Wade, her boss, agreed.

"The US Fish and Wildlife Service is used to seeing Irene Seibold's thirty cows in the bottom. Seeing four times that number with big calves could be disturbing," she said.

But the Montana fence had to be finished first. The fire crew was idle and Jeanne Wade put them to work on the fence, a job they did not relish. When finished, their part was not much better than that built by the Montanan.

Up to now, I had dealt exclusively with Jeanne Wade and Laura Dupree from the Sierra Vista Ranger District. The decisions to cut the number of cows and to fence off all the perennial waters had been made by the two agencies without consulting the four ranchers in the watershed. That part was a done deal. But the details of how to make changes in grazing management on the Seibold allotment were largely up to us, within those limits. We did not agree on every item, but we listened to each other and negotiated consensus solutions, with the understanding that adjustments would be necessary depending on results, and as always, the rainfall.

ii

October rolled around and Jeanne Wade sent a memo to everyone that I planned to put a lot of cows in the Redrock bottoms, but only for a short time. The "short time" part of the memo didn't register with the US Fish and Wildlife Service, or more likely, was not understood. The first week I got a worried call from Laura that the fishery people had seen the cows and were panicky and pissed.

Laura and I met in East Redrock pasture the next day to have a look; the fishery biologists did not show even though she sent them an invite. I was learning that the Endangered Species Act protocol had the US Forest Service dealing with me, the alleged creator of the problem, and the US Fish and Wildlife Service clamping down on the US Forest Service, the agency responsible for solving it. Early on, I sent a letter out explaining my commitment to conserving topminnow habitat and asked for a sit-down meeting with both agencies. The best possible solution for all, I said, would be if topminnow populations recovered and the species was removed from the endangered list. I pledged to work cooperatively toward that goal, but I would not go out of business as they seemed to want. But both agencies ignored my request.

In addition to controlling the number of cows in the pasture, the US Forest Service limits the maximum amount of forage consumed to 45 percent of this year's standing crop. Walking with Laura through the tall grass, I had no idea how much was there, even less how much my cows had already eaten. I suppose I could have asked them, but I was not "cowboy" enough to speak cow.

"We'll stretch out this one-hundred-yard tape, and I'll show you," Laura said. We were on a grassy bench above the creek. Laura was dressed in a fashionably pressed, pickle green uniform with a floppy hat. She carried a clipboard, an ominous sign I thought to myself.

"Take a step and look at the first grass plant next to your right toe and decide whether it has been grazed or not."

I looked down and said "No."

"No, no, not like that. You have to get down and really look at the leaves and stems," she said. Up to now I was beginning to like Laura. She kept bees as a hobby and I loved honey.

"Well," I said, looking up. "This here plant has one stem nipped off."
I plucked the stubble and held it up.

"Okay, that is a 'Yes." Now we take another step."

"This don't seem like cowboy work." I struggled to my feet and walked down the tape.

The next grass plant was a side-oats grama with all the seed spikes marching down the stem in single file, as beautiful to me as a long-stemmed red rose. I wondered if these were left side-oats or a right side-oats, but I hesitated to ask. Laura did not seem to be in good humor.

"No nipping here," I said hopefully. By now I'd figured that "No" was good for me, and "Yes" was bad.

"Okay, that's a 'No,'" Laura said, putting a mark in the "No" column.

An hour later we'd finished. Laura tallied up the "Yes" and "No" marks, and pulled out a graph. On the horizontal axis, she located the number of grazed plants out of the one hundred we had looked at. Reading up to a regression line drawn in the middle of the graph, she looked over to the vertical axis and read off the percent of the total grass that my cows had grazed.

"Eighteen point eight percent utilization here," she crowed.

We repeated the test in three more places. My gobbly cows had eaten on the average, something less than 20 percent of the total. They were not breaking the law. I breathed a sigh. I was liking Laura better again.

"Where did you get the graph?" I asked. The other methods of estimating utilization that I had tried took a lot longer.

"This was developed fifty years ago on the university's Santa Rita Experimental Ranch." Laura pulled out a faded copy of the journal article and handed it over.

"Keep it," she said, opening the door to her bright green US Forest Service truck. "Do this every week or so and when your cows get to 45 percent you can 'head 'em up and move 'em out."

Laura's magical graph silenced the complaints. Armed with a degree in range management from the University of Arizona, she had clout, and could back it up with ciphers to one place to the right of the decimal point. When I moved my cows out, they had gobbled somewhat less than 45 percent—less than the biblical allotment of half and half.

Many ranchers believe that the 45 percent use threshold had been pulled out of some Washington bureaucrat's file cabinet, or some other more personal space. In fact, the science behind the cipher is sound. A grass plant has to replace about 30 percent of its root system every year to stay healthy. If more than 50 percent of its leaves and stems are grazed off, the plant's root building system shuts down. The threshold effect is dramatic, but reversible. When the stems and leaves grow back, root building begins again. But repeated removal weakens the plant and it may die, or be crowded out by weeds and brush. This is overgrazing.

Applying the method over my pastures, I began to make eyeball guesses on the percentages. With time and experience, I could guess what the percent would be by looking at the plants and knowing the cattle count, time in the pasture, and season of grazing. While Laura's method was seemingly precise to the decimal point, to me it had only four meaningful categories: none, light, medium, and heavy. Riding the pastures, my eyeballs began to itch when the utilization got to the heavy side of medium: Time to move.

In any given autumn, I could find places in the pastures where all four categories existed simultaneously: heavy around water troughs; light or none on mountaintops; and medium most everywhere else. The decimal-point precision assumed by the US Forest Service and the grass-huggers did not exist out on the watershed, except at the exact place and time of the measurements.

Utilization surveys had other limitations. It had to be done in the fall after the grasses had completed all their growth for the year. Only then could anyone be certain what 100 percent growth would look like. Also, the 45 percent threshold had been developed on midwestern range with deeper soils, higher rainfall, and different grass species.

Still, the utilization concept was useful. It forced me to get off the horse and look closely at the grasses and soils, and think about what utilization meant to the watershed and the cows. Over time, I learned to estimate how much the cows had taken over the whole pasture in the same way people like Bob Hudson had done for years. Also, Rich consistently guessed the "eyeball" utilization lighter than I did, and he was right more often than I. This I attributed to the fact the ranch was his sole source of income. Lower utilization meant the pastures might run a few more cows for a longer time.

Laura's grass counts got me past the agency's heartburn over cows in the bottoms that first winter. But my upland pastures also needed summer rest. And with one herd and four big pastures—Corral Canyon, Red Bear, Moonshine, and Oak Grove—I now had the flexibility to defer summer grazing in one pasture every other year so the grasses could regrow and recuperate.

Ranching is a season-driven occupation that requires constant vigilance and continual adjustment. Every January, every permittee meets with the US Forest Service to pay their grazing fees and go over their grazing plans for the coming year. Sometimes, office-bound agency people try to rigidly enforce the movement of cattle on such and such exact future date, but Mother Nature sets the calendar with its seasons and rainfall. Flexibility is required to meet the actual conditions on the range. Ranchers and range managers cry out for more flexibility, but too often the rigid, top-down bureaucracy has resisted, like old machinery rusted shut. I was lucky—and our watershed was lucky—that the Sierra Vista District range people gave us some leeway on moving dates.

I thought the old Seibold Ranch could run more than fifty cows with our new grazing management, but the endangered topminnow in Redrock Canyon was a hot-button issue so I didn't push for an increase. When we started resting the creek bottoms all summer, the fall grass clippings in East and West Redrock pastures averaged two to four thousand pounds per acre. At the 45 percent allowable use, we had lots of grass to harvest with our cattle and our weaning weights jumped a hundred pounds each.

Many ranchers focus on the number of head they run, but the beef business is a game of pounds sold and price per pound. On a one-hundred head basis, the extra one hundred pounds per calf netted us an extra fifteen thousand dollars. On some years, depending on the market and rainfall, that amount could double. We would have needed thirty more cows to get that same amount and I was pretty sure that my upland pastures would not be able to sustain that increase (except during exceptionally wet years), nor would the US Forest Service approve it.

iii

Sometime later, the US Fish and Wildlife Service demanded that the US Forest Service reinitiate consultations over not keeping to the guidelines spelled out in the formal consultation documents. By this time, Laura had taken over the trails division and Bill Edwards had taken her place as the district's range conservationist. Bill also had a degree in range management and had done the once-every-ten-to-twenty-year vegetation monitoring in the watershed. Six foot tall with a military bearing, Bill was an officer in the military reserves and certified for fire control management. Over the years I knew him, he had been called up twice for the war in Iraq. He made quick decisions about people. I had gone out with him when he made the initial evaluations, the only rancher, he said, who bothered to understand what he was doing, why, and how it could affect them.

"Jerome and Sally Stefferud were making their fish counts and found the exclosure fencing had been breached at Pig Camp Spring," Bill said. "The cows pooped inside and ate grass."

"Well, that's what they do," I replied, not sure whether he was seriously concerned. He was. At Pig Camp, a storm had toppled a tree and crushed the fence. I had chased the cows out and fixed it a week or so after it happened, although I couldn't be sure of the dates.

"Here are the official terms and conditions that have to be met for you to continue grazing in Redrock Canyon," he said, passing the papers across the conference table.

I had seen these before. Some made sense, like grazing the bottoms only during the winter. Others seemed imaginary, like cows stomping on or drinking down a minnow; having a biological monitor in the stream when working on fence (I had probably been in double jeopardy fixing Pig Camp spring by myself); checking stream banks for trampling and browsing on trees and shrubs. In their attempt to be inclusive and quantitative on all possible events that might occur in the watershed, the fish biologists had become nonsensical.

Surrogate means a stand-in or substitute for an event that cannot be measured directly. Twenty fish was their imaginary threshold for "Harm" to the species in Redrock Canyon and events like a downed fence were deemed "Surrogates" for those "twenty dead fish" even though no dead fish were ever found. These events were *assumed* by the fish biologists to have harmed more than twenty fish, and therefore we, US Forest Service and rancher, were out of compliance with the terms and conditions and subject to severe penalties. But they had no data linking cause and effect of these supposed misdeeds; only opinions, and these came from studies on other species of fish living in different habitats. The threshold number of "twenty" minnows was little more than a wild ass guess, it seemed to me.

"Bill, you better come out and show me how you measure trampling and browsing," I demanded. "If you can measure stuff as vague as this, I'll be damned."

We met at the water gap fence over the creek between East and West Redrock pastures, beneath an enormous ash tree where a pair of gray hawks had fledged their young last fall. Skims of January ice winked back the rising sun and the willows and cottonwoods spread their naked branches over the banks. Rainfall that year exceeded the average by half and the creek was still running strong. That summer, I had seen a great blue heron stalking the shallows and kingfishers perched on willows, the brilliant blue-white-colored birds taking their share of the minnow population.

"Here's a level stretch to measure trampling," Bill said as he strung out the hundred yard tape on the stream bank.

"I figured you'd choose this one. They all drink here. Aren't you supposed to measure the effects over the whole stream? What about the other half mile of streambed where it's too brushy or rocky for the cows to get to?"

We walked along counting footprints, discussing the finer points of bovine podiatry, like dew claws and whether a hoof drag counted as one or two tramples. I had already moved the cows out and today their hoof prints had faded.

When we got to the browsing, we examined willows and cottonwood shoots for nibbles. The US Fish and Wildlife biologists had decreed that if 15 percent of branches examined had been nibbled, we had "Harmed" more than twenty fish and were therefore in violation. Nibbling was another surrogate indicator. But here again, they had zero linkage of the event to cause and effect, let alone to a specific percentage of nibbled branches at a single point in time.

"What about deer?" I asked. "This canyon is full of white-tail and they browse more than cattle. You mean to tell me that you can distinguish a deer nibble from a cow nibble?"

"Not really," he said.

"So the cows get blamed for all the nibbles. Good thing we don't have elk in the canyon."

"I don't make the rules," Bill muttered.

"This is Bullshit, Bill! Surely you and I have more important things to do to help this watershed. I'll fence this area off so we can keep the cattle out of here because these asinine tolerances that can't be determined with any accuracy are assumed by the so-called experts to Harm more than twenty minnows. They don't have a shred of data to link numbers of nibbles or footprints with dead fish. They just want to get rid of cows and this pasture is critical for weaning my calves in the fall," I ended, shocking myself with a conclusion that many ranchers had already reached.

"Looks like you are within the limits anyway," Bill said.

"Hell yes!" I said. "That's because we moved the cows ahead of schedule."

"By the way, thanks for getting me out of the office," Bill replied lamely as he drove off. . . .

I turned and walked back through the gate, as mad as a Gila monster with someone standing on its tail. To my left, the water gap was up and tight, the juniper stays bobbing in the clean current as it entered the canyon. Downstream a hundred feet, a granite reef twenty feet tall turned the stream back to the opposite bank. I climbed the dark rock and sat down to cool off.

Bedrock mortar holes the diameter of my fist had been worn into the rock where a long-vanished people had made their granola from walnuts and acorns. Spear points, rock scrapers, and pottery shards scattered along the creek were clear evidence of continuous human occupation of Redrock Canyon for hundreds and perhaps thousands of years.

The granite on which I sat was older still, ancient almost beyond comprehension. Up until nine thousand years ago, Southern Arizona had been a rich grassland that supported vast herds of grazing mammals; horses, camels, mammoths, sloths, tapirs, antelope, and their attendant predators. They had trampled and grazed the stream bank plenty and the fish in the creek coevolved and survived. If Bill Edwards and the US Fish and

Wildlife Service had been around then to count hoof prints and nibbles, they would have freaked out, I thought, flipping a pebble into the stream and watching the ripples spread and disappear. The difference was that the ancient mammals moved on to graze, drink, and wallow elsewhere, allowing the plant's natural recovery process to take place.

They stayed for a while, used the landscape and moved on, migrating to better pastures. That's the simple genius of Nature that I was trying to replicate here with my cows. Stay a while and move on, so the watershed could renew itself as it had countless times over millions of years. Stay and move on, so that this nit-picking that Bill and I had done this morning would not be required. Or better said, so that the watershed would heal up and I as a rancher could also thrive; or as Diane and I had hoped: "Do better than break even."

The Endangered Species Act seemed designed to do away with my use of the canyon. Perhaps that was not the intent of the law, but the clumsy, adversarial way it was being administered by the agencies made it seem so. But agencies are made up of people, and the people who were driving the process wanted me and my cows gone.

In a light bulb moment, I understood that the Redrock Action Plan to improve the rangeland and riparian corridor was not the ideological end game for the fish biologists. The non-binding conservation recommendations to the US Forest Service in the formal consultation documents concocted by them spelled out my sudden enlightenment:

1. Remove all livestock grazing from the watershed;
2. Work toward acquiring all private lands, especially Cott Tank (on Bob Hudson's San Rafael allotment);
3. Build a dam near the western forest boundary to isolate the watershed from outside influences;
4. If grazing is continued, treat all allotments as a single unit.

I climbed off the granite reef and walked downstream to the confluence of Moonshine Canyon with the main stem of Redrock where I had had my first and only direct encounter with the fish biologists, Sally and Jerome Stefferud. At the time, they were making the annual fall fish counts by dip netting through a long narrow pool. A middle-aged married couple, Sally was short and had the look of a person used to working outside with her gray hair drawn back into a bun. Jerome handled the dip net with a well-practiced dexterity. Their backpacks lay on the stream bank stuffed with data books, collection vials, and water bottles. I had introduced myself and stepped down from my horse to see what they were doing. The conversation went something like this:

"Hi, I'm Richard Collins, the grazing permittee. Have you found any topminnows?" I asked, looking at the wriggling fish and other critters crawling in their net.

"We think so, but we will have to confirm the identification in the laboratory," they replied. "There are other species of minnows in here, long fin and speckled dace, maybe mosquitofish."

"So you have to kill the critters you are trying to save?"

"We have a permit for scientific purposes," she replied.

"Seems sort of like cutting the legs off the mule so it fits into the stall," I mused.

"The drainage down from Oak Grove Spring to the windmill is heavily grazed; your cow droppings are fouling the water," she fired back.

"That's approved on my grazing schedule," I said. "The cows have to come down from the foothills to get a drink. That poop and stomp makes fertilizer, good for the grass. Anyway, I'll be moving them in East Redrock pasture soon."

"We're camped in that pasture at Pig Camp spring," she said. "The cows won't bother us, will they?"

"I can wait a few days until you're done," I offered, as they turned back to the specimen jars.

"Hey. Hey. That's a giant water bug." I said suddenly, pointing to a dangerous looking two-inch-long insect with claws scurrying across their net. "I've read that they eat minnows and frogs. Does the bug have a permit too?" I was hoping for at least a smile.

"That's natural predation," they replied, unimpressed with my entomological lore.

"Have you noticed all the deer grass and new trees coming back since we switched to winter grazing?" I asked, hoping to make a connection between their work and mine.

"We have to keep going," they said, shouldering their packs and turning away.

I had spent a lot of time thinking about Redrock Canyon, riding up the streambed and into the uplands several times each week. Not that this was a hardship. I loved it. This is what I wanted to do, to make the watershed work for my cows and the plants and other animals in it.

The fisheries people spent a good bit of time chewing on the same questions and landscape, only from different angles. But we never had a sit-down discussion to see if we had any shared goals, even though I asked for one. The law, or the way the agencies administered it, made no provision for that to happen. We had a chance that day to start talking but they were not interested in a conversation with an arch-villain cow owner. Perhaps I was guilty of levity on an issue they deeply cared about. I should have remembered that biologists are generally humorless about their work. Self-reflection was not in the US Fish and Wildlife Service's handbook. And neither was collaborative, cooperative effort, apparently.

During the several formal consultations between the US Forest Service and the US Fish and Wildlife Service, I, as one of the ranchers grazing the watershed was given the status of an "Interested Party." That allowed me to make written comments to the documents that flew back and forth between the two agencies, which I did. But they were ignored or dismissed with a few perfunctory statements. As far as I knew, the decisions were made by the husband and wife team of Sally Stefferud, employed by the US Fish and Wildlife Service, and Jerome Stefferud, representing the US Forest Service and supposedly the other interested parties, including me.

From the rock on which I sat, the application of the Endangered Species Act was an adversarial proceeding. In a court of law, or when publishing the results of a scientific study in a peer-reviewed journal, one member of a husband and wife team should recuse themselves from the deliberations; to sit out of the decision-making process to avoid any favoritism. But for topminnow and Redrock Canyon, their assessments and opinions were accepted as gospel, regardless of conflict of interest, or outside contrary information. Only they had "truth-based" knowledge about the watershed and its minnows.

People on both sides of the grazing debate contend that such decisions should be based on the "best available science." But often the "best science" is that which supports the preconceived notions of one side or the other. Part of the problem is that few people understand how science works. The best science requires qualified practitioners who are unbiased toward either side and disinterested in the outcome of the study. But in today's polarized debate over grazing, such people are scarce as a circus without clowns.

Aldo Leopold, the father of the conservation movement, wrote that the general public believes that science has all the answers, just as the prudent scientist knows that he or she does not. Leopold understood that the scientific method cannot consider every possibility, given the vast number of ecological determinants and connections in a watershed, many of which are still unknown even today. A hunch based on long-standing familiarity can sometimes provide useful insights even though it may run counter to the existing scientific dogma.

The next spring, I fenced off that section of the creek bottom along with fifty acres, and put a new water trough on the Kunde Mountain slope on the opposite side of the road so the cows had full access to the rest of West Redrock pasture. Bill Edwards had backed me up with the agencies. The US Forest Service correctly deemed it a "riparian pasture." We pastured a few steers in it to make them "grass-fed beef" that we sold for a premium, or as a hospital pasture for a recovering prolapsed cow.

October and November sped by and we weaned on schedule, December first. That day, Manuel Murrietta had arrived at the corrals before dawn with his best horse. By the time I arrived, he was separating calves from cows. He brought in twenty pairs at a time, and started them trotting around the corral in a tight circle. Now and then, a cow would peel off for the next corral. Before long, all the cows had left and the calves were still circling dumbly in the center. He opened another gate and pushed the calves in, and then repeated the process until all the cattle had been sorted. Looking over the tops of the rolly-poly calves decked out in their winter coats, I felt like my gamble had paid off. They had gained so much weight that now it took only ten to make a dozen and they brought top dollar at the sale.

8

Fences, Fires, and Drug Mules

The pleasurable part of my ranching enterprise lay in working cattle on horseback and selling fat calves in the fall, seeing the country renew itself with the changing seasons and weathers. The payoff came due in December like a Christmas present with the sale of fat calves, the fruits of a year's labor and thought. But fences were absolutely required to make everything work and fence building had to be the hardest job on the ranch.

The Canelo Hills soils are thin and very old, supporting a toupee of grass covering a skull of rock or caliche. Rolls of barbed wire measure one-quarter mile in length and weigh almost one hundred pounds. The wire is strung between brace posts built in the form of an H. An H-brace requires two wooden posts sunk in the ground thirty inches deep. Holes are excavated with a shovel and digging bar that has a point on one end and a spade on the other. The toupee of dirt is scraped away and a hole chipped in the ground with the spade end of the bar while the rocks are pried loose with the point. When enough loose dirt and rock has collected in the hole, the digger switches to the shovel or an empty coffee can to reach-down and scoop-out. In easy ground digging the holes might take a couple of hours, but in caliche it may take all day.

Round posts eight inches in diameter and eight-feet tall are US Forest Service standard issue, pressure-treated against rot. The posts are dropped in the hole and leveled up while dirt and rocks are tamped around them with the bar. A four-by-four-inch horizontal timber is locked between slots sawed into the upright posts and secured with spikes. Then, top-to-bottom cross wires are strung between the posts. In the center where the wires cross, a stake is inserted and twisted until the H is pulled together solid. The longer the horizontal member, the more tension the brace can withstand. Once the H is secured, the tops of the posts are sawed off at an angle to prevent rainwater from collecting and rotting out the posts from the top down. The H-brace is a marvel of cowboy ingenuity in applied physics, the same basic design that holds up tall buildings.

When the braces have been dug in, the right-of-way is cleared, and the bottom wire is strung out and tightened until it sings like a banjo. Abel Murrietta builds the best range fence in eastern Santa Cruz County, maybe the whole state. He walks the bottom wire and drives steel T posts in the ground at twenty-foot intervals. The post driver is a steel pipe with weights welded to the top. His crew from Sonora calls it a *chucho*, meaning a biting dog in border slang. Bragging rights are won by the number of strokes, or bites, it takes to bury the post two feet in the ground. On one daunting stretch in Redrock Canyon, two men pounding the chucho in tandem took thirty-seven bites for each post. Where the fence goes over solid rock, Abel uses a jackhammer to make post holes.

On US Forest Service land, the bottom wire is barbless and placed sixteen inches above ground so that wild critters can crawl under. Calves can also squirt through, but find their way back to their mommas even-

H-brace with gate.

tually. The top wire is thirty-nine inches high so deer can leap over. Abel stretches all four strands separately for maximum tension. On each T post, the wire strands are attached with a wire clip. Once, I built a fence by stretching all four wires at once. That saved time, but a year later it sagged and I had to re-stretch it. Built Abel's way, a range fence may last a century.

Cowboys usually ride with fencing pliers and a coil of smooth wire to make repairs or put wooden stays in the fence where it crosses an arroyo. These water gaps get washed out in downpours and have to be rebuilt every time we go into a new pasture. Even so, cattle do get through. On the big ranches, the manager may send a cowboy to work on the neighbor's round-ups to get back the strays. But with honest neighbors who ride their country, the truants are eventually returned home. Down on the border, neighboring ranchers from both sides of the line once traded work during roundups. But with the new border walls, getting cattle back home has become more dangerous and difficult as the cross-border neighborliness disappeared.

Animals will usually bounce off a tight fence when they run into it. But loose barbed wire can be a death trap. Once, I lost a gelding to wire cuts when a midnight thunderstorm frightened him into a sagging fence. After that, I rebuilt my horse corrals with pipe. To the rancher, a well-built fence is a work of precision that will last for generations. Lots of US Forest Service boundary fences still in service were built by the Civilian Conservation Corps during the Great Depression of the 1930s. Nowadays, some are sagging and we have to prop them up every year. Looking at a rancher's fences will tell you a lot about his or her husbandry practices.

One newly minted ranch owner grumbled, after several months of the real cowboy routine, that this was not what he thought he bought into. He had pictured himself riding over splendid landscapes on a handsome horse, gazing at his herd of slick, fat cows. Another whinnied that his ranch had turned him into a plumber instead of a cow man. Myth has been called an extension of reality, but a cowboy's work would be mostly a handful of dirty, difficult jobs if it wasn't for the horse and the cow.

Pastoralism, in its pure form, described a nomadic culture where people followed the unhindered movement of the herd across an arid and untrammeled landscape, chasing the grass and rains without the re-striction of fences. For the plains Indian tribes, that herd was bison. In

East Africa, the early Maasai had a deep affection for their cattle, drank their milk and blood, and protected them from lions. The herdsmen gave them pet names, sang lullabies, and told stories about them; cows were the people's special gift from God. In *Rawhide Ranching on Both Sides of the Border,* Robert L. Sharp's cow camp men didn't drink cow blood, but they retained and retold stories about their encounters with cows and the watersheds they rode. Their narratives describe with real affection the vast landscapes where they lived and plied their trade. Many such stories have been lost or passed over because their language was a vernacular unfamiliar to the literati. One had to be part of the cow camp culture to understand what they were saying and the feelings expressed.

The old men who are also old-time cowboys still lament about the loss of the open cattle range, where a cowboy could ride all day and not have to open a gate. Andy Adams in *Log of a Cowboy*—perhaps the most authentic portrayal of the early cowboy's life—rode herd for five months in 1882 behind three thousand steers from Brownsville, Texas to the Blackfoot Reservation in northern Montana without crossing a single fence. Novelists Owen Wister and Larry McMurtry exploited that life and the landscape crossed in their romanticized novels *The Virginian* and *Lonesome Dove*, without bothering to understand either one. But they make for decent reading if one is not troubled by the lack of authenticity.

Evolutionary biologists, Edward O. Wilson among them, explained the cowboy's natural attraction to the stream-crossed open space as a product of long-term cultural evolution starting way back when humans came swinging down out of the trees and started walking upright. Cowboys have long known this to be true. Open, grassy pastures with water are much preferable to dry brush thickets.

Except for sheep in high mountain summer pastures, nomadic pastoralism in the Western United States is a thing of the past. And good thing, too. Uncontrolled grazing from the 1880 through the 1920s devastated the southern Arizona range. Today, one can still see its ruin south of the border on the communal *ejido* ranches in Sonora. Here, the community owns the land and each resident family has the right to graze their cows. How many is usually decided by the number each family needs to make a living. Often, all the cattle are run together in giant pastures with only perimeter fences to hold them. The ejido system was instituted after the Mexican Revolution of the 1910 and 20s when many large haciendas, including those owned by foreigners, were seized by the government and parceled out to the peon communities who lived on and worked the land. But as Mexico's population grew, more and more cattle came in until the grasslands had been grazed past the ecological tipping point, converting them into thorn scrub, cactus, and bare dirt.

Our C6 Ranch had pastures ranging from 320 to 3,000 acres. We fenced traps around water troughs to hold cows during roundups. We split Crittenden pasture to keep cows away from mountain mahogany during the winter. Big ranches have bigger pastures but the principal is the same: To control the timing and duration of grazing and to mimic the natural movement of herbivores chasing the rains and seasons. This preserves watershed health and keeps our cows away from the toxic plants.

Even so, in the rural west, the spirit of pastoralism is deeply ingrained in our myths, just like the false notion of limitlessness. But to ranchers who take the time and trouble to see, the watershed has taught us that ecological limits are not only inescapable but indispensable, if we are to thrive over the long haul. "Don't Fence Me In" was a western ballad that expressed a pastoralist's yearning for freedom from limits. But nowadays, songwriter Kris Kristofferson said it better: "Freedom is just another word for nothing left to lose."

ii

The word *exclosure* is a verb converted into a noun. Every time I type it, the computer underlines it in red. The verb is to *exclude*, which means to keep out. "Exclosure" is Forest Service bureaucratese for the fence barrier that keeps out whatever is not wanted within.

The fish biologists staked their topminnow recovery effort on exclosure fences around the headwater springs and perennial springs and other wet areas in Redrock Canyon. In some places, exclosures amounted to wishful thinking based on the hope that if cattle were excluded from damp areas, they might hold water year-round and topminnow would take up residence. One such attempt on the C6 Ranch was on upper Oak Grove Spring.

"This is a terrible place to build a fence," Bill Edwards said. Bill was at that time the Range Staff Officer from the Sierra Vista Rancher District. "It won't be up very long. The first good storm will wash it out."

"That's if the Mexican backpackers don't cut it first," I growled.

We were standing on the edge of a steep ravine in Red Bear pasture looking down into Oak Grove Canyon at a shiny barbed-wire fence stretched between green steel posts driven into the hardpan and cobble by Abel Murrietta and his crew. Five deep arroyos tumbled off the Mount Hughes ridge and sliced into the main stem of the canyon at the base of a steep hill. The fence crossed each arroyo with water gaps placed at right angles to the current. In the canyon bottom, patches of deer grass sprouted between the rocks in a formation the fish biologists called a "stringer meadow." A wisp of wind swept over the face of the steep hill on the other side of the canyon, the grasses nodding to it.

At the east end, a yellow jacket seep called Oak Grove Spring had been piped to a drinker one hundred years ago in a vain attempt to water a handful of cows, but it only held water during the monsoon or a wet winter. Perhaps back then, the weather had been wetter and it watered cattle occasionally, but not now, nor during the two decades that I had been looking at it. And probably never again with global warming looming, according to the US Forest Service hydrologist.

Even so, the US Fish and Wildlife Service compelled US Forest Service to fence it off to see if excluding cattle might miraculously make the water flow and create new topminnow habitat. But the idea was a pipe dream and a power play. By forcing the exclosure to be built, they demonstrated that the Endangered Species Act gave them the power to enforce even dubious projects such as this.

"It's dangerous, too, Bill," I continued. "A flood will strip the wire off the steel posts, and string it downstream to snag a cow or horse or deer. Or the animals will be trapped in the canyon bottoms during a cloud burst when they can't get out. Even Abel's water gaps will wash out here."

We walked up the canyon rim and looked down to a well-worn footpath that ran west toward Highway 82.

"The drug traffickers have a trail in the bottom of the main canyon so the Border Patrol helicopters can't see them. They've already cut the fence." I pointed to the gaping hole, frustrated and feeling riled up. "I see them walking through here all the time."

"There's not much I can do about that," Bill said ruefully.

"You know, Bill, we rotate the cattle so Red Bear pasture only gets grazed for about four months out of the year and it gets rested during the summer every other year. The cows drink on the new pipeline so they don't come down here much anymore." I stopped as my frustration was mounting and the useless fence wasn't Bill's doing.

But the installation perhaps served another purpose? Perhaps, the US Forest Service would get fed up dealing with the problems and cancel our grazing allotments. Then there would be no need for a fence. But to be more charitable than I felt at the time, perhaps the fish biologists truly believed that if the disturbance of grazing were removed, the watershed would revert in a few years back to the water flow of centuries ago.

Months later, Chris Peterson, owner of the Redrock Ranch, and I walked Oak Grove Canyon with covey of seven specialists from a trio of agencies: US Fish and Wildlife Service, Arizona Game and Fish, and the US Forest Service. Chris and I had learned that an outcome might be more forthcoming if we had them all corralled at the same time and place. Halfway up the dry canyon, we bumped into a troop of south-of-the-border backpackers hot-footing it in the opposite direction toward the highway. We had disturbed their lunch break on the way to Tucson, Phoenix, or Las Vegas to find work, or to deliver drugs.

But I was glad that we had gotten the office-bound agency folks away from their paperwork to confront reality out here on the watershed. The truth was that they all yearned to be outside in the clean air putting their boots to the ground instead of sitting in the office pushing paper or attending meetings. The watershed and its creatures were what they had dreamed about when they declared their majors in college, studied hard, and paid a high tuition to attain their degrees. I, on the other hand, was out here every day and every week. One of them, in an unguarded moment, said he envied me my job.

I had given up their kind of life decades ago for less money, little convenience, and no security. But I was my own boss, responsible to my family, the local community, and my conscience. And to the land. Especially to the land and the animals I placed on it. Now and then, I felt the disgust of not living up to the standards I had set for myself: satisfied when things turned out right.

I lived a season-driven life following the changes in Nature's moods; witnessed amazing sunrises and stunning sunsets; struggled through grueling droughts and experienced the blessed relief of the monsoon; witnessed the astonishing creativity of plants, animals, and landforms. On days when I got whiffy from working in the corrals, I had the full pleasure of a hot soapy shower that night. People who live and work inside don't get dirty enough to fully enjoy being clean. I worked with interesting people, including some on this hike. I traded colleagues and co-workers for friends and neighbors. I rode horseback over challenging country with cowboy-rancher peers whom I admired and learned from. I knew the pleasure of physical work, not as arduous so as to exhaust the body, and not so routine as to deaden the mind. The complexities of the watershed and our enterprise fully occupied my body and mind with a spirituality that went above religious convictions. But I digress.

Sometime after our excursion, the head hydrologist of the US Forest Service voiced his opinion in writing that Oak Grove Canyon would never collect enough perennial water to make fish habitat. But the time, money, and annoyance had already been spent and the topminnow was no better off. And the damage was already done.

Who then would remove the wire snares?

iii

June, 2011. Few climes lack a lean season. On the Arizona borderlands ours falls during the dry months of April through June. By noon the temperature had already reached one hundred degrees. Even our resident mockingbird had stopped its cheerful song and perched open beak and panting in the shade of the barn. These were the relentless, nosebleed days, the kind that dried out the sinuses and curled the hair on the back of my neck. Our last rain fell on December 22, a wonderful one full inch, followed by a light snow that dusted the bald knob of Mount Wrightson to the west. But now, the landscape had long since lost its graceful touch. The grasses had shriveled and did not have much strength. Our cows started to resemble the framework of abandoned wickiups. In May, we moved half of the cattle off the ranch to the farm.

That last rain concluded the wettest year in Sonoita for decades; twenty-one inches fell at our house, even more at higher elevations. The Canelo Hills turned as green as the Amazon. But so far this year we've had no moisture: zero, zip, zilch, *nada*. Adding to the fire fuel, January's subzero temperatures killed many mesquite trees. The combination of heavy

Monument fire. Courtesy *Tucson Daily Star*, Dean Knuth, June 13, 2011.

grass left over from last summer and the current drought created a perfect storm for wildfires, to the grim delight of the Mexican drug cartels.

Two days ago, I noticed a puff of smoke rising from the south end of the Huachuca Mountains, thirty-three miles southeast of my ranch head-quarters as the crow flies. This morning it had ballooned into a towering mushroom cloud billowing over Montezuma Peak. By midday, the winds were strong enough to blow Christ off the cross, driving the smoke plume eastward into New Mexico. A month ago, that same offshore wind from California pushed smoke our way from the massive Murphy fire west of Nogales. The air smelled barbecued.

No one has officially stated who started these fires, but the drug cartels were prime suspects. They have done it before as a diversionary tactic. The Park Service and the Border Patrol both said today's fire had started just across the line in Mexico at the edge of the Coronado National Monument near Smuggler's Ridge. The Murphy fire started on the border along known drug trails that stream up from west of Nogales toward Tucson. Both had to be human-caused because the sky has been cloudless for months.

Later that morning, I drove south on Highway 92 headed for the fire, dragging a stock trailer behind my truck. Friends had livestock that had to be moved out of the fire's path. Just before reaching the turn-off to the monument, I bumped into a blockade of police cars and fire trucks, their emergency lights flashing. The high-jumping flames had topped Montezuma Peak and were racing down Ash Canyon eastward into a subdivision of lovely homes overlooking the San Pedro River Valley. Through binoculars, I saw flames bursting through the windows of one house just before the roof collapsed. Next door, the chapel of Our Lady of the Sierras was already a smoldering ruin. Firefighters had tried to stop the flames by cutting a fire break across the steep hill behind the church. Giving up, they now trudged in single file over to the next ridge, masked and roped together for safety. Nature has many ways to humiliate its most adventurous creature—drought, fire, and flood foremost among them. We sure could have used a little flood.

On the way home, I parked on Three Canyons Road, looking west into the maelstrom. The intense combustion created tornado-like winds that drowned out the scream of sirens and tossed burning embers skyward, spreading the fire in a downhill rush of flame and smoke. The fire now raced unchecked down the mountain toward the strip malls lining Highway 92. Sky-crane helicopters circled the firestorms like a squadron of gigantic miller moths, each helicopter dangling a refilling tube from its belly. Swooping down into the billowing smoke they released their two thousand gallon load in a single massive spray on the fire's leading edge. Relieved of its eight tons of water, the aircraft bobbed up out of the smoke clouds and circled back to the parking lot to refill.

A motorcade of thirty Border Patrol trucks—I counted them—rushed past me to help with the on-ground evacuations, each truck carrying four patrolmen. If the drug cartel bastards did set this fire as a diversion, they succeeded beyond their wildest imagination, destroying sixty homes and businesses and costing millions of dollars to fight. I called home to Diane and warned her to watch for drug mules coming up on our side of the Huachuca Mountains through the San Rafael Valley toward Sonoita and Highway 82. To the east on the San Pedro River, the water gap in the border wall would be breached tonight by drug mules hurrying toward Interstate 10 at Benson. The gatekeepers were otherwise occupied.

The *Arizona Daily Star* cited immigration data about how the illegal border traffic has slowed down so much that the Border Patrol officers were getting bored. With fewer jobs available in the United States because of the recession and tons of publicity over deportations, fewer illegal immigrants are now jumping the wall and many already here have gone back home to Mexico.

Politicians claim their anti-immigrant policies are working. Perhaps so, but the drug cartels don't read gringo newspapers. A mile south of our house along a Forest Service road, the brush is littered with yellow rope and black plastic used to wrap marijuana bales. I show the Border Patrol the evidence and ask why they don't stake out night patrols on these drop spots. "Too dark and too brushy," they reply. But they do drive by and park there during the day. I go to community meetings and tell them what I see, but the Border Patrol seems glued to the upholstered seats of their pickups, at least in our area. Their checkpoint on Highway 83 going toward Interstate 10 and Tucson shuts down for inclement weather, like schools on snow breaks, while the drug scouts keep watch. The borderlands would be a lot more secure if the Department of Homeland Security had developed a competent

horse cavalry instead of pissing away a billion dollars on electronic surveillance that could not see through dust storms or down into the arroyos.

Back-country, border-crossers are a different breed these days. Used to
be that most of them were honest country people returning to a job in El
Norte or new immigrants looking for work. Nowadays, they are mostly drug
packers from Mexico's cities and towns. Some, perhaps many, are still honest
people, driven by poverty and cartel coercion into carrying drugs. An elderly
gentleman from Nogales, Sonora, who has a green card and does yard work
in our town claims that half of the young men in his barrio are so employed.

"*No hay otro trabajo,*" he said with a shrug. There is no other work.

So we have had to become more cautious. Used to be that when I saw
someone lying under a tree I'd ride up to see if they needed help. Now I stay
back. Last week in my Red Bear pasture, I watched a Mexican Fed Ex delivery
of cannabis destined for America's Heartland. Through binoculars I counted
ten men trudging up a ridge, their foreheads cut by tumplines that supported
the black rectangular bales on their backs. The leader carried a long gun.

Still, it is impossible to anticipate every encounter. Four days after the
Coronado Memorial fire, I rode out to check water lines in Dark Canyon
pasture. The horse saw them first, shying away from a juniper thicket. My
cow dog Ben heeled up behind the horse and whined. Sis wagged her tail and
walked toward their camp, following her nose to a half-empty skillet of beans
and chorizo. Too late to turn away, I called out, "*Buenos días, amigos,*" to the
two men rising up on their elbows. I told them I was looking for cows and
they pointed uphill where I'd already seen a small bunch grazing peacefully.

"*¿Son dos caminar solo?*" I asked, inquiring if they were walking alone.
Yes, they replied, we going to Tucson to find work.

I rode around the thicket to get a better look. At first they said they
were from Nogales, but when I asked where they had crossed the border
they replied Santa Cruz, a three-day walk directly south at the end of the
San Rafael Valley. I asked where they were from in Mexico. "*Tijuana,*"
the one in the red cap replied. That's a long way from here, I mused,
asking them why they didn't cross in California. "*Es muy difícil ahora,*" he
answered, complaining how hard it was to cross into Southern California
now. (Operation Gatekeeper border enforcement started in 1994, pushing
illegal border traffic into the wildernesses).

"*¿Son burreros?*" I asked, and instantly realized that was a stupid question, asking them if they were packing drugs.

"*No, no, señor,*" they quickly replied.

I didn't see marijuana bales, but they had full shoulder packs leaning against the tree, along with a gallon of sweet tea, a milk carton of water, and a half-empty jug of mescal.

"*Buen viaje, señores,*" I said, and roweled the horse up the hill toward the cows.

People meet in the tangled brush on a sharp hillside twenty-five miles from the border: one, a rider on horseback with a pair of cow dogs; the other two, Mexicans bedded down in a thicket with full mountaineering packs and hiking boots. They greet each other. The conversation is casual, not threatening. The rider asks questions.

Beyond that, what else could be known? That the rider is not Border Patrol; that he is obviously a gringo looking for cows; that he speaks some Spanish. That he is exposed like a snail on a plank as he rides off. That his cell phone does not work in Dark Canyon. Beyond these things, neither could tell for sure if the other was armed. Neither could be certain of the other's destination or intent. But my friendly salutations were wise. Mexicans are a congenial folk, generally speaking.

What could be guessed? That the overly curious gringo cowboy might bring back the Border Patrol? That the Mexicans were going to work, as said? That they were drug mules on the way to make a drop on Highway 82? That they might be "Go Backs," headed back to Santa Cruz with the payoff money? The Border Patrol says that "Go Backs" are the most dangerous border crossers that you can run into because they carry the drug money back to the cartels.

Lately, I've thought about carrying a pistol. Chris Peterson on the neighboring Kunde Ranch carries a hog-leg, six-shooter strapped low on her hip when she is working outside. She says that the gun enlightens the drug mules that she is not an easy mark in case they get careless ideas. My son Rich sometimes carries, especially when he is afoot working on our pipelines that the burreros use for footpaths. He also travels with cow dogs that give warning if someone is approaching.

A friend whose ranch has five miles of border fence has carried a .38 caliber Smith and Wesson ever since the border heated up a few decades ago. The pistol has a two-inch barrel and sits neatly on his right hip within easy reach but out of the way on horseback. Nowadays, the border in his area is fenced with vehicle barriers made of railroad track, twenty-foot-long top rails waist high supported by cross rails at each end. Running parallel to the new barrier is a dirt road for Border Patrol trucks. A sagging barbed-wire fence erected in the last century sits behind the new one, a gloomy reminder of more neighborly times. Back then, ranchers from both sides worked together to keep their cattle on their home ranges. Nowadays, when cattle occasionally slip through the barrier, getting them back home is more difficult and dangerous.

The new fence has stopped most cross-border vehicle traffic, although the cartels will sometimes push the rails aside with a tractor or use a flatbed tow truck to drop a drug-loaded pickup over it. They painted one such truck Forest Service pickle green for camouflage. The Border Patrol trucks stir up clouds of dust and they do not help maintain the roads. Even so, my friend prefers the present situation to the past. Before the vehicle barrier, drug and people smugglers made their runs in broad daylight almost every day, cutting the barbed-wire fence and speeding over the ranch roads often with the Border Patrol in hot pursuit. Now, the drug mules hop the barrier at night and stay to the canyons and mountain trails where they cannot be seen. This rancher's family homesteaded this land three generations ago and he has no intention of leaving it. When asked about Trump's new border wall he says emphatically: "No Thanks." What we have is working okay and the wall would permanently scar the land.

My judgment on the gun carry question is that a pistol is like any precision tool that must be used regularly to stay proficient. And I don't take the time to do so. Also, I have no experience in judging the level of threat I might be facing as a Border Patrolman presumably would. At a certain critical juncture it may be impossible to tell, like when a desperate immigrant lost and out of water jumped at me from behind a juniper thicket. After I got my panicked horse turned around, I tossed him my water bottle and led him to the highway on horseback. Like most ranchers, my first impulse is to help. In an interview given several years before he was murdered by a border crosser, rancher Rob Krentz remarked: "Well, if they asked me for water I'll still give them water. I mean that's just my nature."

Late last fall in Sonoita the weather turned cold. Down south in Mexico the pot crop had been picked and packaged for delivery into America's Heartland. One morning Diane looked up from her desk in time to see seven men dressed in black sprinting down our fence line, a scant hundred feet away from the house. She ran to lock the doors and dialed up the Border Patrol who surrounded our house with white and green pickups fifteen minutes later, red lights flashing. But the Go Backs had already faded like smoke into the Canelo Hills. Later, the officers found five hundred pounds of marijuana stashed by a windmill on the Tunnel Springs Ranch a mile or so away. We have the advantage of a nearby Border Patrol station at the Sonoita crossroads. For others who live in more remote areas, the response time is often several hours or days. Now I keep a loaded gun in the house, but Diane refuses to touch it.

"I don't do guns," she says.

Even so, I know that I may bump into drug mules who would shoot first if I threatened them. That danger is minimized by cartel standard operating procedures. The business organization that employs drug mules values secrecy, maneuvering through the borderlands with as little publicity as possible. The last thing they want is more military on the border getting in the way of their shipments. But if one of the delivery boys is spaced-out on meth or heroine or pot, or hates gringos for whatever reason, this undercover edict by the drug bosses could be meaningless. Rob Krentz was armed, and I suspect that carrying a gun wouldn't do me any good either.

Borderland ranching has always been risky, mostly because of the terrain, weather, and working with livestock. The weather is still the rancher's biggest hazard: drought, thirst, heat, and cold—especially drought when the land burns up, the grasses wither, and the cattle become a tapestry of bones. But today, a new menace looms just across the border in the form of Mexico's criminal cartels, a threat that exists in service to America's insatiable appetite for illegal narcotics and cannot be stopped by higher, stronger, or longer walls.

9

More Horses and a Dog

As we rode into the new millennium with the addition of the Seibold and a couple of leased pastures, we needed more horses. Through the Quarter Horse Association, I learned that the Bird horse had been raised on the Dean Reeves Ranch in Eagle Butte, South Dakota. Taking a chance I called information and got the telephone number.

"Yes," Mrs. Reeves replied, "we still raise horses. Matter of fact, we're having our annual sale the second week in September."

The Reeves sale catalog listed seventy-six horses, most of them raised on the Reeves Ranch, and fifty-one foals weaned right off the mares. Their stallions carried the bloodlines of the legendary stallions Peter McCue and King P-234, renowned for siring rugged cow horses that worked for a living. Dean's sons, Jim and Tom, grew up horseback, breaking colts and riding bucking horses. Tom went professional, qualifying for 18 trips to the National Finals Rodeo. In 2001, he was crowned World Champion Saddle Bronc Rider.

The Reeves Ranch lay thirty-eight miles south of Eagle Butte so isolated that their chickens roosted with the burrowing owls for companionship. Diane and I drove the rutted dirt road on a mid-July day to have a look-see. Dean Reeves was a middle-sized bear of a man in his mid-fifties with a tight, round belly and hair sticking between the pearl snaps on his shirt. His wife Emma Lou had the dark hair and high cheek bones of Native American heritage.

"Come to make an early pick?" Dean whinnied as we got out of the truck.

"I have a good gelding at home sired by Sir Fancy Bird and I'd like to find another one or two like him," I whinnied back.

"The Bird horse died in a blizzard a few winters ago so we don't have any of his offspring, but we've got several by T. J. Blue Cowboy that are just as good. Maybe better," he said. The sale horses were tied all around the outside of the arena, a kaleidoscopic assortment of colors from gray to bay, sorrel to paint, dun, palomino, and coyote-colored buckskin. The grays showed the coloring of Reeves' reference stallions, T. J. Blue Cowboy and Roan Bar Country. Jim Reeves rode a big gray gelding that caught my eye with his soft eye and easygoing attitude. When Jim roped a steer, the horse squatted on his hocks and took the jerk without a flinch. Jim took the rope off the critter and the horse walked easy-like back to the roping box, completely unruffled by what he'd been asked to do.

"That's Jim's pick of this year's three-year-olds," Dean said. "He's a T. J. Blue Cowboy."

A thunderstorm boiled up on the afternoon horizon. Rain drops big as marbles started hammering the ground, turning the arena dirt into a mud bog.

"You better get a start for Eagle Butte, Dean warned, looking up at the darkening sky. If the gumbo gets too wet you might be here for days."

We got up the first hill and then ran into a real downpour. I switched to four-wheel drive and gunned the truck, but it was like driving into wet cement. We sat in the cab with golf ball-sized hail bouncing off the truck roof until Jim showed up with a giant tractor and pulled us back to the headquarters.

Emma Lou put two more places on the dinner table that seated fifteen, all cowboys and Reeves offspring. The pot roast nested in a pan of lovely gravy, áu natural, brimming with vegetables from her garden, followed by sour-dough bread and cherry cobbler to die for. Sleeping accommodations were arranged when Dean said: "You folks take our bedroom upstairs. Me and the missus will sleep in the basement. The other house is full of cowboys."

I've lived in cities and towns where the people next door are strangers. But in ranch country neighborliness is a constant. We felt at home with these thoughtful people in a countryside that many would consider Nowhere.

That September, we bought four geldings, including the big gray called T. J., a fast-running son of the famous Windy Ryon that Dean had misnamed Apache; Tuffy, a four-year-old bay; and a dark bay gelding with a flowing mane and forelock that had been Emma Lou's favorite. When asked her why she had decided to sell him, she replied with a sigh: "Can't keep them all; this is what we do." When Diane wrote out the check, Dean Reeves called us aside and said if we ever wanted to sell T. J. to call him first. "That's the easiest horse we've ever started," he remarked.

ii

A year or two after I brought the Reeves's horses home—time gets away
when you're having fun and getting things done—I back-rode Moonshine
pasture on T. J. with my cow dog Troy. Our job that day was to find a dozen
heifers that we had missed when we moved the main herd into Oak Grove
pasture the week before. Of all the jobs on the ranch, I like back-riding the
most. Back-riding is like a solitary Easter egg hunt writ large, with cow critters for colored eggs. Even though I've ridden this country for years now,
I find something new every time I go a-looking; a concealed arroyo or bird
or flower I hadn't noticed before. Or I may run into an old acquaintance,
like the lost stub-tailed cow that will have an early calf next year.

When I first started on this ranch, back-riding was more of a pain.
I'd find a few head and then have to drive them five miles to the corrals,
then ride back and look for more. Now, with money from the Canelo
Hills Coalition (more on this soon), we've fenced holding traps around
the water troughs in each pasture. Now, when I find a cow or two, I can
hold them in the traps for a day or so while I go looking for a few more.

Fall is my favorite season for prowling, especially after a good monsoon.
In southern Arizona, too much rain is usually just about enough. That
summer's monsoon literally swam into the Canelo country. Never had I
seen the hills so green, the canyon flows winking back at the rising sun.
The grasses were tall and seeded out; side-oats grama and plains lovegrass
on the steep hillsides, green sprangletop and blue grama in the bottoms.
The hummingbirds and buzzards had gone south, but graceful Northern
Harriers returned. The hawks swooped over the rolling contours of the
grassland hillsides, looking and listening for the rustle of mice or voles.

Today in Moonshine, a stream of water rushed over the slick granite,
collecting in pools deep enough to bathe in. At the edge of the pools,
clusters of red monkey flowers attracted hummingbirds and bees; not the
backyard honey bees, but the big, black, solitary, ground-nesting bum-
blebees that bustled and shouldered their way from blossom to blossom.
By autumn the cows looked well-to-do, building lumps of fat behind their
hip bones. As we drove them to the corrals the week before, their calves
frolicked in front of the herd.

Over the past year T. J. had developed a lot of what horsemen call "rate." Rate means that the horse will move up when asked for speed and quickness to catch or block a cow, then settle down after the action is over. Manuel Murrietta had seen it first, roping steers. "This is one good, big, gentle horse that tries hard to do what you ask for, every time," he remarked.

"Yeah, and he is smarter than a dictionary" I added, pleased with my purchase.

T. J. and I topped over a low ridge, circled around a hill and peeked into a wide ravine split down the middle by the creek. On the far side, a mesquite thicket covered the slope that led up to the yellow, lichen-covered rock pinnacles on the mountain top. I stopped to glass the hillsides for cattle. T. J. stood as still as a tripod on a spotting scope. A half-dozen deer bounded over the top and disappeared in the juniper thickets. Above, a Red-tailed hawk soared on the thermals. Suddenly it wheeled and plunged downward like a four-foot winged blade, disappearing behind the ridge. On the trail Troy-dog sniffed at coyote scat, hiked a leg and drenched it with squirts of pee.

Around the next turn, the canyon opened into a grassy basin, golden in the soft autumnal light and we stopped again by the stream. Troy crouched under T. J.'s neck to bite stickers from his paws. A covey of Mearns quail flushed in low, scattered flight and then dropped into the grass and started to call the covey back together with a quiet peeping. The dog watched the harlequins with a certain disdain, then resumed biting stickers. A cow dog, his business was not with such small, feathered foolishness.

We climbed on. Around the next turn I saw the heifers scattered over the middle reaches of the canyon, grazing up behind a pipeline drinker we had installed with Canelo Hills Coalition money. T. J.'s pace quickened and climbed to get around them. One-by-one we pushed them toward the canyon trail that went up to the holding trap in the next saddle a half mile ahead. After our weeks and months together, the horse anticipated our moves. Or perhaps I had given him cues so subtle that I myself was unaware; a slight shift of my weight in the stirrups, a gossamer touch on the reins.

Troy-dog was cued differently. A border collie from the plains of New Mexico, he had the highest I.Q. in dogdom. Troy had started herding sheep as a yearling and then graduated to moving sheep in a feedlot at two

years old. He operated on voice commands and instincts bred into his behavior by selection pressure for herding over a hundred generations. He
crouched low and stalked the cattle like a leopard getting ready to spring,
eyes locked on the heifers who eyed him nervously and turned away from
his stare. He stopped, one front paw lifted and looked back at me.

"Go on," I said.

Troy leaped ahead and started the heifers moving with a few deft nips
at their heels. The cattle went up the canyon at a trot while Troy-dog
silently crisscrossed behind the herd to keep them moving. Suddenly, a
maverick split off the bunch and made a dash toward the juniper thickets
on the ridge-top five hundred feet above.

"Look back."

Troy sprinted around the errant critter. He stopped the heifer with a
sharp bite on its nose and then pushed her back to the herd, nipping at
her heels. The rest of the way, he took one side of the herd and I took the
other. He had no preference; nor did I. Our idea was utilitarian, to do the
job the easiest and quickest way.

Starting up the last ridge before the fenced trap, my saddle slipped and
I stepped down to reset. Nature called and I dropped my chaps and made
water, then mounted and followed on. By the time I got to the trap, Troy
had the heifers penned and was crouching low in the entrance like a closed
gate, tongue lolling out. He looked happy, proud-like.

We were two head short. A cow trail came down from the high ridge to
the west. Tracks and shiny mounds of cow poop declared that the missing
pair had watered here earlier and gone back up. T. J. and I started for the
trail and Troy leaped to follow. "Stay Troy," and the dog melted down
into the open gate.

The trail was a quarter mile up 45 degree slopes on a narrow ledge.
T. J. labored up, slipping on the loose scree. His one fault was environmental. He was raised on South Dakota's flat-land gumbo and had not
yet adapted to our mountain country. Even so, T. J. would develop into a
decent rock horse, not the best, but good enough.

On top, I reined up to let T. J. blow and catch his breath. The air
smelled of wet juniper and horse sweat, a fog of cowboy perfume that
lodged in memory like a childhood dream. The morning air was so

clear the beyond became visible. To the southwest lay the tiny town of Patagonia; farther on the twin cities of Ambos Nogales on the Mexican border. To the northwest, Mount Wrightson still slumbered in its appalling permanence, surrounded by the black clouds of last night's storm. Five hundred feet below us sat the snowbird mansions built in the Rail X Ranch Estates, one complete with a swimming pool and covered *ramada*. The subdivision was gated, meaning only that the backpackers coming up from Mexico entered from the rear instead of the front gate on their way to Tucson to find work or drop off drugs.

Ahead the ridge flattened out and we rode to an empty water trough where the two truants were lying down, chewing their cuds with a sideways grinding of their lower jaws. A collapsed, ten-thousand-gallon water tank squatted a little ways downhill from a big sheet metal apron. The apron had a gutter on the lower end to collect rainwater. At the low end of the gutter a big pipe had been attached to funnel rainwater runoff over the lip of the big tank. Good place for a drinker, but when the US Forest Service had it built decades ago, the contractor had neglected to put the gutter above the lip of the tank so that the water spilled out on the ground.

"They forgot to use a transit and level," Rich said when he first inspected the contraption. Water does not run uphill, not even for the US government. Our annoyance was not that ranchers make no mistakes; we do, me included. The difference was that we have to live day-to-day with the results while the agency person goes back to the office until next year.

"Time to go" I said to the heifers as T. J. moved behind them. The trail to the trap descended in switchbacks across the face of the bluff. T. J. skidded down the mountain in short, slide-steps, iron shoes nicking on the granite boulders. The cattle saw the other heifers below and bawled. At the bottom, Troy-dog slunk to one side and let the others in and I stepped off to close the wire gate.

Inside the trap, a new water trough sat in the fork of the saddle between the two pinnacles of Moonshine Mountain split by the divider fence between Corral Canyon and Moonshine pastures. The high elevation of the trough drew cattle up out of the bottoms of Oak Grove, Moonshine, and Corral Canyons pastures (see map 1). Uphill a little ways from where we stood, a five-thousand-gallon storage tank connected to the new pipeline to insure that we had reserve water if the Mexican backpackers or hunters cut the lines. Another big improvement thanks to the Canelo Hills Coalition.

The heifers went back to their narrow-minded business of grazing. An hour later we would move them to the windmill at Oak Grove corrals. I pulled T.J.'s saddle off, hobbled his front legs and turned him loose on a thick carpet of grass. I leaned back against the saddle and pulled a bag of deer jerky out of the cantle bag. Troy-dog laid down and commenced to bite stickers again after he gulped his share of the dried meat.

10

Canelo Hills Coalition

Our Canelo Hills Coalition came together in the winter of 2001–2002, spurred by a dense dust cloud of acronyms: FWS, ESA, FS, NEPA, BA, EA, and BO. Harm and Harass, Incidental Take Statement, Surrogate Indicators, like water witching or worse. Reasonable and Prudent Measures and the Terms and Conditions of a nonnegotiable deal. Reinitiation of Consultations, a chance to tighten the screws against cows. A barely comprehensible legalistic, pseudoscientific, dehydrated language created by a bureaucracy to supposedly save endangered species. But nowhere did it suggest that people get together and talk about their visions and goals for the shared watershed. The Endangered Species Act, a law that contradicts itself by erecting barriers against the most powerful human engine for change—collaboration and community effort.

Reading the formal consultation documents wore me out. Written in the passive voice and jargon of the professional expert, it was empty of any expression of the watershed's true value, its multiple beauties, incredible intricacies, a coherence that when respected could allow me to continue grazing. Only lawyers and bureaucrats could reduce the workings of the watershed to such limited possibility.

Conservation recommendations; those nonbinding, not-so-gentle hints of what the US Fish and Wildlife Service would really like the local US Forest Service to enforce. Redrock Canyon had been through this mill more than once since the 1991 Redrock Action Plan. In every go-round, the recommendation to eliminate grazing had been repeated, after the US Forest Service had been scolded for not counting hoof prints and nibbles exactly on schedule, or having a cow in an exclosure for a short time, or a fence knocked down by a flood.

"Bob, it looks to me like Fish and Wildlife is treating Redrock like a single unit, not four different grazing allotments," I said. Bob Hudson, manager of the Vaca Ranch, leaned his elbow over my pickup bed as we talked. "We should do the same, we all have the topminnow and we share the creek."

"Not if you are talking about combining our operations. We've got different cattle, different ways of doing things. I'm already winter only, and the rest of you graze it year round," Bob said.

"I've already gone to winter only in the canyon bottoms on the old Seibold place. John McDonald on the Papago has only one pasture in the watershed and he uses it mostly when there is natural water in the canyon. Chris and Larry Peterson have taken ten years of non-grazing use on the Kunde," I said, pausing to gather my thoughts.

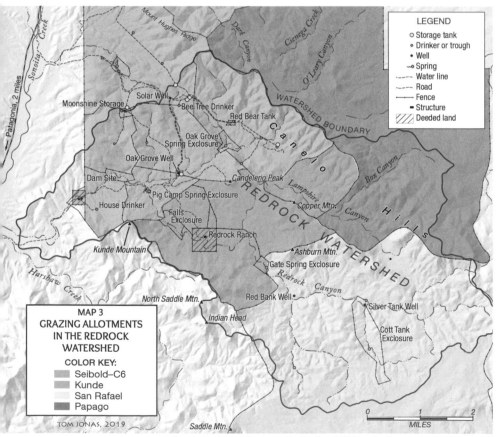

Map 3. Grazing allotments in Redrock Watershed.

"But I agree about not combining operations. You got Herefords. I like the F-1 crossbreds. But we use the same grazing management. We all rotate our herds around to rest the pastures. We need to tell the agencies that the whole watershed is doing that. The second thing is to get our own vegetation monitoring going," I continued.

"Yeah, they are killing us with those spot-checks made a decade ago," Bob scoffed. "This is now, and we cut back our herds way back when. The US Forest Service's head biologist is so anti-cow he has set up every rancher in the forest to cut cow numbers any way possible. Even the range conservationist told me that."

"We'll go to the University's Cooperative Extension Service. They have the range scientists who know this stuff," I said. "I've already talked to Dean Fish. He thinks the range science program would go for it. We need to fire back," I said. "Their science is sloppy, but the way the Endangered Species Act is written and administered lets them get away with it."

"Agreed, but will the fish people believe our monitoring? They will probably call us liars if we find something different from theirs," Bob said.

"We need the Sierra Vista Ranger District to buy in. Do the monitoring with us. They have to be partners to make this work."

"Being a partner with the people that stabbed me in the back? That's going to be hard to swallow," Bob said. "Let me think it over for a day or two."

"They are setting us up to close the whole canyon to grazing; period, end of story," I concluded. "We can't afford to hire lawyers to fight that battle for us. At least I can't."

Earlier, when I first heard the rumblings that the US Forest Service wanted to cut cow numbers again, I called Wendy Glenn of the Malpai Borderlands Group, asking if we could join up. The Malpai ranchers' coalition in Cochise County had pioneered collaborative work on their watersheds with state and federal agencies to return fire to the landscape for ecological restoration. Wendy listened carefully, but declined, saying that our ranches were separated by a hundred miles and located in different biological zones, the Chihuahuan versus the Sonoran deserts.

We needed our own coalition, Wendy suggested, because the problems are almost always local and are best solved by local people with local knowledge working with the agency's local people. I felt much the same way, but the Endangered Species Act and the way it was being applied in our watershed blocked any homegrown participation.

I then asked a group of experienced range managers and conservationists to take a look at my allotments and help me come up with a vegetation monitoring plan. Sure, parts of the Redrock watershed needed help, but the government agencies tried to make a case against my Crittenden and Corral Canyon pastures, most of which were not even in the Redrock drainage.

When they found out that I was asking for objectivity, not a whitewash, there was an astonishing circling of the wagons. Dean Fish and Kim McReynolds from the University of Arizona's Cooperative Extension program were the first responders. Others included Dan Robinett, a range conservationist whose botanical knowledge and integrity commanded respect from both sides of the debate. Jeff Simms, an open-minded fisheries biologist for the Bureau of Land Management, agreed to look at my riparian areas. Phil Ogden, emeritus professor of range at the University of Arizona, lent us his wisdom of accumulated science and practical experience.

George Ruyle, the university's extension specialist in range joined up after taking a horseback ride. We entered from the Rail X side and rode up on the last water trough on Tom Hunt's old pipeline. The rangeland around it told the story of long term, heavy use.

"What's going on here?" George asked suspiciously.

"This was the only permanent water in the pasture for the last thirty years," I explained. "Until I took the new pipeline over the saddle," I said, pointing east to a low spot between the hills two miles in the distance.

"Dan Robinett did the engineering. Afterward, we strung out the pipe one 500-foot coil at a time. Every section had to be pulled in place by hand, or by this here horse I'm riding. Bird busted his hinges on the first coil. After he got used to it, this big bay-roan bastard pulled two sections at once." I reached down and checked just to be sure I wasn't riding him on a loose cinch.

"It goes to twenty thousand gallons of new water storage at Red Bear pasture," I continued. "Now we've got three new permanent waters in Corral Canyon pasture and one in Red Bear. The drinker just ahead Rich named 'Pain-in-the-Ass' water. It's in the lowest point of the pipeline and leaked a bunch until he installed a good pressure valve."

The new water system was a collaborative venture. I had gotten a grant from the Arizona Department of Environmental Quality (ADEQ) to help pay for the pipe, and factored in some extra money for new fence and erosion control. Why was ADEQ interested in watering my cows? The state's money came from the Federal Clean Water Act. The feds were interested in reducing "Non-Point Source Water Pollution." Think of a sewer pipe emptying into a river. That's point source pollution. The rest is nonpoint source, and mostly comes from soil eroding off watersheds. Erosion is a natural process. Taken far enough, it can create a national park, like the Grand Canyon. I didn't want Redrock to become a Grand Canyon on my watch.

Yet all watersheds, even the Grand Canyon, are naturally stabilized by vegetation to hold back the soil and rain, to keep water on the ground while it soaks in. In the same way that a cement parking lot has more runoff than a lawn, heavily grazed pastures have higher rates of erosion, more soil loss, and less infiltration of rainwater into the ground. Grazing management that increases vegetation and ground cover helps hold back water and topsoil. That means less sediment going down the creeks and rivers. People who study soils say that it takes at least a thousand years to make one inch of topsoil. And all life on earth depends on that first few inches.

Some US Forest Service folks liked our project too. Early on, I decided to just keep working and working until we found those people and left the others grumbling on the sidelines. Laura Dupree did the archeological and biological clearances to ensure that I was not trampling anything ancient or rare. Our local Sierra Vista Ranger District kicked in two ten-thousand-gallon fiberglass storage tanks to supply water to troughs at the end of the new pipeline. Even so, I did the work out on the watershed.

Would the US Fish and Wildlife Service buy into the project? Would they understand that getting more livestock waters in the uplands would spread the effects of grazing over the whole twenty-thousand-acre watershed, rather than to have the cows camping out and denuding the bottoms? The cows could graze a while and be moved on; graze a while and move on. Would the agency buy into a project that also helped cows?

Reading their documents, one would think so, because they cited references that listed erosion and sedimentation in the streams as bad for native fish. Think of gills and how they breathe. But the project would help our cows, and cow critters were the culprits in their view.

One foot of top soil over caliche.

ii

The Canelo Hills Coalition first met on my back porch in the spring of 2002; Bob Hudson, John McDonald, Chris and Larry Peterson, and George B. Ruyle, head of the University of Arizona's Range Science Program.

"Is everyone in for the long haul?" George asked. "This is at least a five-year commitment."

"What are we committing to?" Chris asked.

"Intensive vegetation monitoring on each ranch, set up and done by our Sustainable Rangeland Management Program, but only if each of you actively participates. We will set up monitoring sites in every pasture and read them in the fall. You'll have to go with the range technicians and help. It takes one day to read two to three sites, and depending on the size of the ranch, you'll have six to twelve sites." He paused.

Dr. Ruyle was not a big talker and this was a long speech. George was in his fifties, trim athletic physique, pencil mustache, and rimless glasses. He had earned his MS in range ecology from the Berkeley hotbed of environmentalism, and moved on to a doctorate from the more agriculturally minded Utah State. He came to Arizona as the university's extension specialist in range and had advanced to head up the entire range science program.

"My staff and I will analyze the data and report what we find. Good or bad. No papering over the results."

"What about the creek bottom, will you monitor that, too?" I asked.

"We will monitor the vegetation only in the creek bottom pastures, but not the creek itself, or the fish. That's up to the US Fish and Wildlife Service since there is an ongoing formal consultation," George replied.

"What will it cost us?" Bob Hudson asked.

"Four thousand dollars a year," George answered. "We have to charge you something but this is only a part of the total cost. There will be three to four people in the field for three weeks every fall, plus office time to collate and analyze the data and write reports. The ranchers will have to provide transportation to your range sites."

"We've got the horses and a place for you to stay overnight," Bob Hudson offered.

"Another thing. The US Forest Service has to participate by sending its range staff to help with the monitoring," Dr. Ruyle insisted.

"I already have a letter of support from the new Sierra Vista District Ranger, Steve Gunzel," I said.

"Having our own data should keep the environmental activists off our backs," John McDonald said. John, the owner of the Papago allotment, was a lawyer.

"Another good thing about monitoring is that all the agencies want some kind of evaluation," I added. "They like to see a whole watershed working together. We will be in a good position to get grants to pay for the new waters and fences we need. There is money out there for this kind of stuff."

"I'm in," Bob said. "But just one thing. I'm busy with the ranch and I don't want a bunch of meetings just for the sake of getting together. If they are necessary, that's fine."

"Hudson's Law," I said. "No meetings unless we need one . . ."

Monitoring for the coalition ranches would not begin until 2003. George and his staff had lots of previously scheduled field work, including mine on the Crittenden and Seibold allotments. Also, the US Forest Service had monitoring records that went back to the 1950s. They had to be found and analyzed to see if the methods used over the years would allow comparisons with the new data to be collected.

Of all human endeavors, science most loves the litany of routine. To be valid, conclusions have to be based on consistent methodologies, applied by experienced practitioners who also analyze and interpret the collected data. Armed with a healthy skepticism, but with a willingness to be surprised, cooperative extension's team of range evaluators had done this before on other landscapes in Arizona.

Even so, George felt that we were on the right track with the rest-rotation grazing management, and grazing in the bottoms only during the winter. And the data seemed to show it. Compared to the 1990s US Forest Service data, the ratings on my pastures had improved from "fair," to uniformly "good," with an upward trend in 2001. But Dr. Ruyle cautioned that single year comparisons might only reflect differences in rainfall one year to the next.

Monitoring by the coalition would be for five consecutive years, giving us solid baselines on which to measure future trends. This would be important with global warming and climate change affecting our rainfall, whether for worse or for the better. As ranchers, we rolled the dice every year, anyway. Like agrarians the world over, we were inherently optimistic but we had to operate with a built-in resilience to roll with the weather cycles. Otherwise we would have dropped out and done something easy a long time ago.

The next step. I went to Elizabeth Boettcher, the ADEQ's administrator of my previous grant and explained our coalition to see if they would fund what we needed to do. She liked the way the US Forest Service and I had worked together before and liked even more our new watershed-wide approach. I explained that each ranch would have to operate separately and we needed to improve the whole ranch, not just the pastures in Redrock Canyon.

"We are in the business of erosion control state-wide, and not just in special problem areas," she relied. "Do you have a list of projects with costs?" she asked.

"Not yet, but we can put them together with a little time," I replied.

Over the next months, each ranch reviewed its needs for water improvements and fencing. Together the four ranches encompassed fifty-five thousand acres, including the twenty-thousand acres in the Redrock Canyon watershed. New pipelines, storage tanks and troughs, refitting existing wells with solar panels, drilling and equipping three new wells added up to the lion's share of the total cost; 425,000 dollars. We had to put up 40 percent in like-kind contributions of labor, materials, transportation, and the monitoring.

ADEQ accounting and reporting requirements were stringent, and no one was equipped to take on those tasks for the whole coalition. Each rancher had to submit paid receipts and pass inspection before being reimbursed. Fortunately, the not-for-profit Coronado Resource Conservation and Development District took on those responsibilities. ADEQ was delighted because they had to deal only with one entity for accounting and reporting, instead of four.

ADEQ also required that we spread the word among other ranchers and parties interested in watershed conservation. During the life of the grant, from 2003 through 2007, we held open meetings where we presented results, including things that worked well and some that did not. Each time, the university scientists presented their monitoring results with data and interpretation.

Even so, some ranchers have been leery of outside monitoring of their range because in the past certain groups had tried to use the data to put them out of business. Some still are, but the Canelo Hills Coalition showed how by working together with the US Forest Service vegetation monitoring could be an avenue to identifying problems that could be solved. Many times, the data demonstrated the rancher's compliance with regulations. Also, monitoring can give protection from lawsuits by anti-grazing groups who often have no reliable data to back up their claims. Sometimes in fact, their so-called evidence has been unscientific and downright dishonest.

These activities saw the light of day when southern Arizona rancher James K. Chilton, Jr., won a counterclaim against the Tucson-based Center for Biological Diversity for "willful, malicious, or fraudulent" conduct. The center had sued the US Forest Service over the renewal of Chilton's Montana US Forest Service allotment, arguing that his grazing practices harmed an endangered fish called the Sonoran chub.

Their evidence of Chilton's alleged overgrazing, published on their website, included photographs of hunting camps, old mining roads, recreational sites, and several pictures that were not even on the allotment. On cross examination, the photographer admitted that one picture showed the trampled and trashed scene of a big party that he had attended the day before.

In response, Chilton had hired a leading range scientist from New Mexico State University to do comprehensive vegetation monitoring over his whole ranch. His results and testimony helped to unveil the center's fraudulent tactics. Taking a page from the center's game book, Chilton filed a counter claim. In a jury trial, Chilton was awarded six hundred thousand dollars in damages in a verdict that was twice upheld on appeal, including to the Arizona Supreme Court.

In the Age of the Anthropocene, our watersheds and its creatures indeed need advocates, but the center's main tool is the lawsuit, which stifles cooperation and collaboration. They are proud of how they do in the court room, but are short on accomplishments out on the land. They seem to be a holdover from the days of confrontation spawned by Edward Abbey's provocative prose, but without his extraordinary literary flair.

The center's lawsuit-based approach promotes tribalism between those who use natural resources—we are all users—and concerned citizens who want to protect our watersheds. The center claims for themselves what they would deny to others: that only they know how to protect and honor the land and its creatures. But real conservation out on the watersheds requires getting sweaty and dirt under the fingernails. The center mostly threatens and files lawsuits to condemn others. If successful in the courtroom or not, the center's legal expenses are often reimbursed under the Equal Access to Justice Act.

The act, originally intended to support veterans, the disabled, and small businesses, gives the center (and other environmental activists groups) large financial incentives to practice combat biology in the courts. In a recent landmark analysis, Lowell E. Baier, a conservationist and legal authority on environmental litigation, noted that reimbursement for legal fees in lawsuits involving the Endangered Species Act now range from $150 to $625 per hour. He further pointed out that "environmental groups have been the most aggressive in reaping larger awards at exorbitantly high rates."

The center promotes their self-proclaimed image of rescuing animals and plants from rapacious ranchers and farmers. But as self-sacrificing advocates, they don't measure up. Internal Revenue Service filings showed that the center's executive director/CEO, Kieran Suckling, was paid $206,807 in 2013, while compensation for its four founding members amounted to $676,850. The Center's six-year average of legal returns from 2008 to 2013 amounted to $969,365 per year. In 2014, the Center received $1,260,754 in legal refunds. Most ranchers and farmers do not have the resources to defend themselves against all that money.

Moreover, the Act has paralyzed America's public land management agencies, Baier argued. The listing of the jaguar with much of southern Arizona as critical habitat is a recent case in point. The preponderance of expert scientific testimony clearly showed that the jaguar's critical habitat is one hundred fifty miles farther south in Mexico. It only rarely visits the United States and does not stay or breed here. Nonetheless, a naïve judiciary ruled otherwise on thin evidence presented by the Center. Part of the problem is that judges, while they may be learned in the law, are not fluent with basic principles of ecology and the way science works to reach a reasonable conclusion. A solution might be a cadre of judges who also are trained in how science reaches conclusions coupled with some common sense, in the same way that juvenile court judges have special qualifications.

The tragedy of the jaguar ruling is not the critical habitat designation—the cat is not a real threat to livestock or people in the southwest. But the loss of hundreds of hours and thousands of dollars of the US Fish and Wildlife Service's budget hurts, when they have other really important stuff to do.

And guess who paid the bill: you and me.

Meanwhile, a lone male jaguar had recently appeared in our nearby Santa Rita Mountains. Dubbed "El Jefe," it was photographed by the University of Arizona Jaguar Survey Project several times over more than a year. When the university's survey ended, the center sponsored a tracker with a highly trained dog to follow the big cat around its haunts, in what amounted to a publicity stunt. With its acute sense of smell, sight, and hearing, coupled with an intimate awareness of its surroundings, the jaguar had to know it was being pursued. Eventually, the cat was photographed no more and probably left the mountains, perhaps afraid of being followed, or to search for a female jaguar in Mexico. Whatever its reason, a private citizen tracking a rare, endangered cat with a hunting dog should have been barred by the Endangered Species Act as "Harassment," specifically prohibited by the act's wording. Instead, the environmental activists used the situation to up their image in the popular press, while the US Fish and Wildlife Agency remained irresponsibly silent.

Even so, the center has one program that shows they understand the Earth's most serious problem. Each year they pass out thousands of free condoms embossed with pictures of endangered species. They target the unusual donations around colleges, perhaps because in the United States students are among the most fertile and sexually active groups. (Among the campus stallions, one may suppose that condoms embossed with jaguars are in greater demand than those with Gila topminnow or the Pima pineapple cactus.)

The center's effort is an effective gimmick to momentarily prod awareness of humanity's massive contribution to species extinction and habitat destruction. The world's human population is now over 7 billion and adding 144 million more each year, while more and more wild species are having a hard time surviving in less and less habitat. By the middle of the century, when we have smothered the earth with 11 billion of our kind, perhaps there will be no wild habitat.

11

Toward a Practice of Limits

The words *inexhaustible* and *limited* are contradictory terms. Both cannot exist in the same object at the same time; if one is true the other must be false. Even my best cow horse can't go in two directions at the same time. Luddites, some ecologists, and the cultural critic/conservationist/writer Wendell Berry, like to point out that petroleum supplies are limited and ought to be used conservatively, or not at all. People who promote solar panels to make electricity claim the sun's energy is inexhaustible. But what about at night? Perhaps ocean waves will someday provide all the energy we need, but can we find ways to store it? Every energy source has its limitations.

Graduation commencement speakers extol the unlimited opportunities ahead for the graduates. But NASA's first photographs of our earthly home taken from outer space forever shattered the notion of human limitlessness. Here was our gorgeous, blue-green globe reefed in white clouds travelling alone in the darkness of the universe. That image defined our ultimate limits as humans. Yes, space scientists fantasize about populating another planet, but who would want to leave eastern Santa Cruz County, Arizona, for Mars or the Moon?

The notion of limits comes hard to the American mindset, especially to people in the West. The politics of limitlessness was encoded in the giveaway of land by the Homestead Acts. The open space that starts just outside our cities and towns seems to imply freedom from urban/suburban confinement. I felt that pull from the open desert next to my family's farm when I was a child. Most modern science is driven by the refusal to accept limits. Science and technology insist that there is always a better deal to be discovered just around the corner. The trouble with this conviction is that going around the next corner leads ultimately and inescapably back to home ground. The cartoon philosopher, Pogo the Possum, voiced this paradox as: "We met the enemy and he is us."

Ironically, ecology—a science that looks into the connections and competitions between plants, animals, and the physical environment—forces us to accept the fact of earthly limits. We do so reluctantly, and try to dodge the consequences of our waste and greed by insisting that the doctrine of limits applies to everyone everywhere except to us.

"I sure wish those city people would quit tearing up the countryside with their damn ATVs and trashing it with plastic," I grumble like a cornered coon, ignoring for a moment that ranchers use ATVs and drink Aquifresh from plastic bottles.

To those of us who live on the land, knowledge coming straight out of life is generally more useful and convincing than that coming from the printed page—unless it happens to affirm what we have already decided. If a study finds that grazing may promote grassland health, ranchers embrace it as "Good Science." Most fisheries biologists would label the same study as "Bad Science" because it validates cattle grazing. But science in its pure form is supposed to be unbiased. The problem is that scientists are also human. And it is human nature to surround ourselves with people who believe as we do. And in so doing, we close our minds to other possibilities.

Even so, most ranchers I know accept the necessity of limits to grazing on our watersheds. During prolonged drought, the only way out is to sell cows. But sometimes the reluctance to do so is a question of when, how many, and what price. And while we dilly-dally, the watershed and our cows suffer. Two reasons for our hesitation are that we look mostly at our cows and think about how much work and time we have in the herd. Also, we quite naturally think in terms of a human time scale.

A single cow can produce only one calf per year. The rancher's livelihood, and consequently our thinking, are closely tied to this annual cycle. In any case, most people and cultures I know about do not think beyond five generations: Back two to our parents and grandparents; forward two to our children and grandchildren. But most of the time we are thinking in the present tense.

"*Numero Uno*, Now."

The cattle debacle that decimated southwestern rangelands from 1883 to the 1890s was caused by rampant overstocking during a severe prolonged drought followed by torrential rains. Even so, a few visionary ranchers like Colonel Henry Hooker on the Sierra Bonita and Colin Cameron on the San Rafael looked back and recognized that years of continuous overstocking the range was damaging their land. They and a few others looked ahead and sold down their herds to save their ranches. In our time, farmer and philosopher Wendell Berry, has looked ahead, informed by human culture but guided by ecological science. Mr. Berry had the audacity to say that if a watershed is used with care not to exceed the ecological limits, it can provide a good living for generations to come and be virtually inexhaustible. Berry was writing about farming and forestry, but the principle is the same for ranching. This common-sense outlook, call it a philosophical or spiritual paradigm if you must, is the polar opposite of the zero sum game played by Garden of Eden activists and contrary backward-looking ranchers.

The important word here is *care*. And care implies *affection*. I cannot conceive doing what I do unless I liked livestock and healthy, working landscapes. I think that applies to all good ranchers who live on the land. People who call ranching an industry are selling it way too short; perhaps they spend most of their time in the corrals, sale barns, or cattleman's clubs. An industry implies making a product with machinery. Ranchers make their livelihoods from the land and working with living creatures. Our responsibility is to preserve the land's innate capacity for self-renewal if we want to be in for the long haul.

But, unlike cows and ranchers, watersheds do not operate within the confines of the present but within the longer reaches of perpetual time. The structure and function of a watershed is ancient and complex, the full workings of which is probably beyond human comprehension. Even so, we understand that like healthy human cultures, a watershed lives by the sum of its components. The accommodations and competitions between its elements work to achieve the resilience called "sustainable." If used with care, a watershed can absorb change, thanks to an intricate system of checks and balances that act as shock absorbers. But when used beyond its tipping point, bringing a watershed back into health can be difficult in the extreme. By then, the rancher has already gone belly up or has sold out.

Once I asked a range scientist who was also a life-long rancher how can we know when we are getting close to the limits with our grazing on a watershed, pasture, or ranch. He showed a startling photograph of one pasture completely taken over by the uneatable sweet resin bush:

"When you go this far, it's too far," he said.

"We need more warning than that," I replied respectfully. His example sounded like a walk in the Grand Canyon, say, and stepping off the Bright Angel Trail going downhill. Once you've taken those first few wayward steps, it gets harder to return to safety. Even so, I was to learn that no single early warning sign exists, in the way persistent rises in blood pressure and cholesterol indicate that a heart attack may be just around the corner.

The stated purpose of range monitoring is to document changes in the vegetation and soil cover of the watershed over time. As such, it forces ranchers and grazing managers to look more closely and more often at their basic resources of grass, soils, and water. Hopefully, we will recognize the signposts of approaching limits before we fall off the cliff into sweet resin bush, snakeweed, or whitethorn.

Monitoring is a decisive step toward the practice of limits on grazing—limits which are both unavoidable and indispensable if ranchers are to stay in business over the long haul. Monitoring illuminates the boundaries that have to be recognized and adhered to if we are to keep rangelands healthy. It can tease out long-term trends in rangeland and riparian health, provided the measurements are consistently carried out for a long time. Like all good field-based science, monitoring is data driven and data rich. It is impartial and does not take sides. The US Forest Service's snapshot evaluations done every ten to twenty years to meet the requirements of the National Environmental Policy Act (NEPA) are perhaps a little better than nothing, but not by much. Some ranchers call these "drive-by shootings."

Another pivotal benefit of monitoring with the caretaker agency is the building of mutual trust. Animosities usually disappear when you spend a few days with your adversary crawling around on the ground looking at grasses and soils, especially if each party goes into it with open minds and a willingness to learn from each other.

The good news is that watersheds, especially the riparian bottom lands, are resilient, thanks to aforementioned system of checks and balances.

Ranchers, more than most folks, live in the present and are convinced by what we see. Our lives are lived next to Nature, rather than in statistics and textbook theories. We believe that knowledge-based truth does not come packaged exclusively in scientific journals and learned conferences. The rancher does not have to master the detailed science of monitoring, but he or she should know what the results mean in terms of watershed health and to the caretaker agencies. As a practical matter, monitoring is too important in today's environmental age for the rancher not to be involved. Those who choose to ignore it do so at their peril.

So how many ranches are paying attention?

Kim McReynolds is a rangeland specialist for the University of Arizona Cooperative Extension who works in southern Arizona. She occasionally gets a panicky call from a rancher:

"The Forest Service is threatening to cut my cow numbers. Can you help me?"

"Bring in your monitoring data and I'll look at them," she says.

The phone goes silent for a moment.

"But I don't have any," the rancher replies.

Today, Kim and her staff monitor the rangeland on seventy-five ranches in her area. Ranchers who do not participate are not necessarily an "endangered species." But they are perhaps becoming "threatened." The new generation of ranchers want to see how their primary crops— grass, water and soils—are getting along. For the youngsters, Kim and her colleagues have another approach. For years, she has put on the Natural Resource Conservation Workshop for Arizona Youth. Atop Mingus Mountain, in the Prescott National Forest, high schoolers discover nature by conducting hands-on projects on water, wildlife, soils, and plants.

That experience has changed many attitudes and a few lives. My grandniece, a vivacious teenager from New York City, got the message and changed her university plans accordingly. The emphasis is on how to use our watersheds with care, staying within limits. And I am happy to report that our Canelo Hills Coalition gave scholarships to students who otherwise could not attend. Kim's conservation clinic for youngsters is a corrective to what Aldo Leopold complained about in the *Sand County Almanac* written in the 1940s: "The education actually in progress makes no mention of obligations to land over and above those dictated by self-interest."

Recent commentaries on battles between activists and ranchers over grazing on public lands in the West have pointed out that the adversaries have been engaged in a phony zero-sum game, explained as follows: The natural resources "pie" is of one fixed size, and what is gained by one side is automatically offset in equal measure by the losses to the other. Thus, if cattle were banned in Redrock Canyon, the activists would control the watershed and be accountable for the health of the whole.

But the zero-sum concept ignores the watershed's absolute importance in the overall communities of life. Upper elevations like mountaintops, rim rocks, and ridges form the watershed's common boundaries, while water and gravity do the essential work of shaping its topography and creating its soils. A simplified definition might be a topographical formation where all the water that drains off to a common outlet like Redrock Canyon. But a watershed is much more than the sum of its nonliving parts. Its biomass and to a lesser extent its biodiversity varies greatly with the seasons and weather, its slope and exposure to the sun. These factors create different soil types that give rise to upland range, riparian bottoms and the myriad vegetation types such as grasses, shrubs, and trees.

Also, a watershed like Redrock Canyon participates in a much broader arrangement, both human and natural. It defines the natural boundaries of Place. The town of Patagonia, Sonoita Creek Nature Preserve, Patagonia Lake, and other downstream users, including ranchers and recreationalists depend on it. Above all, the watershed should not be dammed and poisoned to the dubious benefit of a single species, as proposed by the US Fish and Wildlife Service and the Bureau of Reclamation—more on this later.

But astonishingly, the Endangered Species Act is not designed to look at or even care very much about the watershed as a whole living entity. Instead, the act drives single species management decisions and a blinkered focus on small areas, aided and abetted by Garden of Eden activists like the Center for Biological Diversity who seem to make a profitable business out of lawsuits to keep the zero-sum game in play.

ii

In 2003 when Canelo Hills Coalition ranchers started monitoring their rangelands, George Ruyle and his staff outlined the process, using standard Forest Service methods so we could compare our results to theirs. Like most field-based ecological studies, the process proceeded from small *sample plots* of rangeland that would be studied intensively in order to develop general statements about overall condition of each pasture and ranch. Sample plots were required because studying every acre would be impossible, even on a relatively small watershed like Redrock Canyon with twenty thousand acres, not to mention all four ranches at fifty-five thousand acres. I was generally familiar with the need for sampling, having used sample farms to study the distribution and severity of a disease called river blindness in coffee plantations in Guatemala when I worked for the Centers for Disease Control right out of college. The affected area spread over a whole mountain range and was highly variable in terms of its people, vegetation, terrain, altitude, and rainfall. Also, it contained over one hundred villages so we had to select a few representative areas to study rather than try to cover them all.

In rangeland monitoring, the size, location, and characteristics of the sample plots were crucial to how well, or not, they represented each pasture, ranch, or the watershed. George and his staff selected most of the same monitoring sites established by the Forest Service in the 1950 and 60s so comparisons could be made of any changes that might have occurred over the decades. In general, the sites included different soil types, elevations, slopes, vegetation, and distances to cattle water, fences, and roads, both in upland and riparian bottom lands. In the Redrock watershed, the soil and ecological types were sandy loam bottoms (in the creek), shallow uplands, shallow hills, and limestone uplands. "Shallow" refers to the depth of the top soils. Also, the soils were very old, having been formed from weathered rocks millions of years ago. In addition to the Forest Service sites, George added several near the new water lines and drinkers.

Most range grasses grow better in sandy bottoms and shallow uplands. These areas were more accessible to cattle and most of the monitoring sites were located there. Shallow hills and limestone hills also grew good grass, but had steeper slopes and cows spent less time grazing them. Each site was staked and located on ranch maps by GPS so they could be found and revisited each year. Selection of monitoring sites also required detailed knowledge of how the grazing had been managed over the past several years; numbers of cattle and seasons of grazing use, particularly during the immediate past season.

Monitoring of rangeland vegetation, like much of ecological science, requires haystacks of data to discover a few needles of understanding. The reason is that the ethics of the scientific method does not admit speculation, or even common sense, unless it is backed up by mountains of objective data. In addition to the detailed monitoring protocols carried out every decade or two, the Forest Service has an "Ocular Method" of evaluating rangeland where the range conservationist rides the landscape once a year to get a general impression of range condition. Such cursory inspections often do not hold up to more thorough scrutiny. Yet, they find their way into biological assessments and popular press as "proof" of overgrazing, as in the fence line photographs where cattle have grazed one side but not yet the other (see Paul S. Martin, 2005).

The following are a few of the aforementioned needles of understanding developed over the twentieth century by range scientists and used today by ranchers and agencies to evaluate and manage grazing.

iii

In the 1980s, I had an introduction to range monitoring on the Santa Margarita Ranch with Dan Robinett of the USDA Soil Conservation Service. The ranch had had the same manager for thirty years, and I thought it made sense to document a starting point for the new absentee owner who was not a rancher, as I was not at that time. Only much later did I understand the intricacies of rangeland ecologies, the forthright culture of ranching, and the husbandry of the land and livestock. The very richness of that way of life as I later discovered it makes me irritable now that I did not know more at that time.

The Santa Margarita Ranch was big; five thousand acres of deeded land and thirty-five thousand acres of State of Arizona grazing lease. The manager had stocked it conservatively and the ranch was in good shape when we took over. His philosophy was to sell down the cow herd during a drought, a practice that had preserved its range condition. It also helped that we were in a four-year-long wet weather cycle.

"First, we'll have to set up permanent monitoring sites," Dan said, as he studied the topography and soils maps for the Altar Valley. The ranch ran from the Sasabe Road at two thousand feet elevation to the top of the Baboquivari Mountains at over five thousand feet. Dan selected sites in the lower, middle, and upper elevations. At each site, he drove a two-inch diameter pipe in the ground to capture rainfall and poured in a little oil to prevent evaporation.

"Each year when we read the sites, we'll drop a ruler in and measure the precipitation," he explained.

Next, Dan took photographs and stored them in a permanent file. This was before the digital age and the prints were black and white. Today, they look like sepia prints from a pioneer's museum, but they still tell the story. Dan read the sites each year in the fall or winter; after the growing season was over and before the plants got so mangled that they were hard to identify. Dan was a fountain of botanical knowledge. He recognized hundreds of species on sight, and could recite their growth habits and whether the cows liked them or not. In the lower elevations, Dan pointed out the snakeweed and burroweed that can move in when the range is overgrazed for a long time.

In the lower country, Lehmann lovegrass grew thick and tall, especially next to the highway. Lehmann was a drought-resistant African grass that had been imported decades ago to stabilize road cuts and reseed grubbed-out pastures. Without the native, natural factors such as insects to control it, the imported grass had thrived and crowded out native species. Today, Lehmann is accepted by ranchers as a fact of life, while it is demonized by the biodiversity people. But the grass is not an actor in environmental morality plays. Like any species, it naturally exploits available niches on the landscape.

This difference in human perspectives of a plant illustrates cultural differences among players on the natural resources divide. To a rancher, Lehmann lovegrass on his or her range is looking at reality and making the best deal possible, while the biodiversity advocates wring their hands, lament its vigorous take-over tendencies, and try eradication. Yes, ranchers would prefer to have native perennial species and can manage their grazing to promote that mixture, but they have to play with the hand they have been dealt. Dan, as far as I remember, was too smart to wade into this philosophical shoot-out but he did point out that Lehmann lovegrass did the important job of protecting the soil from erosion by generating a ton of litter. Depending on your perspective, a Lehmann lovegrass pasture could be classified as in "excellent" condition for watershed protection, "good" for cattle when green, and "poor" for biodiversity.

"The most important attribute to measure is litter," Dan mused during the few times we worked together. When he first said that, I figured I'd do okay as Mom always complained about how I didn't clean up after myself. But Dan was talking about plant material that covered the bare soil and slowed down erosion. Dan's litter could be a live plant, broken leaves and stems, dead plants, or cow poop. The metal frame he used for monitoring had a pointer welded on one side. Every time Dan took a step on the transect line, he recorded whether the pointer landed on litter or bare soil.

After he had looked over the ranch, Dan suggested a different pasture rotation. The manager had worked the ranch pasture by pasture, keeping the same cows in the same places all their lives.

"Cows will use the range better if they stay in the same pasture," he believed. "They'll know where the waters are and won't get lost."

That practice was an example of T. N.'s claim to me years later that adaptation to the environment was a critical factor in a cow-calf ranch. The old manager took that truism to the extreme. But leaving the old ladies at home all the time also made them into "bottom huggers," cows that never got out to rustle feed from the hillsides and mountaintops, with the consequence that the easy places in the pasture never got rested.

Dan's idea was to winter all the cows in the high mountains, move them down through the middle pastures in the spring, add in the bulls, and then go to the lower area when the Lehmann had greened up. "The topography of the ranch's watershed gives you a natural downhill rotation," he said. That way, the native grasses at high elevations got the summer growing season rest, and Lehmann got hammered when green and the cows would eat it. Another advantage of Dan's herd rotation was less stress on the cattle; the calves could be processed in branding traps as they were moved down into the lower pastures with their mothers instead of driving the herd long distances to the main corrals.

But the old manager was right that his cows didn't appreciate the change in scenery. They walked the fences for a few weeks before spreading out over new territories. A few of the older ladies repeatedly found their way back home and had to be culled. Both he and Dan were correct in their assumptions as far as they went. The difference lay in that the manager was thinking mostly about the welfare of his cows, while Dan was more concerned about grass and soils. But if the grass and soils are healthy, the cows will not have to go on welfare.

iv

In the fall of 2003, George Ruyle and his monitoring crew started work on the four ranches in the Redrock watershed. Katie and Walt Myer had dug through old US Forest Service files to unearth data and reports dating back to 1959. As promised, the US Forest Service sent three range staff to help. They would work with Katie, Walt, and others from the university's Cooperative Extension Service, who were proficient in modern-day methods of rangeland monitoring.

As promised, I went along to help them locate the old monitoring sites and to learn what I could. I didn't expect to become a certified range monitor, but I needed to understand the process and how the caretaker agencies would use the analysis. Also, I looked forward to learning enough rudimentary plant identification to show off to city slicker friends.

The process they used was similar to Dan Robinett and Laura Dupree's walking along an established transect line. The sampling unit was a forty-square-centimeter frame made from thin metal rod. Katie called it a "quadrat."

"What's that?" I queried.

"The sampling frame," she replied, tolerantly. "We'll walk a hundred steps and put down the frame a hundred times." At each step, Katie peered into the frame and identified each plant and estimated the densities of the three most common species. This routine gave an inventory of the plant species at each site, and which ones were the most common and contributing the most to overall biomass. Like Dan's, her frame had a pointer welded on the base. At each step, she noted whether the pointer touched litter, live vegetation, bare ground, rock, and so forth. This measured the percent of the ground that was covered and protected from erosion when it rained.

My job was to mark down the data points on printed forms. Clipboard in hand, I followed Katie as she worked down the transect line, calling out the data:

"Frame," and I made a mark. "Litter," and I made a mark. "Sideoats grama," and I made a mark. "Wolftail," and I made a mark, and so ad infinitum, until we finished the entire transect or I called time out to sharpen the pencil.

The amount of grass produced at each site was estimated by clipping all the grass found in standard-sized frames and putting it in paper bags. Back in the laboratory, the bags were dried, and the contents weighed and the amount of grass extrapolated to "pounds of dry matter per acre." This estimated the amount of grass available for cows to eat, with leftovers to cover the soil.

The monitoring had to be done during my favorite time of the year, after the growing season was over in the late fall or winter, but before the plants became bedraggled and seedless. We hit the ranch roads just after dawn when the air was crisp and clean, the sky indigo, and the plants glistening with dew.

I also enjoyed the company. Katie and the others pointed stuff out, like pedestals around isolated plants where the roots were holding to the dirt while the rain eroded the soil around it. Or a rare plant out of its normal range. They looked at the same ground I did, but with better-informed eyes. Having seen many other ranches, they could place my pastures in the continuum of rangeland conditions seen over the region.

The US Forest Service folks seemed happy to be out of the office and doing field work. Dressed in their pickle green uniforms, they blended nicely with the juniper trees. We worked in teams of two, with one person reading the frames and the other, always me, relegated to putting dots on printed forms because I could not correctly identify all the species.

We had nine transects on my ranch. Crawling around on the ground looking at plants and soils for five days made acquaintances out of the US Forest Service people who I had sometimes viewed as adversaries. The monitoring process served to build up a measure of mutual trust and respect, even though it did not seem like cowboy work. After George and his staff had analyzed the data and written the reports, the US Forest Service and I could sit around the table and discuss a given situation. We didn't always agree, but we worked from the same starting points that we had all helped to collect and define.

Logic insists that the time of the year and the immediate past grazing history will determine how a pasture looks on any given date. The fisheries biologists seemed to make their inspections at those times when cattle had just come out of a pasture, or during the dry spring when every living thing was stressed. From those limited eye-ball evaluations, they inferred that the watershed was being abused. Had they come when cows had just gone into the pasture, or in the fall after the rainy season, perhaps they would have been less alarmed?

As we reached the first decade of the 2000s and the condition of the riparian bottoms and upland pastures steadily improved with new growth, they still had nothing good to say. Each time, they fell back on outdated data and generalizations that didn't apply to topminnow in the Redrock watershed. Any grazing was bad. That conclusion was the beginning and end of the story for the US Fish and Wildlife Service.

CF 2 - East Redrock	2004	2006	2007	CF 2 - East Redrock Production Crittenden Clay Loam Upland 2006 = 3800lbs./acre
vine mesquite	7	14	10	
1 - 10%				
green sprangletop	3	1	4	
20 - 30 %				
sideoats grama	12	6	7	
cane beardgrass	0	1	1	
plains lovegrass	0	0	0.1	
20 - 30 %				
blue grama	0	2	1	
hairy grama	0	0	0.1	
sprucetop grama	8	14	7	
0 - 2% threeawns	0	2	0.1	
0 - 10%				
curly mesquite	10	10	10 (38)	
annual grasses	2	2	2	
Forbs (10 - 20%)	3	6	10	
Similarity Index =	45	58	52	

Note: In 2006, the site made 1700 lbs per acre allowable use (45%) for cattle. Also, a site with a modest S. I. can grow large quantities of perennial native grasses.

Grass production and similarity index.

v

The next fall, 2004, Katie brought her entire family to the monitoring party. Her father, Walt Myer, taught range science and soils at the university in addition to running the family ranch. Sister Jenny, like Katie, had a bachelor's degree in range. Nick Cline, Katie's husband, a cowboy who worked at the Marana Livestock Auction, was like me, good only for making marks on data forms. Mrs. Myers stayed in Bob Hudson's guest house and sat with Sarah, Katie, and Nick's infant daughter.

With 2004 monitoring in the hopper, I had annual data starting in 1998, the year before I began the pasture rotation. Ground cover with litter and live vegetation showed a steady trend upward over the years. And the land *looked* better. In the bottoms, new cottonwood, willow, and walnut saplings sprouted above the heavy summer growth of grasses and weeds, shading the water. The stream had begun to re-build its banks and started to meander. That year, the C6 Ranch had a barbeque to celebrate another milestone. The Forest Service issued our new ten-year grazing allotment. It was a long time in coming, and long overdue.

The National Environmental Policy Act of 1970, NEPA, was a landmark environment law. It required that any time the feds contemplated taking an action that spent federal dollars on the forest, the US Forest Service had to analyze the possible effects of the proposed action on the watershed and the adjacent communities. In our case, the action was the reissuance of the ten-year grazing allotment. At the same time, the US Forest Service must develop and analyze alternative actions, including cancellation of the allotment and taking all the cows off the land. When the analysis has been finished, the public is asked to comment and choose which alternative they prefer. After all the comments are in, the US Forest Service's district ranger selects the alternative that best fits the needs of the watershed and rancher. The law and its application are complex in the extreme. So much so that universities offer graduate-level courses in NEPA. According to US Forest Service regulations, the Canelo Hills Coalition could not begin to do its work without NEPA clearance on what we proposed to do. The new wells, pipelines, and fences paid for by the ADEQ grant were on hold, even though they would help us meet the requirements of the Endangered Species Act. A bureaucratic rule threatened to cancel our work. We were stuck in an environmental Catch-22.

For the past several decades, the US Forest Service had been mired in a massive backlog of overdue NEPAs on their grazing allotments. Allotments had to be renewed every ten years, and a new NEPA analysis was required each time, even if the rancher's management and cow numbers did not change. In some cases, an allotment could not be transferred to a new grazing permittee unless a current NEPA was in force. Often, the occasion of a new NEPA analysis gave activists an opportunity to reduce the numbers of cattle or cancel the grazing permit. The uncertainty over the stability of a rancher's grazing privileges frightened bankers and threatened to close off financing. In 1993, President Clinton's secretary of the interior, Bruce Babbitt, promised to curtail public land grazing by burying the ranchers in paperwork. He was no doubt referring to NEPA and the Endangered Species Act.

When I inquired about when our analysis would be completed, the replies said that US Forest Service staff had higher priority stuff to do. When the head of the Coronado National Forest wrote asking me to comment on the new overall forest plan, I wrote back to say that future planning was a fine thing but execution of your current duties was woefully lacking, and we were about to lose our ADEQ grants. The range evaluation part had already been done by the coalition (with US Forest Service participation) and I had proposed the same stocking rates as before. But now the biologist, archeologist, recreationalist, cultural specialist, trails and roads department, wildlife, law enforcement, and general public had to chime in with their opinions.

In 2003 and 2004, something changed. Someone upstream in the bureaucratic pipeline must have started kicking butts and taking names. The NEPA analysis was taken out of the hands of the head biologist and assigned to Rick Gerhart. Rick was a wildlife biologist who dominated the paperwork, rather than vice versa. He assigned the tasks to new staff members with deadlines for completion. On our C6 Ranch, a different biologist looked at the field data and made note of the marked improvement in range and riparian conditions as a result of our management. The public comments ranged from support for what we had been doing to removing all cattle. Topminnow and the damage grazing allegedly would do to its habitat formed the basis for the "Remove the Cows" comment.

The US Forest Service chose to continue our management unchanged. In the final report, every written comment was published, including mine. Sally and Jerome Stefferud, the fisheries biologists for the US Fish and Wildlife Service and the US Forest Service who had by then retired, repeated their objections to any grazing. And they extended their complaints to areas on our ranch outside the Redrock Canyon watershed. In one, they had camped near a drinker in Crittenden pasture and complained of being attacked in the middle of the night by my herd of wild cows.

vi

Grass monitoring on the coalition ranches cost four thousand dollars a year, a noteworthy sum on a 215-head ranch like the C6. In those days, four thousand dollars would buy two replacement bulls or four bred cows. The US Department of Agriculture had a program that funded collaborative work between a rancher and an academic. George and I wrote a proposal and a year later, we were funded. In the grant, I included the training of a local person in the field techniques of grassland monitoring so that we could continue the evaluations when the university finished our five-year project.

Jim Koweek, a local nurseryman, mandolin player, and cowboy was the ideal candidate. After graduating from the University of Arizona, Jim and his family moved to Sonoita where his wife Annette taught science and math in the Elgin school. Jim day-worked on several ranches but his heart was in plants, the mandolin, and music. A moment of clarity about his true calling came courtesy of a horse he bought from Bobby Sharp off the San Rafael Ranch. Bobby

Grass monitoring in the shadow of Kunde Mountain.

claimed that the gelding was good, except that "once in a great while he might buck a little." Jim rode him out the first week; no problem. Second week was okay too until the last day when the horse threw a hissy fit. Jim recalled that just before he hit the ground, he was struck first by a moment of clarity: "That it was a whole lot more fun to sing about this cowboy stuff than to do it." After that he got serious about the mandolin and the botanical side of ranching.

About the time the Canelo Hills Coalition started our monitoring, Jim had sold his nursery business and was looking for something else to do. To learn the range grasses and monitoring techniques, Jim worked side-by-side with Walt Myer and Katie Cline and the university team for two seasons until they certified the accuracy of his work. After our five-year program ended, Jim continued monitoring on the coalition ranches. He eventually wrote a practical guide to plant identification, beautifully illustrated with photos so even an amateur like me could tell the difference between Emory and Mexican oaks or the various species of grama grasses.

After we completed our intensive monitoring, George Ruyle recommended reading one-third of the sites each year, or doing the whole ranch every third year. Rich and I talked it over and decided to have Jim read one-third of the upland transects each year except for East and West Redrock. These two pastures had topminnow habitat and were critical for

George Ruyle explaining monitoring on the Rose Tree Ranch.

our fall grazing schedule and weaning calves. So we did them every year with Rich and I trading off as scribes.

The US Forest Service liked Jim's work so well that they hired him to do monitoring on other allotments around southern Arizona. The Sierra Vista Ranger District had forty allotments and could not cover them all and still keep up with their office work.

In 2005, the Arizona Department of Agriculture started a modest program to fund water, fencing, and erosion control. The idea was to help keep working ranchers on the land and slow down the conversion of deeded acreage into ranchettes. The program was competitive and gave priority to ranchers whose allotments had been cut and who were monitoring their range as part of a regional improvement effort. The

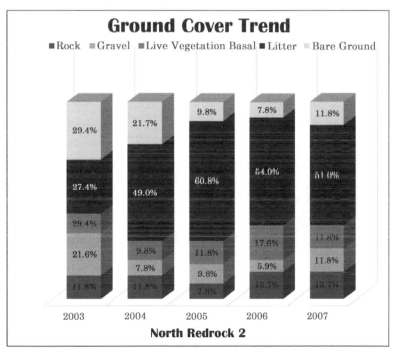

Percent soil surface cover on transect North Redrock 2

- There were significant changes in bare ground and litter between 2003 and 2005.
- Ground Cover has been stable since 2005.

Vaca Ranch, Five-Year Ground Cover Trend.

Canelo Hills Coalition qualified and opened its membership to neighboring ranchers. Soon, the coalition covered over one hundred thousand
acres and the headwaters of the Babocomari River and Cienega Creek.

But between the ranchers and the US Forest Service, not all was sweetness
and light. One example was a ranch on the border near the San Rafael Valley.
In the 1990s, the allotment had been cut by 25 percent. Three generations of
that family had lived on the ranch and depended on cows for their livelihood.
The US Forest Service claimed a large pasture needed to be divided and a
new well drilled to improve the pasture rotation. The US Forest Service's
carrot was to restore the cuts when the new improvements had been installed.
The rancher followed through with the help of a grant negotiated by the
Coalition, but the number of cows allowed stayed the same.

This experience exemplified how the US Forest Service sometimes
fails to follow through on its end of the deal. The rancher compiles and
conditions improve, yet the number of cows permitted by the Forest
Service stay the same. This also happened on the Vaca and Open Cross
ranches. Such lack of follow-through remains a recipe for conflict and
mistrust between the caretaker agencies and ranchers, even today in the
midst of collaborative projects like the Canelo Hills Coalition in Redrock
Canyon. The long-standing practice of reducing cow numbers seems
strongly embedded in US Forest Service culture. But unbiased, long-term
rangeland monitoring can help find the right balance, when coupled with
cooperative attitudes by agency and rancher.

vii

Our funding agencies required that the Coalition spread the word to our neighbors about what we were doing. In 2005, we held an open house at the Sonoita Fairgrounds and invited everyone to attend. The extension service's range riders laid out the monitoring data, using the US Forest Service's "Similarity Index" technique as a guide, with the coalition's data and the US Forest Service approved methodology. The results showed startling differences from the agencies' earlier assessments that said our range conditions remained "low" with similarity indices mostly "Poor" to "Fair."

The Similarity Index conveys the likeness of a monitoring site to its hypothetical potential. In theory, the vegetation at each site has a "climax state" of historical vegetation species before any disturbance such as grazing or fire has taken place. That state is the most diverse plant community that that site can achieve, given its unique characteristics of soil type, rainfall, slope, and sun exposure. Katie's monitoring data was then scored to express the percent likeness that our sites had to the theoretical climax plant communities.

For example, the theoretical climax plant community is considered to be 100 percent. If a site is rated at 86 percent, this means that it has reached 86 percent of its potential. The US Forest Service has translated the Similarity Index into a grading system of "Poor, Fair, Good, and Excellent." (More recently changed to "serial stages 1, 2, 3, 4" to remove bias.)

For the eighteen sites in the Redrock watershed, cooperative extension's results rated one site as Fair, eleven as Good, six as Excellent, and none were Poor. Science and nature do not take sides by placing our moral interpretations on natural phenomena. But by the US Forest Service's own rating system, 94 percent of our upland vegetation communities were in "Good" or "Excellent" condition. The one site that rated "Fair" was located near the confluence of Redrock and Lampshire Canyon on the old Kunde Ranch, even though it had not been grazed at all for more than five years. Here, the effects of long-term heavy grazing had long-term damaging effects. This rangeland would take a long time to heal. Overall, Katie's data showed that range conditions had improved markedly in Redrock with the changes in stocking rates, grazing management, and more waters; significantly better now than the values repeatedly cited by the US

Fish and Wildlife Service during the ongoing consultations under the Endangered Species Act.

Unlike physics and mathematics, a theory in the ecological sciences is seldom carved in stone, applicable in all places and for all times. Hypotheses do not become theories until they are repeatedly tested against observations out on the watersheds. Frederic Clements, a Nebraska soil scientist, observed in the 1920s that if an undisturbed plot of tall grass prairie was burned or grazed, the vegetation would return to its original mix of species. The time required under Nebraska conditions was three to five years. In more straightforward terms, nature would heal herself if freed of outside disturbance, including that caused by grazing. Clements postulated that every undisturbed range site had a unique climax suite of vegetation specific to its soil type and fertility, exposure to the sun, and weather conditions.

Rangeland monitoring works from the minute study of small plots of land carefully chosen to reach general conclusions about the condition of the whole watershed, pasture, or ranch. For this reason, range scientists are less apt to be mistaken on small matters than large ones. While small samples are a practical necessity, their accuracy on western ranges is often limited by extreme variations in the terrain-topography, spotty rainfall over the landscape, and large variations in soils and vegetation types.

Despite its development on the Great Plains with its fertile soils and abundant moisture, Clements's climax vegetation theory was applied by government evaluators uncritically throughout the much more arid and rugged terrain of the American west, and has guided US Forest Service rangeland evaluations into the twenty-first century. But in the desert southwest, the theory didn't hold water. The rainfall here was less than in Nebraska by one-half to two-thirds, our soils were thinner and less fertile, and the topography rugged, mountainous, rocky, and deeply creased by arroyos. The regeneration time was in the neighborhood of twenty years, if it happened at all. A different standard for comparison was required to assess rangeland health in the southwest.

Nowadays, ecological site descriptions have provided that comparison. A simplified explanation is that range scientists divided up local western landscapes into different ecological sites based on their unique existing native plant communities, soil types, rainfall, topography, and the ecological processes of water and mineral cycles, and energy flow. On the Sonoita landscape, Dan Robinett identified and described many of the ecological sites. One afternoon, he took us to a site on the Empire Ranch where a diverse suite of native perennial grasses stood tall and wavy in the dry breeze. This site had been grazed for years by cattle under a rest-rotation scheme. A thick stand of live plants and litter covered the ground. The soil showed little sign of erosion.

Here, we could actually see what a healthy site looked like on our home range; identify and clip its grasses, dig into its soil. Not far away was a windmill and storage tank where cattle drank when in the pasture. We were looking at a real-life situation from our local neighborhood, seen in real time, the land being used with care, rather than an abstraction from a textbook taken from an entirely different realm.

In spite of its irrelevance to the arid western watersheds, Clements's climax theory has permeated the thinking of conservationists for almost a century. Its durability, I think, can be traced to a preconceived notion held by Garden of Eden activists: Nature will heal Herself if humans just get out of Her way. According to that misanthropic definition, climax vegetation on a plot of land made that site *pristine.* Pristine means something "in its original state." But through common usage, it has come to mean "untouched by humans, or virginal." These are terms that describe human *sentiments* about a place rather than its *physical and biotic attributes.* The activists have been good at selling these half-truths to the general public who are moved more by sentiment than reality.

The reality is that we humans have been around for thousands of years. In my part of the world, *Homo sapiens* migrated over the Bering Straits about twelve to thirteen thousand years ago and eventually reached the southwest. Just thirty miles from Redrock Canyon, archeological excavations at Murray Springs and Lehner Ranch uncovered slaughtering sites of bison, horses, and mammoths used by the Clovis people more than nine thousand years ago. In Redrock Canyon, rock scrapers, chipping tools, grinding pedestals, and pit houses show a continued human presence going back more than three thousand years.

The preservationist's view of the Sonoran desert before Christopher Columbus was a vast, highly variable terrain teeming with wildlife and plants, and all but empty of people. Yet, anthropologists estimate on the basis of much evidence that thousands of Native Americans lived in the borderlands region when Father Eusebio Francisco Kino showed up in 1687 AD. Some were wanderers or raiders, others lived by hunting and gathering, and many farmed in the watersheds of today's Santa Cruz and San Pedro Rivers.

Kino and others brought livestock in droves and they prospered in regions that had lots of grass and water, the same places where grazing mammals had flourished centuries before. Our local watersheds with their unique collections of plants and animals had co-evolved with grazing pressures for at least twenty million years, including cows for the last three centuries. Grazing was not and is not the natural enemy of wild nature and the environment, the complaints of preservationists and grass-huggers notwithstanding. Grazing by my cows, *properly managed*, returned the watershed to its original state and made it pristine by definition.

viii

Even so, science-based monitoring on small plots is not the only source of truth-based knowledge about the watershed's condition. To know, in the true sense, is to *see*. This source of knowledge can only come from constant, long-term contact with the landscape and cattle, week after week, year after year; riding the watershed and watching the herd in all seasons and weathers; learning through experience what works well or not so well in managing the land and the animals; taking into account market economics and family needs; all of these factors conditioned by the weather—hot, cold, dry, drought, and once in a while wet. Such deep knowledge comes only from long experience, paying attention to what the land and cows are saying and acting on that knowledge. During my twenty-five years in the Canelo Hills the land and the livestock have taught me a lot, but I still have more to learn.

The best practice may be to complement practical, experience-based knowledge with science-based rangeland monitoring. The first comes naturally to the cowboy or rancher who stays out on the range and pays attention. The second requires technical expertise coupled with lots of experience. For a few years, the Sierra Vista Ranger District helped provide the second method of evaluation with their range conservationists, but as the years went by, their participation faded as other parts of their jobs took priority. Nowadays, Jim Koweek fulfills this function with the help of the university's Cooperative Extension Service and ranchers' participation.

Most ranchers use the day-to-day surveillance as a forward-looking tool; deciding where to go next with the cattle during the grazing year. Science-based monitoring gives a view of where we've been; like the scene in a rear-view mirror, as one rancher put it. According to George Ruyle and co-inquisitors, most ranchers do it to ward off anti-grazing lawsuits and agency cuts in cow numbers.

Either way, the rancher's guiding principal should be to maintain the land's innate capability for self-renewal, to paraphrase Aldo Leopold again. Conservative stocking rates and good grazing management are ways to sustain that capacity. It is the rancher's responsibility to preserve it if he or she wants to prosper and continue ranching for a long time. Most of us take that job seriously.

12

Taking Better Care

During the drawn-out maneuvering over topminnow, exclosures, and NEPA, life on the C6 Ranch trotted cheerfully along. Rich came up with new ways to manage the outfit. When he first started work in 2004, he took a week-long course on bovine reproduction. That experience focused our attention on keeping the cow herd more productive through pregnancy testing and examining teeth. A few weeks after weaning the calves, we brought the cows to the corrals, put them through the squeeze chute where the veterinarian thrust her hand up the cow's rectum. If the cow had bred back that summer, the fetus could be felt by reaching down through the intestinal wall and picking up the uterus. Unless she had a

Moving cows on the C6 ranch.

good excuse—weaned a late calf, for example—the open ones went down the road to the sale barn.

As cows age, they shed teeth. The high silicone content of range grasses grind down the enamel and the teeth start to fall out by ten years of age or so. The squeeze chute also serves as a dentist's chair, in addition to an obstetrical couch for pregnancy testing and prolapse repair. As a recipient of several dental implants myself, I felt some sympathy; perhaps I shouldn't be chewing grass stems?

The dental exam consists of running the cow through a narrow lane into the squeeze chute, a mechanical contraption that can be pulled tight, thus holding the cow mostly motionless allowing for more invasive procedures, cranking open the cow's mouth and rubbing a finger across the lower jaw (cows have teeth only on the lower jaw). If she has all her teeth, and has a calf inside her, she stays. If she has lost only a few teeth and is bred, she gets another year. No teeth, and she is a "gummer," unable to graze efficiently. Even if bred, she is unlikely to raise a decent calf on our rough country. Other ranchers who operate on irrigated pasture or easy winter range might buy her.

Cows with defective udders or teats, cancer eyes, prolapsed uteruses, cripples, and those with bad behavior also made the trip to the sale barn in Marana. Culling is a heartless process, and I occasionally saved back one or two old girls out of sympathy, empathy, or maybe it was nostalgia. I had watched them being born on the ranch where they lived useful lives. One crippled heifer I especially remember had slipped jumping out of the trailer when I unloaded her at Rail X corrals and broke a front leg. Cows have an incredibly high pain tolerance and she merely picked up the leg and hopped over to the feed trough and commenced to eat. Tom Hunt and I moved her into the chute where we splinted the leg with a plaster cast and steel braces. Stumpy healed up and lived out a full life, hobbling along with the herd, raising a calf every year.

During the first years, we sold our calves through the local sale barn or the video-TV auctions put on by Superior Livestock Company. A Superior representative would film the calves a month or so ahead of the sale date. The auctions were held at big cow towns like Fort Worth, Texas, or Denver, Colorado, where thousands of cattle would be offered to many buyers with lots of money, all bidding against each other as they watched the videos. Premiums were paid for calves that had their vaccinations and had been weaned off the cows for a few weeks, a process called preconditioning, or backgrounding.

Weaning a mammal off the teat is, like birth, a stressful experience. I oftentimes wonder why over the long march of evolution, mammals did not come up with an easier plan for reproduction; like protozoa, for example, where they simply divide. According to ranching tradition, weaning involved the sudden stripping away of calves from the cows and their protective herd environment. The procedure took place in dusty, crowded corrals. A cowboy on a sorting horse or men on foot separate cows from calves; steers went one way, heifers the opposite. Immediately after weighing, the calves were crammed into giant trucks and hauled away to some unfamiliar, scary place. The stress from fear and separation anxiety lowered the calf's immune response and when they arrived at their new destination, pasture or feed lot, they went off feed and lost weight. Some came down with respiratory diseases, like the flu or pneumonia. At times, as many as 10 percent may die.

To lessen that fear-related stress, Rich devised a fence-line weaning routine that took advantage of the sensory bonds between cow and calf based on their unique smell, sound, and sight. (All moos may seem the same to you and me but each calf knows its momma and vice versa). He lined the corrals with narrow net wire fencing and filled the feeders with dry hay. After sorting the calves off the cows, he turned the cows back into the adjacent weaning pasture while holding the calves in the corrals.

For the first day or two, the cows and calves hugged the fences and bawled an unrelenting twenty-four-hour serenade, the cowboy's equivalent of a rock concert. When the cows got hungry, they left to graze in the pasture. As their rumens filled up, the pressure of a full, un-nursed udder drove them back to their calves where they rubbed noses through the fence, but still unable to nurse. Comforted by the presence of their mommas and a familiar setting, the hungry calves gradually begin to eat hay. By ten days or so, the pairs had forgotten each other and we could move the cows up on the mountain for the winter. After three weeks, we send the calves to the buyer, unstressed and already eating out of feeders.

Our heifer calves drew the attention of Doug Ruppel, manager of the thirty- thousand-acre Babocomari Ranch. Once a Mexican land grant, the Babocomari watershed began on the flanks of the Canelo Hills and ran east toward the San Pedro River with the Babocomari River flowing down the middle. The Brophy family had owned the ranch since 1934 and practiced sustainable grazing management even before that became a catchphrase. Ben Brophy and Doug saw a strong market for high quality bred heifers. Each summer and fall, Doug scoured southern Arizona ranches for the biggest and best heifer calves. He pastured them over the winter and bred them the next spring to high quality Black Angus heifer (low birth weight) bulls. After breeding, the heifers grazed happily on good native grass until the next year when they were offered for sale as bred two-year-olds.

One year, Ben and Doug sponsored a clinic by Dr. Lynn Locatelli, a veterinarian specializing in low-stress cattle handling. Breeding success in their artificial insemination program was tightly linked to keeping the heifers under low stress, as were good health in general and getting good weight gains on pasture or in the feedlot. Doug targeted ranchers whose cattle fit their specifications, plus a vaccination program to jump-start their immune systems, calves for which the Babocomari paid a premium. Rich took the course and that fall Ben and Doug bought all our calves, including the steers.

Their program worked well while the market held up. Doug had selected the best stock and confirmed that they were pregnant, so the buyer would not be buying a "pig in a poke." The heifer calf he paid $750 for in the fall might bring $1,500 to $1,800 a year and a half later. Doug claimed that Rich's heifers sold themselves, while buyers clamored for more.

The Babocomari was all deeded land. As such, the ranch had been able to restore fire to their watershed, unshackled by agency restrictions. Each spring the Babocomari burned the coarse giant sacaton grass to freshen it up and set back the mesquite brush and whitethorn. Fire had been a vital force of renewal for grasslands for the last twenty million years until government agencies deemed it undesirable. Archeological evidence showed that natural burns took place about every eight to twelve years. But at the beginning of the 1900s, the US Forest Service trotted Smokey the Bear out of its cage and stopped the renewing flames.

Nowadays, ranchers are striving to restore fire but the Endangered Species Act and housing development often blocks the way. On the Malpai Borderlands in extreme southeastern Arizona, ranchers had to wait for seven years while dueling herpetologists argued about the possibility that fire would kill a few rare rattlesnakes. When the burn finally happened, post-fire surveillance found that the snakes knew how to hide from the flames. They too, had evolved with fire. In 2001, a June lightning strike on my Crittenden pasture sent a rush of flames into oak and juniper brush on the north slopes of Monkey Canyon on the Sonoita side of Mount Hughes. The US Forest Service had to act quickly because the fire could have spread to houses, including mine.

Ben and Doug's bred heifer program worked well until 2008 when the great recession hit in the middle of a local summer drought. The Babocomari had little grass left on its whiskered pastures and the heifer buyers had their credit lines canceled because of the currency crisis.

Ranching is nothing if not cyclical, whether the ups and downs are caused by weather, market prices, or credit crunches. When all three kick in during the same year, the wreck is on. One old-time cattle speculator claimed that until you have declared bankruptcy a time or two, you could not claim to be a real cowman. The Babocomari Ranch had deep pockets and survived, but to our dismay, they stopped the local heifer buying program.

Taking a page from the Babocomari book, we switched our Crittenden pasture for developing yearling replacement heifers too big to interest the Canelo Hills mountain lions. Also, heifers grazed the deep canyons and high Mount Hughes ridge better than cows because they were younger, lighter, and did not have a calf to raise. Because heifers ate less forage than cow-calf pairs, the US Forest Service allowed us sixty-five heifers in place of fifty pairs. Rich figured out that we could breed the heifers with artificial insemination, and sell the excess over what we needed on the C6 to neighboring ranchers. Young bred cows adapted to rough country still had a good market in our area.

ii

In 2004, Rich started building his house in the mouth of Redrock Canyon, a mile east of the confluence with Harshaw Creek and five miles from Patagonia. Most of our deeded land was in the flood plain and Santa Cruz County required a hydrological study to prove that the house site would be above the hundred-year flood level. Upstream, just inside the forest boundary, a granite outcropping intruded into the creek bottom on the north side. During a hundred-year flood, the water would be pushed to the south, inundating our sacaton grass bottomland and lapping up against the hillsides. Rich turned the problem into an advantage by anchoring the house foundation into the south-side hill and elevating the porch three feet on concrete pillars. The elevation gave the house a wrap-around porch rulered by a salt cedar railing and windows with sweeping views of the creek, corrals, and flood plain.

In 2006, he moved in, the whole shooting match, as they say, glad to be out of the camp trailer parked under a nearby juniper. Every morning when he walked out the front door, he was already at work, no commute required. Kunde Mountain to the southeast loomed over the homestead, a lichen-yellowed, granite escarpment. To the north, Moonshine Mountain bulged on the skyline. Redrock Creek sliced between the two, a canyon choked with mesquite, ocotillo, and hackberry that opened up to the rest of our country south of the Mount Hughes ridge.

Rich and I divided the work with Rich taking the larger Redrock Canyon side, and me on the Crittenden pasture along Papago Springs Road. We still worked together when moving cattle, trailering horses back and forth the twenty miles between Sonoita and his new homestead. Now and then, Diane would ride too. She had claimed Tuffy, the Tom Reeves horse, for her mount. Perched like a perky sparrow on the shiny bay gelding, she, like T. N., preferred to ride at the back of the bunch. Years later, when we retired Tuffy to my niece's farm in Oregon for her young daughters, Diane took over T. J.

The longest cow drive we had was six miles, putting the cows away for the winter up on Red Bear pasture. Six miles is not far as cattle drives go, but we had to lace two hundred cows through mesquite thickets, climb a couple of rock-strewn ridges, and thread the needles through a couple of wire gates located in the canyon bottoms. That distance would take less than a couple of hours on flat ground, but ours took a full day, what with throwing all the cows together, driving them up the mountain, and returning on sore-footed horses.

Over the years, the Basinger family, Tyler and April, Mike and Julie, Cotton and Pat helped us a bunch on that drive. They ranched not far away in Elgin and Tyler was the best farrier in the county. His son, Shawn, was in veterinary school in Colorado specializing in equine medicine and they were eager to work together when Shawn graduated. And so were we all. The Lord allegedly created the world and all its creatures in six days and then went on vacation. But horsemen wish the Almighty had taken more time with the design of the horse's legs. For a big animal so powerful and flighty, their legs and feet are held together by a fragile and complicated network of bones and tendons. Tyler and Dr. Shawn working together would be a blessing to the local horses and horse people.

That winter, Rich met Jacklyn Ann Crawford through the intermediary of Sam and Jennifer Donaldson, whose family owned the neighboring Empire Ranch. Jennifer ran barrel-racing horses and so did Jackie. Barrel racing involves running the horse around a clover leaf pattern of barrels set up in the rodeo arena. The rules are simple: Do not crash into the barrels and the fastest time wins.

To the horse, the event makes sense only when running between the barrels. All horses are born to run, but when asked to slow down and crank its body a full turn around the barrels and then accelerate to top speed for the next barrel, most horses don't understand. At first they go blasting by and miss the turn; or they turn too soon and knock over the barrel. But if the horse is started slow around the clover leaf pattern and then speeded up gradually over a period of several years, a few get the hang of what the rider wants. A winning barrel horse is a tribute to both the adaptability of the horse and the patience of the trainer.

The event has no counterpart in ranch work, but the ladies love it nevertheless. The best horses command six-figure purchase prices, and the professional racers may earn as much every year. But like jackpot roping, local barrel racing is largely a social event for showing off riding skills and the equine athlete. Jackie had a decent barrel horse and a good job in Tucson as a paralegal. But the commute to town killed two hours each day, and left little time for the barrel horse, except on weekends.

Rich and Jackie were married on May 5, 2007. To finance the honeymoon, that spring Rich took on a fencing contract for a two-mile stretch of Abel Murrietta–style construction. Not a walk in the park, but he finished it before the Cinco de Mayo wedding date.

The wedding was held at our C6 Ranch headquarters, out on the grass in front of the house facing northwest at sundown. Pastor Steve Lindsey from the Canelo Cowboy Church presided. Steve had recently given up ranching for the clergy, and I suggested to Rich that he should confirm Steve's legal authority to tether the knot. A quick check with county clerk confirmed that Reverend Steve was duly ordained to solemnize their vows, and together Rich and Jackie pulled the marriage license.

A brisk, dry wind blew out of the west all that day, but graciously backed off as the sun dropped behind Mount Wrightson. Steve read the required ritual; the bride and groom repeated the vows, exchanged rings, and embraced. After a short, leisurely honeymoon in New England, they took up residence in the Redrock Canyon house. Jackie's commute time increased to three hours per day, but it was in the nature of her upbringing in a military family to tough it out.

Rich and Jackie in Redrock Canyon, 2007.

iii

Spring is inventory time when ranchers brand and count the new calves. The ritual of branding carries a burden of tradition dating back to the ancient Egyptians. The root word for "brand" is "burn," meaning a hot iron is applied to the animal's hide, creating a unique, permanent scar reserved to its owner. Lost or stolen, a branded cow or horse can be returned. The practice was brought from Spain to Mexico and then to the American west. Our cattle carry the C6 brand on the right hip.

Traditionally, cattle are herded into corrals and the calves sorted off into a separate pen. The rancher may hire the local high school football team to do the mugging. A cowboy neck-ropes the calf while the football team wrestles it to the ground. One person drives his knee into the calf's neck and holds the top front leg back while another one sits on the back end, holding the top hind leg back while pushing the bottom leg forward with his foot. A third person hovers over the calf with a pocket knife to castrate and notch an ear. A fourth cowboy applies the branding iron and vaccinates. There are almost as many variations on this routine as there are ranchers. Some rope the hind legs to avoid the choke hold. If the football team is playing an away game and the rancher is short on help, one cowboy can rope the calf, dismount and tie it down with a pigging string while the horse backs up to hold the rope tight. This is how I learned to rope and tie calves as a teenager in Paul Cornelius's auction pens.

All these methods involved lots of labor, dust, and noise, which creates a ton of fear-related stress on the calves, not to mention the choking and pain. Sometimes a calf (or cowboy) breaks a leg; rare but it happens. Even so, the whole hullabaloo is so strongly entrenched in ranching lore that it has been widely viewed as a rite of passage for aspiring cowboys.

Some ranchers nowadays push the calves into a small squeeze chute where the calf is loosely held by the neck. The chute is tipped on its side to immobilize the calf during branding and castration. Rich preferred this method especially when branding solo. He could work a dozen cows in the corrals, sort off the calves, and take his time. Afterward, each calf immediately returned to its momma for comfort, reducing its stress from separation anxiety. But one old-timer when told of a new, easier way to brand, snorted contemptuously that it did not honor the ranching tradition. . . .

In 1999, on my horse-buying trip to the Reeves ranch in South Dakota, I stumbled on to the Nordfork for branding. Jim Reeves claimed that every year he branded over seven thousand calves on his three-year-old horses, each one dragged to the fire on horseback.

"That's a lot of calves," I commented. "You must have a big ground crew."

"Big enough, but we use Nordforks."

"What's a Nordfork?"

Jim reached in the back of his pickup and pulled out a metal frame that looked like two open toilet seats hinged in the middle. One end was tapered into a V with a two-foot-long handle welded to the apex. The other end was a wider V that opened to let the calf's head pass through. A fifteen-foot-long rope, broken in the middle by a rubber bungee cord, attached the broad V to a heavy spike hammered into the ground.

Jim explained as he laid the contraption out on the ground: "As the heeler drags the calf past the Nordfork, the ground man drops the broad V over the calf's head and follows it up until the small V catches the calf behind the ears and the rope tightens up. The heeler then faces and holds his dallies while the ground crew goes to work. The rubber bungee stretches so the calf doesn't get hurt. When you're finished, the heeler throws slack in the rope at the same time as the ground man lifts up the handle and the calf jumps free."

"So, those four horses I just bought from you must savvy the Nordfork. I'd better take a couple of these gadgets home and give 'em a try." I said. "But tell me, why do you call them Nordforks?"

"Don't rightly know. Maybe somebody named Nord came up with it," he replied. "There are a bunch of Norwegians living up north of there."

Before I left, Jim gave the name of a local welder where I could order them. Later on, a bit of detective work led me to the Idaho rancher Nord Hill, who in 1991, fabricated and tested his tool and has been making and selling them ever since.

Back home, Manuel Murrietta had graduated that year from Cochise College and started work on the C6 Ranch. We had a handful of late calves to brand so we gave the Nordfork a test. As advertised, it eliminated the hassle of flanking and tying each calf down. With me roping, Manuel branded, vaccinated, and castrated the calves while the Nordfork and my heeling horse held them without a struggle.

The next spring, we took the Nordforks to Bob Hudson's Vaca Ranch. We unloaded our horses at daylight and spread out over the thousand-acre holding pasture where Bob and his vaqueros had gathered the pairs into the day before. The cows seemed to know the drill, and began bawling up their calves. We moved them into a net-wire trap, and set up two Nordforks. Fernando Valenzuela, his son Gerardo, and Manuel were the designated heelers, while the rest of us became the ground crew.

Bob kept the cows in with the calves during branding to reduce the stress of sorting. This also allowed the calves to mother up immediately after branding. Even so, the mixture of cows with calves, branded and unbranded, made catching two heels more challenging, and Bob wanted the best heelers on horseback.

Fernando rode a rangy roan gelding to the edge of the herd, softly swinging a sixty-foot rawhide riata for a rope. He eased up to a calf and picked up two hind feet, took several dallies around his saddle horn, and towed it easily to the Nordfork without a struggle. During that whole day, I never saw the *vaquero* miss a set of doubles or get in a hurry.

Manuel Murrietta heeling as Sands Ranch branding, May, 2015.

Gerardo and Manuel also roped, using their nylon twines. With three heelers, the ground crew had a hard time keeping up. Now and then, one roper would have a calf heeled and on the ground, waiting for an empty Nordfork. I had seen these two cowboys win more than their share of fast times at the local rodeos, but today they moved at a more deliberate speed, schooling their young horses on how to pull and face up, giving them time to do everything right.

Cowboy custom has ranches trading work with neighbors during branding. As the seasons passed, the use of the Nordfork spread around southern Arizona ranches. The last branding I attended was in 2015 on the Vera Earl/Empire Ranch owned by Ian Tomlinson. By then, Manuel had quit the rodeo circuit and graduated to become the cow boss on the largest ranch in the region. Over the last fifteen years, he had refined the Nordfork routine into an outstanding piece of cowboy ingenuity. With his experienced crew, a calf could be worked—branded, vaccinated, and castrated—in less than one minute. This saved labor as well as stress on the calves and cowboys. It kept to the old tradition of using horses for roping and branding. In fact, the Nordfork had become a good training tool for both aspiring cowboys and young horses.

Ian and Manuel disallow any catch except two hind feet. This enforces precision on the part of the roper and virtually eliminates injuries. The roper and rope horse learns to move calmly through a large herd, setting up a calf for a good throw instead of charging at the cattle swinging a loop like a windmill in a hurricane. The apprentice cowboy learns to position the horse, how to dally to the horn, and move off with the calf easy-like. The calf only feels a belly drag over soft ground to the branding fire where the Nordfork is dropped over its head and catches behind the ears as the horse comes tight on the rope. The bungee cord stretches so the calf is immobilized and can easily be turned over to brand on either side.

On the Vera Earl Ranch, every hand gets to take a turn at roping. This makes for a happy crew and trains the next generation of cowboys. And the aspirants have ace heelers and horsemen in Manuel and lefty Harvey Jacobs as a role models. At the entrance to the Sonoita Fairgrounds is a larger-than-life-sized bronze by Deborah Fellows of a rancher mounted on a fine looking horse. On the pedestal below, bronze plaques list the names of each year's winner of the prestigious Sonoita Ranch Horse

Competition. Manuel's name and brand appears on four of the fifteen plaques, riding horses he had raised and trained.

Manuel Murrietta schooling a three-year-old colt, Nordfork Branding, 2015.

13

Habitat or Species?

As the years rolled into the new century, we improved our grazing management to promote watershed health, grew enough grass to feed the cows and calves, and accommodated the Gila topminnow. The National Riparian Team paid us a visit and declared our operation was a good model for how to manage grazing in creek bottoms. Even the US Fish and Wildlife Service started tossing a few compliments our way.

In 2007, I received out of the blue a bombshell letter from the Bureau of Reclamation inviting me to comment on a dam they intended to build across Redrock Canyon. The dam would allegedly act as a barrier to non-native fish swimming upstream from Patagonia Lake located ten to twelve mostly dry stream miles to the west. The fish biologists worried that these illegal immigrants would reach Redrock's waters to prey on and out-compete the endangered Gila topminnow for local habitat. Mosquitofish, another minnow species, was the main threat, but other worrisome predators included sunfish, bluegills, bull frogs, and bass.

Item #3 of the "Conservation Recommendations" by the US Fish and Wildlife Service's Formal Consultation Documents had finally surfaced.

Locally, mosquitoes forced the United States Calvary in 1867 to move Fort Crittenden out of the Sonoita Creek bottom to a more healthy foothills site, probably because mosquitoes transmitted malaria although they didn't know it at the time (malaria transmission by mosquitoes was not discovered until 1897). Since World War II, DDT had been used for mosquito control until Rachel Carson exposed DDT's deadly collateral effects on birds and wildlife in the book *Silent Spring*. That book, perhaps more than any other, kick-started the modern environmental movement. But without DDT, the mosquito plagues worsened. Mosquitofish had been imported from Africa as a biological control agent to eat the mosquito larvae that inhabited our marshes, lakes, and streams. But they also eat and out-compete other watery critters, including topminnow. As cosmopolitan today as house sparrows, they have become an aquatic version of Lehmann lovegrass in the eyes of endangered species biologists.

Our West Redrock pasture had been chosen for the dam. The Bureau's write-up as required by NEPA ran on for 192 pages and described its effects on the watershed in great detail. The dam would be constructed between two rock outcroppings that narrowed the channel to a dozen yards. Across this reach, the concrete dam would be five to six feet high. Mud, silt, and gravel behind the dam would eradicate fifteen hundred feet—over one quarter of a mile—of gorgeous, healthy sandy loam creek bottom. I had fenced this reach in 2002 for a riparian pasture that I needed for weaning calves and other special uses. Now it would become a barren mud and gravel bar.

The creek bottom held the accumulated watershed wealth of sandy loam soils where the water run-off collected to bring forth abundant life for many species. In 1998, after I stopped summer grazing, the creek bottom, this quarter mile had exploded with renewed botanical vigor biologists call "ecological release." Willows, cottonwood, ash, and walnut saplings had grown to heights of ten to fifteen feet, to form a green canopy that covered the stream bed in dappled sunlight and shade. Gradually, the stream channel had narrowed and started to regain a sinuous path between the canyon walls. Bank-side vegetation was capturing sediment and rebuilding the stream banks. Deer grass grew to knee-high on my horse. Reeds, rushes, sedges, and watercress reappeared.

Water clear as gin tumbled over the rocks and filled shallow pools for minnows and other aquatic creatures. At night, raccoons and coatimundi scoured the backwaters for crayfish and frogs. One year, a pair of Western Kingfishers had migrated in to catch minnows, nest, and raise their young. As the winter gave way to early spring Phainopeplas, a black silky flycatcher, nested in the elderberry trees. Nearby Patagonia is called an "Important Birding Area" by the National Audubon Society. This designation attracted winter migrants of the two-legged variety. When a pair of gray hawks nested in the ash trees at Pig Camp spring, the birders migrated to the Redrock Creek bottoms.

During the dry spring months, this area still kept the memory of water. The creek bottom remained a verdant corridor in a landscape otherwise wilted by drought. In fact, over the entire ten-mile length of the Redrock Canyon, only three places—Cott Tank tributary, Gates Spring, and the Falls—had dry season natural water. Now, it seemed that my West

Redrock Creek upstream from dam site.

Redrock pasture might be added to that list. The US Fish and Wildlife Service had started calling it the "new, near-perennial reach," a self-contradictory term that expressed how the stream was recovering under our new grazing management without saying anything good about us.

In the summer when the monsoon burst over the watershed, the creek's personality changed to a storm-driven flood. A low wall of red-tinged water surged past Rich's house and onward to Sonoita Creek, only to recede and clear the next day. Morning glories and monkey flower bloomed in the canyon bottoms, attracting brightly colored butterflies and bees. Vermilion-colored and ash-colored flycatchers foraged on insects rising above the water. Javelina wallowed in the backwater where whitetail deer embedded their heart-shaped hoof prints in the mud.

At October's end, Rich and I herded our cow-calf pairs into the Redrock Creek pastures. At the time, the calves weighed four hundred pounds and still nursed their mothers. We put them through at the Oak Grove Spring corrals where we vaccinated against bovine viral diarrhea, pasturella, and leptospirosis, diseases that could cause considerable losses after weaning. In an average rainfall year, they put on another hundred pounds grazing in the bottoms before being sold at weaning. With the dam, these natural season-driven changes benefitting many species of plants and animals, including our cows, would be jeopardized by a scheme unlikely to rescue a single creature—the Gila topminnow. Astonishingly, the US Forest Service's final review passed over the Bureau's project with a "Finding of No Significant Impact."

After the dam, the zealous saviors of topminnow would visit our barren reach of the stream now and then to make surveys on which to write long-winded reports. But we had to look at the wreck every day. And when this misguided example of environmental heroism collapsed and the topminnow disappeared, they would probably fall back on cattle as the excuse.

Who then would take out the dam and restore the watershed? Not the Bureau of Reclamation; they are in the business of destroying watersheds with dams and irrigation schemes. Not the US Fish and Wildlife Service; they are in the business of enforcement, not restoration. Not the US Forest Service; they are handcuffed by the formal consultation process of the Endangered Species Act. Once a Biological Opinion has been issued, no matter how flawed, the US Forest Service was shackled by the Endangered Species Act from trying other solutions out on the watershed. Locked in by a bureaucratic preordained process and fearful of lawsuits from Garden of Eden activists, flexibility to react to actual watershed conditions was foreclosed.

An over-grown federal bureaucracy with a billion-dollar budget and an army of employees, the Bureau of Reclamation had turned the mighty Colorado River into a ditch with Glen Canyon and Hoover Dams. Its waters are now shunted into canals for farmers and city dwellers in the overcrowded oasis cities of California, Arizona, and Nevada. The Bureau's latest mega-project was the 336-mile-long Central Arizona Project canal completed in 1994 that brought Colorado's water into southern Arizona. The canal's construction did so much damage to the Sonoran Desert that NEPA required the bureau to allocate millions of dollars for mitigation and restoration. But that Biological Opinion did not take into account the local watershed users, nor local watershed ecology. Like most big federal projects, it relied on a "one-size-fits-all" approach. Now, that opinion required the Bureau to spend some loose change in little Redrock Canyon to build a dam across a small watershed in Arizona's smallest county under the guise of making amends for their larger sins and misdemeanors. But that dam would destroy a small paradise and restore nothing. I now felt Edward Abbey's anger and remorse.

The bureau's dam proposal differed from Canelo Hills Coalition's other skirmishes with the Endangered Species Act because this time they had to listen to us. NEPA required the bureau to consult with the people affected by their project, and that included the Canelo Hills Coalition ranchers as well as other down-stream users.

Also, the proposal included a new bureaucracy closer to home with a corollary scheme, this one concocted with the Arizona Game and Fish Department. They would "renovate" the creek upstream from the dam by poisoning all waters in the canyon with rotenone and antimycin A, chemicals that kill all gill-breathing animals like fish and aquatic insects. Before applying the poisons, they would net all the fish and frogs, save back any topminnow and other native critters in aquaria, and kill everything else, especially mosquitofish. Bullfrogs would be killed by gigging or shooting. The bullfrogs' "sin" was that they eat minnows. After the waters were "cleansed," and the poison given a few days or weeks to dissipate, topminnow would be restocked. This process—poisoning and restocking—might have to be repeated several times, according to the experts. Bullfrogs, for example, would hop up the streambed to repopulate the springs above the dam. But the plan made no mention of removing the exclosure fencing so that cattle could clean out the headwater springs during the winter and give the beleaguered topminnow the habitat it required.

Although the dam mostly affected me, everyone in the Coalition opposed it. We had learned the power of collective action. We pointed out that a ten-foot-high natural waterfall between the Kunde Ranch and our East Redrock pasture already isolated most of the creek and all of its perennial waters. Chris Peterson and I escorted the project's proponents on a field trip so they could see the falls. On the way, we showed them the mess the dam would make of a beautiful area that we had worked hard to keep healthy and functioning.

"But if we don't build the dam now, we'll lose the funds," the bureau's point man complained. He seemed genuinely embarrassed by a natural solution—the falls—one that did not require a lot of money, concrete, and a big machine. In government bureaucracies, not spending all the allocated money constitutes a cardinal sin, whether or not the project is really needed or wise. Not spending it all now means they will get less money to spend next year.

"Why don't you build the dam in Sonoita Creek upstream from the lake," we countered. "That will cover Redrock Canyon, as well as a lot of other watersheds."

True, the Central Arizona Project had brought non-native fish into the lower Santa Cruz River watershed. But even if the fish made journey from Tucson up the mostly dry Santa Cruz River and into Sonoita Creek, they would have to navigate several miles of dry creek bed to reach Redrock Canyon waters. While this was theoretically possible during a strong monsoon runoff, the odds of it happening were minuscule. And the vertical drop at the falls on the Kunde allotment protected most of the springs from upstream migration.

The dam scheme also didn't guard against the stronger possibility that the non-native fish might swim downstream into Redrock Canyon. Years before, dirt ponds on deeded land had been stocked with bass, blue gill, and catfish. The mosquitofish likely came along as bait.

Two years later, the Bureau of Reclamation dropped the Redrock dam site, perhaps in favor of one in Sonoita Creek, though we did not know. But the poisoning of Redrock Canyon remained on the docket. Arizona Fish and Game Department was the lead agency with legal authority to take the action, but they needed or wanted us to approve.

"We are not the US Fish and Wildlife Service. We are committed to working with ranchers, not trying to run over them," Don Mitchell, their amiable fisheries biologist said repeatedly. Don had done an aquatic survey of the Redrock drainage and knew the landscape. He offered a carrot. The department would pay for new livestock water development and fences if we went along with the poisoning project.

But three of the four ranchers had already been down that road with the Canelo Hills Coalition and we didn't need any more improvements. Chris and Larry Peterson still needed waters and fencing, but they were utterly opposed on moral grounds to the use of chemicals to kill wild creatures simply because a confederacy of bureaucrats and a few biologists deemed them expendable. These animals had equal rights to occupy their homeland in the creek, and I agreed.

Also, our drinking water could be contaminated. Rotenone had been linked to Parkinson's disease, and other ailments. Rich's domestic well was just a mile and one-quarter downstream from the dam site. Also, the town of Patagonia's wells were in the same aquifer. The Bureau of Reclamation's write-up said that both chemicals had low toxicity to humans, but pregnant women, infants, and older debilitated people should avoid drinking the stuff. They had forgotten the golden rule of the watershed. "Do not do unto those downstream what you wouldn't like those upstream to do to you."

Our quarrels with the US Fish and Wildlife Service, Arizona Game and Fish Department, and the Bureau of Reclamation were broader than just bovines and minnows in tiny Redrock Canyon. Our objections encapsulated conservation's current puzzle: Do we attempt to preserve a rare species in a marginal habitat or should we expend the effort elsewhere where it could succeed? More broadly, should we manage our watersheds for a single endangered species, or for overall ecological health to the benefit of all creatures?

For the coalition and other people who work and live in the watershed, overall ecological health was paramount. Our livelihoods and drinking water were at stake. Even so, agencies, some academics, and private organizations believe that society must save all endangered species in every place where they might be able to exist regardless of cost to other wild creatures and human users. The Endangered Species Act codified this requirement in stone. When differences cannot be resolved, the parties turn to a poorly informed judiciary to settle the disputes. That process is extremely expensive and time-consuming. Most ranchers, farmers, and small rural communities do not have the money or patience to put forth their views in court. Meanwhile, with a workable solution in limbo, scientists, users, and preservationists dilly-dally while the watershed continues on its relentless path.

The environmental activists have controlled this debate up to now by turning science into a morality play. Users of the landscape like ranchers and farmers are portrayed as the villains while the anti-grazing posse rides to the rescue of the watershed like the Lone Ranger absent the white horse. But the work of the Canelo Hills Coalition—and other modern-day rancher coalitions—has changed that drama into a reality check. We have shown that the watershed can be grazed without harm, thus providing an authentic, observable example of pristine nature.

In today's world, science has become the new religion and scientists its infallible priesthood. Science supposedly supplies the only truth-based knowledge system. And its workings are above the perception or questioning of those who are not ordained. But the proponents of the exclosures and the dam had filtered in the scientific articles that supported their positions, but missed or dismissed other studies that did not. By inference, their science gave them both practical and moral authority: Grazing should be eliminated in order to conserve a single species. This would allegedly restore "biodiversity" in the watershed even though the required dam would eliminate habitat for other creatures and degrade overall ecological health and biodiversity.

People who rely on science for moral authority suffer from a misapprehension of what science is and how it works. Science does not take sides or proclaim moral judgments: People do. While science can define important aspects of our world, the accumulated wisdom of human experience instructs on how we ought to live in it. Also, the accepted scientific facts of today may prove to be wrong tomorrow. As Aldo Leopold wisely noted in the *Sand County Almanac*:

> The ordinary citizen today assumes that science knows what makes the community clock tick; the scientist is equally sure that he does not. He knows that the biotic mechanism is so complex that its workings may never be fully understood.

Overall habitat health, biodiversity, and topminnow *populations* took a back seat to saving *individual* topminnows under the application of the Endangered Species Act in Redrock Canyon. The law, or its administrators, seem to ignore the roles of ecological connectivity and the physical environment. When repairing a water gap, for example, we had to post a "monitor" to look for dead minnows drifting downstream. If more than twenty floated by, the work had to be shut down, and a call immediately placed to the US Forest Service hot line. Incidental "Take" had been exceeded; topminnow had been "Harmed." But no one, to my knowledge, ever saw twenty dead minnows, or even one, except for those killed by the fish biologists during their stream surveys. They also claimed that cows would tromp on or swallow minnows when taking a drink but provided no data that showed this was in fact true.

Worse yet, the fisheries biologists from both the US Fish and Wildlife Service and the US Forest Service assumed without question that exclosure fencing to keep cattle out year-round would allow topminnow habitat to recover. That miscalculation turned out to be a tragic mistake that contributed to the species' demise in our watershed.

"In the open mind there are many possibilities, but in the expert mind there are few," to paraphrase a Buddhist proverb.

ii

Cienega Creek starts in the Canelo Hills a half mile east of my head-quarters, one of several fingers that drain the northeastern flanks of the Canelo Hills. The fingers converge into a main channel that flows north for thirty-five miles, then turns west northwest, eventually reaching the Santa Cruz River in the heart of Tucson. Bordered on the west by the Santa Rita and Empire Mountains, and on the east by the Whetstone and Mustang Mountains, its watershed is many times larger than Redrock Canyon (see map 2). It has more water, including marshland, springs, and long reaches where water flows year-round.

The Cienega Creek watershed had been the heart of several large cattle ranches since the 1880s. One hundred years later, it faced an uncertain future that included housing subdivisions, mining, commercial development, and grazing on a patchwork quilt of federal, deeded, and state-owned lands amounting to almost 150,000 acres. In 1988, through a visionary program of land exchanges and purchases, the Bureau of Land Management acquired the deeded land and created the Las Cienegas National Conservation Area in collaboration with the local lessee-rancher and the State of Arizona. During the congressional hearing to appropriate the necessary funds, rancher John Donaldson testified to the watershed's unique strength and beauty, saying that, "whether or not my grazing is continued, the land should be preserved from development." The enabling legislation passed in 2000 by the United States Congress mandated that grazing would be continued in concert with wildlife, landscape conservation, and recreational uses. In short, ranchers and the other parties would have to work together.

Cienega Creek had healthy populations of topminnow from the get-go, but the BLM fisheries biologists Jeff and Karen Simms worried about the effects of year-round grazing in the creek bottoms and decided to investigate. By 1996, part of the creek bottoms had been fenced. During the wet summer growing season, the cattle were kept out of the lower (north) creek, but winter grazing continued. In the upper creek, cattle were completely excluded year-round. Topminnow seemed to be thriving in the winter-grazed creek, but declining in the upper reaches.

I first heard about Jeff's work in 2002 and asked if he could show me what a healthy topminnow habitat looked like so I could compare it with Redrock Canyon. "Sounds like a field trip is in order," he replied. Driving up to Empire Gulch where the cattle had been excluded, we parked under the deep shade of a cottonwood-willow forest. Jeff pulled on his rubber boots and waded into the bog with a dip net. The stagnant, stinky water yielded a jumbo catch of frogs, predaceous bugs, and mosquitofish, as well as pond scum and leaf litter. Its undercut banks made ideal habitat for ambush predators like bull frogs and garter snakes.

"Topminnow are on the decline here," the biologist noted. In fact, they seemed to have disappeared, although he cautioned that his survey methods might have missed some specimens.

We drove north to the lower reaches of the creek where a strong stream of water meandered in riffles over limestone substrate, collecting in broad shallow pools with clean bottoms of sand and rock. Here, where cattle had been allowed to graze during the winter, Topminnow were doing well, Jeff said. But he cautioned that more years of study were required to draw any hard and fast conclusions.

In 2010, Jeff and Karen Simms summarized twenty years of careful observations. In the lower (northern) portions of the creek, Gila Topminnow populations had remained stable. In the upper (southern) portion, drought and poor water quality eliminated topminnow from two study sites. Here, topminnow habitat had been reduced by 40 percent from the 1990-baseline when cattle had kept the vegetation pared back and the creek bed open. Reasons for the decline included "dog hair" thickets that had sprouted up and shaded the creek, lowering the light levels, plus increased leaf litter that smothered the pools with rotting organic matter. The litter-driven food chain had replaced the algal-driven food source that topminnow preferred. Creek flows decreased and the pools deepened and stagnated. Dissolved oxygen dropped to less than two parts per million while the lower segment contained twice that amount. An oily scum from the bumper crop of microscopic diatoms developed on top of the stagnant pools, retarding the exchange of carbon dioxide and oxygen with the atmosphere.

Healthy Gila topminnow habitat required disturbance, Jeff and Karen Simms concluded, especially in spring-water ecosystems. Redrock Canyon with its low perennial water flows was a spring-driven ecosystem.

Historically, grazing had provided that disturbance until the US Fish and Wildlife Service forced the US Forest Service to fence out cattle.

The BLM biologists backed up their findings with publications from earlier studies in Nevada, Australia, and Arizona. The latter work by ethno biologists A. M. Rea and G. P. Nabhan noted that all of the biodiversity we have now had been stewarded [disturbed] by native peoples who used these ecosystems for survival—water, food, fiber, irrigation, and spiritual renewal—for thousands of years. Grazing should now be added to that list.

In fact, John Donaldson had provided for healthy topminnow habitat on the Empire Ranch years before the BLM took over. When he leased the ranch in 1975 John did a horseback evaluation of the watershed, surveying its multiple habitats and grasses. Flood draws, marshland, and giant sacaton grass dominated the upper (south) three miles of the Cienega Creek bottoms. Sacaton is a deep-rooted bunch grass that can grow higher than the shoulders of a tall horse in the silty soil overlying the floodplain where water is near the surface. The plant greens up in the early spring and grows tons of high quality forage.

Early on, Donaldson had loosely fenced both sides of upper Cienega Creek in a zig-zag pattern that followed the margins of where giant sacaton grew. After his cows calved in the mountain pastures in early spring, the cowboys moved them down into the sacaton bottoms. The abundant green forage and easy country with nearby water helped the cows heal up from calving and put them on a good nutritional level to take the bulls and breed back. The relatively small pastures concentrated the cows with the bulls which ensured a high percentage calf crop the next year. The calves benefited from heavy milking momma cows and the green grass. The cows pruned the rank old growth and ate the new leaves and stems, rejuvenating the bunch grass plants for the next season. In centuries past, fire, both natural and human-caused, had provided the same ecosystem services to the watershed. Meanwhile, through all this natural disturbance by cows, Gila topminnow had flourished in the creek.

At the beginning of summer rainy season, the wet and manure-laden sacaton bottoms became breeding grounds for swarms of biting flies and ticks, as well as producing excellent fertilizer to rejuvenate the soil. As the monsoon advanced, the cows naturally wanted to leave the bottoms for higher, less buggy pastures. Donaldson's cowboys open the gates and herded them into the lower foothills where grama and other summer grasses had greened up and grown tall.

In 1988 the BLM began a biological planning process that brought together the many other interested parties with Donaldson into the management of the watershed. By that time MacFarland Donaldson, John's son, had joined the ranching enterprise. In one early meeting of the parties, Mac remembers when all the competing interests—hikers, hunters, preservationists, wildlife enthusiasts, bird watchers, ATV and biking clubs—listed what they wanted to do on the ranch. At the conclusion, John spoke up: "I hear what you all want from the ranch, but no one mentioned what the land needed from us."

Even so, after months of meetings, an uneasy but functional truce developed between Donaldson, the Sonoita community, and most of the recreation/preservationist interests. Each January, a Biological Planning Committee met with Mac and John to work out the pasture rotation and grazing plan for the coming year; where the cows would graze, on what dates, and how many. Attending those meetings I listened as Mac pleaded for the flexibility to vary the schedule based on changing weather, rainfall, and cattle market conditions. At first, this horrified the environmentalists who viewed the watershed as a rigid geographical entity and didn't trust the cattlemen to do the right things at the right times. They refused to believe that responsible ranchers like Mac and John Donaldson operated in a constant dialogue with nature and the watershed to protect its health and their livelihood.

But over time the group improved their perceptions of how the watershed functions under variable climatic conditions. Also—and this was crucial—Donaldson and the planners developed a measure of mutual trust that each party to the collaboration would do what needed to be done. To the cattlemen, having so many partners to educate and satisfy, people who had no personal assets at risk, "no skin in the game," was at times frustrating.

Fast forward to 1995. The Center for Biological Diversity threatened to sue the BLM over cattle grazing in the occupied Gila topminnow habitat of upper Cienega Creek. Their premise was that cattle in the creek would damage riparian habitat and result in illegal "take" of topminnow under the Endangered Species Act. Under duress, the BLM and Donaldson agreed to put up exclosure fencing tightly around the wet margins of the creek. Once again, ignorance and prejudice against cows overruled the common-sense observation that showed topminnow was thriving under Donaldson's short-term grazing regime. Agency personnel who did understand were blocked by the Endangered Species Act and the threat of lawsuit from doing anything different. Sealing off cattle from the creek also sealed the fate of topminnow in upper Cienega Creek, just as it had done in Redrock Canyon.

In 1999, John N. Rinne, a research fisheries biologist at the Southwest Forest Science Center, an independent arm of the US Forest Service, noted in a peer-reviewed article that scientific support was lacking for the claims that grazing has done irreparable harm to our native fishes. Of the two hundred articles he reviewed, only eight were done in the southwest, and only four were data-based. Eighty percent were not peer-reviewed, the gold standard for scientific validity. Most were opinion, summary, survey, or review papers that presented no new data and primarily promoted the pre-conceived opinions that grazing was harmful. Rinne said in conclusion:

> Finally, the time has come to remove ourselves from promoting and sustaining the litany about (negative) effects of grazing on fishes and to embrace collection of scientifically sound, defensible information that can be used by land managers. Too often, qualitative, nonscientific data are collected . . . The reliability of these data are low; however their use and incorporation into management and public opinion have been too common.

Science, in other words, is a systematic mode of inquiry, not a compilation of foregone conclusions. Science becomes most interesting when the inquiry discovers something unexpected or new, but the scientist must be open to that possibility. In 2010, Bob Hudson and I rode down to the Cott Tank drainage exclosure in Redrock Canyon where cattle had been excluded for fifteen years. The spring-water pools looked and smelled like open septic tanks with plugged up leach lines.

"This needs to be cleaned out," I muttered.

"They couldn't pay me to graze it now," Bob growled.

iii

In the 1960s, the world had gone berserk with tribal conflict between the nuclear-armed countries, creating the threat of thermonuclear war. During that time, I enlisted in the United States Air Force to fulfill my military obligation. My cowboy skills didn't mesh with any Air Force job descriptions. But my transcripts in veterinary medicine sent me to a hospital in Alabama for training as a triage medic. Triage is a system of priority for medical treatment in a disaster with too many injured people to save everyone. I learned to recognize the frothy, bubbly bleeding of punctured lungs and compound fractured skulls. These people went into one category as beyond medical help. Others with broken limbs and lacerations went into another after I splinted the fractured arms and stopped the bleeding. These might survive if the doctors got to them in time. Fortunately, I never had to practice what I learned, but selecting between who would live or die was a dilemma that stayed with me (as did the insanity of war).

Evolution in nature, broadly speaking, operates on the triage principle, albeit on a much slower time scale and without conscious thought. It determines what species continues on and what species dies out. The Endangered Species Act can be thought of as an attempt to counter the triage of evolution. It seeks to halt the process of extinction, especially that which is caused or abetted by too many humans and our polluting and wasteful ways. Though the act is well-intentioned, the law as it has been applied has not resulted in the recovery and delisting of many species. A system is needed to prioritize what species can reasonably be saved: triage, to complete the comparison.

We need a selection process that concentrates efforts on those species that have a decent chance of making it, instead of trying to save every species in every place where they might be able to exist. Right now, that selection has been left to academic biologists who ascribe to the principle of maintaining maximum biodiversity, saving all species, everywhere. That removes the burden of selection, yet it is not practical or even possible. Right now, Garden of Eden activists and their lawyers think that they are the deciders, producing chaos and the opposite of the intended effect of the act. Somebody needs to decide which species can be saved and which ones have little chance of survival. Nature, driven by natural selection in the Age of the Anthropocene, will otherwise prevail. She may prevail anyway. One danger is that we would select only those species of immediate importance to ourselves. That would leave an uninteresting and monstrous world, like the one that might have been left had the thermonuclear bombs been dropped. . . .

The US Fish and Wildlife Service's opinion that continued grazing in Redrock Canyon would cause Gila topminnow to die out ignored Bob Hudson's common-sense statement that the species had persisted in Redrock Canyon for decades in the presence of cattle. Yet when cattle were excluded, topminnow eventually disappeared. Logic would insist that the role of exclosure fencing should have been explored. Instead, they shifted the blame to mosquitofish and other non-native competitors and predators. They simply could not imagine that seasonal grazing by cows might help the beleaguered species.

Clearly something more complex was going on, and it was probably related to habitat change. Jeff and Karen Simms on Cienega Creek looked deeper than mere associations in time and place. They found that excluding cattle caused the habitat to change to an environment that favored mosquitofish and other topminnow predators and competitors. And they observed and described those changes in detail by comparing areas with and without grazing over the past twenty years.

But in Redrock Canyon the agency biologists believed they already had the answer—cows and grazing had to be harmful. Most of their terms and conditions to minimize Harm and Take of topminnow flowed from that unexamined premise. The Bureau of Reclamation's and the Arizona US Fish and Wildlife's proposals would alter the canyon's environment to allegedly favor topminnow but the exclosures would stay in place. These were recipes for failure based on simplistic thinking and would damage, rather than "renovate," the habitat as claimed. But the actions provided the momentary comfort of environmental heroism and the expenditure of a lot of money. They ignored complex interactions between other species and the topminnow's total environment.

More recently, Douglas K. Duncan, a supervisory US Fish and Wildlife fish biologist, looked deeper into the mechanisms for the persistence of topminnow in the presence of mosquitofish in small habitats. It has long been known, he said, that topminnow tolerates [likes] springheads with high water quality, while mosquitofish do not. The winter grazing that kept the springheads in Redrock Canyon clean and water quality high had, over time, been prevented by the exclosures, although Duncan again failed to connect his observations to that logical conclusion.

The Redrock Canyon-topminnow experience makes a strong argument for changing the Endangered Species Act to focus on habitat health first. In the same way that exercise and proper diet prevents heart disease, the focus on habitat health first should prevent and slow the extinction of species. Extinction, no matter how dreadful its finality, is a natural biological event. Focusing on habitat first would let nature determine which species lives on and which ones pass away. It would relieve humans of the God-like responsibility of species triage. The watersheds are complex beyond human understanding, as Aldo Leopold and other more recent ecologists have observed. Provided that the watersheds are healthy and functioning, we should trust them to do their work. Also, focusing on habitat would leave a place for humans in the watersheds.

As Jeff and Karen Simms concluded after decades of careful study: "If you take care of the watershed, then you will be taking care of fish habitat."

On May 1, 2015, the US Fish and Wildlife Service issued a ruling that finally brought common sense into the use of surrogates for estimating the amount of "Take" that might "Harm" an endangered species. The final rule says in essence that surrogates may be used, provided the Biological Opinion: (1) describes the *causal link* between the surrogate and Take of the listed species; (2) describes *why* it is not possible to know or monitor the amount of Take directly; (3) sets a *clear standard* for determining when the extent of Taking has been exceeded. In the Redrock Canyon-topminnow saga over exclosures, no causal links had been proven, and the extent of Take was vague if not impossible to determine.

The exclosures were unquestionably a significant disturbance of the spring water ecosystems that required spending a lot of federal money. This should have triggered a NEPA analysis that could have unearthed the faults, but the agencies apparently ignored or were exempt from environmental laws. Alternatively, they could have listened to Bob Hudson's common-sense reflection that the grazed headwater springs had "something that topminnow liked."

14

Why in Hell?

Once, I complimented a billionaire on his purchase of a fine ranch with a balanced mixture of summer and winter country, lots of deeded land to go with the grazing leases, good water and range improvements, and a storied history going back to before Arizona's statehood.

"It's no different than buying another yacht," he sniffed. He may have owned the ranch on paper, but his was a partial tenancy shared with the people who worked the range. Only they knew the land and cattle in all their shared intricacies, rode through the hot noontimes and cold winters, the droughts and floods and fires.

Recently, another billionaire swept through our borderland region buying up ranches. His overseer, an experienced cow man, chose them well, plucking up the ones with lots of deeded land and carrying capacity. He also retained the people who worked there and savvied the country and the cattle. They understood the husbandry of growing cattle on the borderlands.

But transfer of ranch ownership does not always happen that way. Ranches of any size and quality cost a lot of money and new buyers are often people who have been successful in other occupations. Some look at the ranch and think that running it will be easy and the skills that made them successful elsewhere will automatically transfer to the watershed and livestock. This can be a recipe for disaster. The land and cattle suffer along with the new owner's bank account. Other buyers are more perceptive and seek out and hire people who know what they are doing, or go slow and learn from the neighbors and the land.

Ranches, like farms and other home places, come in different sizes and quality. The most important amenities on a ranch are good neighbors. I knew this when I started, having grown up in the country, but I really didn't appreciate how important neighbors are until I bumped into a bad one. That experience taught me how to be a better neighbor myself.

The average size of a ranch in our region is about 250 cows, a number that can rarely or barely support a family. An old chestnut reads: "Behind every successful rancher is a spouse with a good job in town." For others less fortunate, the rancher may drive the county road grader or school bus, deliver the rural route mail, and work the ranch on weekends. Another savvy saying: "To make a small fortune in ranching, you have to start with a large one."

And yet one old-time ranch real-estate broker remarked that he never saw a ranch that didn't make money when it sold, meaning that there seems to always be people who want to be part of the ranching tradition. Buyers are seeking a different way of life on a place-based, season-driven landscape that fosters a sense of authentic human attachment to the natural world. They want to escape what geographer-anthropologist Marc Augé called "non-places;" modern cities of concrete, asphalt, and shopping malls, drive-by freeways, airports, Walmarts and Costcos, and the fleeting, shallow social media of the internet—places so slick and featureless that human memory cannot cling to them; places that inspire no lasting sense of belonging. Social critic Gertrude Stein described them as placeless places, where—"There is No There There."

Some ranches sell and resell about every five years. These often have poor water and forage, country too rough to manage well, and are small-sized. These pop up on the realtor's websites usually advertised as a "good" starter ranch. The set carrying capacity on the agency's books plays a role in enticing a prospective new owner to jump in. The neophyte begins calculating the income he or she will have every year "on the average," without understanding that there is no such thing as average on the ranch. Rainfall, topography, poor calf crops, coyotes and lions, disease, dry windmills, and poisonous plants weave in and out of the landscape and the bank account like evil fairy godmothers. Unable to run the stated number of cattle year after year, they sometimes blame the agency instead of the weather and their inexperience.

But some buyers don't care if the ranch pays for itself; they buy in for the lifestyle and scenery, a get-away from town. More and more, new ranch owners fall into this category. Some of them, when they find out how much work is involved, will hire someone else or put the place on the market for the next yearning neophyte to come along and pick up the tab and shovel. This changing demographics of ranch ownership sometimes presents problems for the watershed and the caretaker agencies because often the new owner has no concept of land-use ethics and grazing management.

The best ranches seldom come up for sale to the public unless the price is overly high or the ranch is so huge that few people can pay the price. The good ones are usually passed down to the next generation or are snapped up by a neighbor. Or to a billionaire who may set foot on the property once or twice a year. They may buy a country club vacation residence in town where they can play golf and visit the ranch at branding or shipping time without getting their hands dirty. These are the shiny new people who made amenity ranching fashionable with thousand-dollar Stetson hats, belt buckles the size of hub caps, and lizard-skin boots for lifestyle enhancement and bragging rights.

Ted Turner, another billionaire, had a different plan. He turned two million acres of cattle ranches into bison pastures, claiming that bison, being native to the landscape, would be easier on the watersheds than cattle, horses, or sheep. Also, native critters like elk, pronghorn, deer, with their attendant predators of wolves, cougar, and bear, would have

Ranchland for sale.

more room to roam and a better chance to capture a meal. Ever the en-
trepreneurial capitalist, Turner built up a chain of restaurants called Ted's
Grill that specialized in buffalo burgers and the like. He also bought a
slaughterhouse and processing plant to supply them with buffalo meat.

At first, he claimed that bison would restore the native range by their
migratory habits and tendency to scatter their dung with their whisking tails.
But bison ranchers soon learned that bison, when confined in pastures, ball up
in the same places as cattle and strip grasslands and trample creek banks when
unable to migrate. I recently noticed a help wanted ad in the *Society for Range
Management* for a range conservationist to monitor Ted's buffalo ranches.
Duties included working out pasture rotation schemes and monitoring grass.

That leaves the multi-generational family rancher who ekes out a
living from the land and cattle. All of them are frugal, hard-working folks
and some of them do well if they can run enough cows. Most are good at
marketing their products. Academics and trade publications have recently
sounded an alarm about the ancient average age of ranchers with no one in
the family to take over, as on the Seibold and Kunde ranches. A dearth of
competent cowboys has been another complaint. In my part of the world,
there are plenty of vaqueros in Mexico who know how to do ranch work,
but our borderland neighborliness has been eliminated by the border wall
and our deeply flawed immigration policies.

But ranching is a blue-collar occupation with enough romance and history surrounding it that there will always be people who want in. The life of
the cowboy is lived near to Nature, working with livestock and horses. This
has a strong pull on those who are fed up with grime, crime, and confusion
of city life. People with gumption, a strong work ethic, and basic ecological
understanding of the watershed will survive. The problem-solving types
will be fascinated by the ecological and economic complexities, as I was.

Nowadays, the problem is two-fold. First, the large capital investment
required to buy in. Second, the best way to learn how to ranch (or farm) is
to ranch and farm. The mundane tasks of ranching are not, and perhaps
cannot be, taught in school, our land-grant universities notwithstanding.
On-the-job training and apprenticeships are required. Some wannabe
rancher types will fall by the wayside because of the work, but enough
will stick it out for ranching to survive in the west.

ii

Conservation organizations, after decades of opposition to grazing, have recently awakened to reality: That intact, working ranches are good for the watershed and wildlife. The underlying cause goes back to the Homestead Acts. The homesteader arrived on a horse, leading a mule packed with digging tools, a sack of potatoes and a crate full of chickens or piglets, and driving a milk cow he hoped would freshen soon. He was more likely to be a wannabe farmer fresh from a clerical job or a burned out Civil War veteran. As such, he homesteaded the land with water and the best soils, often the river bottoms or natural springs. There he built an adobe hut for his unlucky, shop-worn bride. Together, they planted potatoes and built a hen house and a pen for the few pigs that survived the coyotes, lions, and wolves. Not many of these folks stayed on the original homestead, but those that did were the very definition of resilience. The others were bought out by bigger outfits that blended the homesteader's lands into larger ranches.

Much of the better land with water had already passed into private ownership—deeded lands—by virtue of the Homestead Acts before the forest reserves were established. This took place in most forest reserves and other public lands (BLM) throughout the west including the Coronado National Forest. But deeded lands were limited in scope, and in order to run enough cattle to survive economically, ranchers needed grazing on public lands. In the second half of the twentieth century when nature organizations and government regulators began work to remove cattle from public lands, some ranchers had no choice except to sell their homesteads. They could not run enough cattle to make a living without their grazing allotments. The explosive growth of the Sunbelt created a strong market for "ranchettes" and ex-burban home sites in places like Sonoita. Subdividers bought the rancher's deeded land, bulldozed in roads, chopped it into small pieces. These were the very same lands with the highest ecological values. But their so-called development, rendered the land useless for ranching and of little value for wildlife.

That slow awakening to the economic reality of public land ranching eventually drove the more practical nature organizations into collaboration with ranching interests. In order to save the best remaining land, they had to save the working ranch. At the same time, and with perhaps equal lack of speed, the ecological principles that guide watershed stability seeped into the ranching community. A natural, though sometimes uneasy alliance developed between ranchers and nature organizations to save these untrammeled landscapes. Even so, Garden of Eden activists remained dead set against the rancher and the cow, untroubled by economic reality and the growing fund of knowledge showing that grazing, when managed well, does not injure the land or destroy the wild. These groups have served their purpose and should now move on to other issues. Their multiple lawsuits, rather than helping species, clog up the system and divert the US Fish and Wildlife Service and other conservation agencies from more important work. To rely on the legal system and lawyers to preserve biodiversity and watershed health has become counterproductive, paralyzing America's land management agencies. Theodore Roosevelt IV, a prominent conservationist and governing member of The Wilderness Society noted in a review of Lowell E. Baier's landmark book, *Inside the Equal Access to Justice Act*:

> This masterful work of scholarship flawlessly proves that today's paradigm of cooperative conservation and federalism in endangered species conservation is a far more responsible endeavor with measurable results than can ever be achieved by combative saturation litigation and court intervention.

Edward O. Wilson, an early advocate of biodiversity, astutely observed that humans (and ants) conquered the earth by working together. What has emerged from the forced marriage has been cooperative watershed groups made up of ranchers, the local community, agency and university personnel, and sometimes conservation organizations. The distinguishing features of these groups are: (1) using local knowledge and local people to define problems and their solutions out on the watershed, (2) agency staff serving as facilitators and collaborators, and (3) one or two ranchers to do the day-to-day work of keeping the organization moving forward. As Bill Edwards remarked to me when we formed the Canelo Hills Coalition, "These collaborative groups are more successful when started and driven by local people."

This approach is in distinct contrast to the old, often dysfunctional top-down approach where the agency dictates what the rancher and local communities can and cannot do. Giant government organizations like the US Forest

Service and Bureau of Land Management are not that good at executing work plans out on the watersheds. Under this new paradigm, agencies, instead of being enforcers, become facilitators and the ranchers get the work done. While this alliance may not work in every situation, in most cases and more and more frequently, the work gets started and the watershed and the local community benefits, leaving the activists and grass huggers to grumble on the sidelines.

The fallacy of the top-down land-management approach forced on western watersheds by a centralized governmental bureaucracy is exemplified by the sheer magnitude of western geography. In my little corner of the world, our Sierra Vista Ranger District has jurisdiction over forty grazing allotments encompassing 274,000 acres grazing about 5,100 cows. The usual staffing consists of one range and watershed person and one range conservationist. But often one or the other will be pulled off the range and moved into other duties like fire control or paperwork in the central office. In our neighboring district to the east, the Douglas Ranger District is even larger, 472,000 acres spread over three mountain ranges with forty-six allotments running 7,500 cows. Also, the standard US Forest Service procedure is to move their personnel around every few years. Just as the range conservationist has learned enough to be useful, he or she gets moved.

We live through our stories, cultural anthropologists say. The collaborative, conservation approach also requires that ranchers change some of the stories we tell about ourselves. We can no longer be the isolated, independent, rugged individualist going it alone against the forces of Nature, and everyone else. The collaborative community approach requires the rancher to work together with other users—including neighboring ranchers—for the benefit of the whole watershed. This approach is not new, although the emphasis on land conservation may be. Historians Bernard DeVoto and Wallace Stegner pointed out fifty years ago that western ranchers who survived and thrived worked together with their neighbors. The Lone Wolf more often ended up foundering, leaving the cooperators holding the reins.

But this does not mean that individual ranches and ranchers should be blended into a single, shrunken, socialistic enterprise, like the *ejido* communities and ranches in Mexico were, and some still are. That would be doomed to fail for reasons of the well-known individuality attached to the western personality, as well as the varied and vast landscapes that ranchers inhabit. One size would not work for all, or even very many. Better that each rancher maintain his or her operational autonomy in the midst of the collaborative watershed community.

Our Canelo Hills Coalition was one such partnership on a small scale. It solved critical problems for the ranchers but the tunnel vision of the agencies' biologists made the efforts ineffective in saving Gila topminnow in Redrock Canyon. But we developed more water, improved our grazing systems and the riparian habitat, calmed the US Fish and Wildlife Service, and stopped a ridiculous dam and poisoning of the creek. The coalition's experience highlighted the need to change the Endangered Species Act and the clumsy way it is administered.

At a minimum, the law should be amended to focus on preserving habitat rather than single species. Also, a pathway is urgently needed to correct flawed biological assessments and opinions without the threat of lawsuits. Such flaws arise from preconceived erroneous beliefs, lack of knowledge about the species and its habitat, as well as changing environmental conditions.

Lowell E. Baier recommended reforming the Equal Access to Justice Act as a more palatable and quicker way of reining in "eco-warriors" who have abused the good intentions of the law and crippled our land management agencies. Among his recommendations are: (1) Transparency on the use of the act, informing Congress and the public the true cost of each lawsuit; (2) Reasonable limits on attorney's fees and legal costs; (3) Restrict organizations eligible to collect based on net worth, including restrictions on wealthy tax-exempt nature groups; (4) End "no fault, sue and settle" litigation where activists sue, and the agency, for example the US Forest Service, gives in because they do not have the resources to fight the claim. This would leave the act in place to represent the people for whom it was intended: social security and veterans claimants, and small businesses including small farmers and ranchers who may suffer from undue regulation by overzealous government bureaucrats and who do not have the resources to defend themselves in a court of law.

After more than two decades of working on projects with the US Forest Service, I found that collaborative conservation has lots of potential for good out on the watersheds. The secret was to find seams where projects would help the US Forest Service to meet its obligatory responsibilities and the rancher's needs at the same time. The agency has a long history of regulation to prevent overgrazing. Nowadays, they have a new bundle of environmental and legal constraints to watch out for.

T. N. had a savvy saying to describe finding the right tool for the job: "That's top drawer!" he would exclaim when our work went according to plan. Several of the US Forest Service people I worked with were top drawer and looked for ways to get the job done. Meanwhile, a few others looked in the opposite direction. But to complete the metaphor, the cabinetry within which agency people had to function was overburdened with rules imposed by a central administration far removed from the watershed. One local example of how rules can inhibit progress: Abel Murrietta no longer bids on US Forest Service jobs because new rules have run up the cost and the new overseers don't have a clue how to build good fence.

Government policies on promotion can create a lack of continuity and follow-through. Agency people who were instrumental to the project get transferred, generating a vacuum. That can stall an ongoing project until someone new gets up to speed. After cycling through this merry-go-round, the rancher and others may be reluctant to get involved again. The agency needs to reward its people who stay out on the watershed with promotion and higher salary. The way it works now is that the top drawer people get sucked up to a desk job in "higher" administration, while the collaborative projects fall to the bottom shelf.

Losing a promising project to bureaucratic procedure seems opposed to the agency's reason for existence, especially today. To quote Lowell E. Baier once more:

> Voluntary cooperative conservation [like the Canelo Hills Coalition and the Malpai Borderlands Group] has emerged as the best response to crippling environmental litigation. In the face of rampant litigation . . . those committed to voluntary conservation have preserved and often prevailed.

Such litigation has often been filed against voluntary conservation efforts, suggesting that perhaps the eco-warriors are more concerned about loss of power than the fate of the species or watershed.

iii

"Why in hell would I give half my ranch to the Natures," the old cowboy thundered, stuffing the slick, colorful brochure of native grassland into an empty feed sack. He had been approached about donating a conservation easement to prohibit subdivision development on his deeded land along the creek. He would keep title to his land and home, the literature said and continue to run cattle, but in the marketplace, his estate would be worth fifty cents on the dollar, or less.

I could not think of any good reason either, at the time. I didn't have plans to develop the magnificent wedge of land alongside Alamo Canyon where we started way back when. But the housing boom had shouldered its way into the high desert grassland and Sonoita and Patagonia were growing. Long-term residents from California and other boom states had seen the value of their homes grow exponentially, while the quality of their freeway-centered lives plummeted. As they reached early retirement age, their homes had increased into the million dollar range and they started looking around for a better way to enjoy their declining years. Some, especially those oriented toward horses, or the Sonoran desert, or the beauty of the open, circling horizons, found their way to Sonoita and Patagonia. As they bought and built their Nests in the West, our property values soared.

I didn't want to see a row of ranchette houses perched along the lip of Alamo Canyon, each one with its well drawing water from the skimpy aquifer like straws in a milkshake, sucking Alamo Spring dry. But we were not in the financial category to give it away, either. We could just sit on the property until our heirs could reap the benefits of such a disaster if they chose to. Any young, growing family has many valid needs, and who were we to force Rich and Jackie into our way of life?

A partial solution appeared when our partner on a piece of investment land out of state decided to sell. We had owned that land through the recession and its value had climbed during the recovery. But the capital gains tax would take away half of that gain. At the time, the Southeast Arizona Land Trust, a local group of like-minded neighbors, was offering to hold conservation easements on ranch lands for ranchers who wanted to preserve their watersheds.

The value of our easement against subdivision was determined by appraising the land before the easement was placed (retail price), and again after the easement took away the rights to subdivide. The difference was construed by the Great Washington Tax Man as a charitable donation of capital assets for the public good—conservation deemed to be a public good—and therefore deductible against capital gains and other income. What we saved in taxes made up for less than half of the donated value of the conservation easement. But we have the satisfaction of preserving Alamo Spring and keeping pesky new neighbors at arm's length. Solitude, even in Sonoita, is a disappearing natural resource, as important to me as clean air and decent schools for the grandkids. We are not ones to force our way of life on others, but this is one situation our heirs will have to live with.

I liked the local focus of the land trust made up of neighbors helping neighbors, so I volunteered to be a member of their board of directors. After a few years, we merged with the larger Arizona Open Land Trust. To date, the Land Trust has over thirteen thousand acres under easements and have brokered many thousands more to conservation buyers, for example, Pima County and the Department of Defense.

To hopefully conserve local water, the trust started a new program to pay farmers with riparian land to pump their wells into dry river beds of the Gila and San Pedro Rivers. This temporarily re-creates short reaches of riparian habitat for wild creatures. The farmers are paid for their water and they can return it to growing crops after their short-term contract expires.

But will it create permanent habitat? Or will it increase the claims on the water by downstream users like cities, developers, and Native American tribes? Theoretically, a developer could, if the practice begins to generate enough water, claim a one-hundred-year water supply as required by law that could justify a new housing development downstream. The developer's forty acres of undisturbed Sonoran Desert might be converted into four hundred new houses. The Land and Water Trust's work is a holding action against the population boom in Arizona's Sunbelt. To quote a slogan from the Salt River Project in Phoenix where I grew up and once farmed: "Arizona Grows Where Water Flows." As Arizona's water flows diminish, as they eventually must, Arizona's population growth will also have to slow down.

The Land Trust also negotiated many of Pima County's recent purchases of ranches for the Sonoran Desert Conservation Plan, funded mainly by voter-approved bond issues to the tune of 192 million dollars. Between 1997 and 2009, the county purchased fifteen ranches, a total of 48,000 acres of deeded land that came with 176,734 acres of grazing leases. In a pioneering step for land conservation and against urban sprawl, Pima County protected a large swath of the Sonoran Desert from the clutches of developers salivating to cash in on the population boom with cheap land. But in an early blunder, Pima County passed up the chance to buy the Rosemont Ranch. Now, we are staring at an enormous open-pit copper mine a little ways down scenic Highway 83.

On the downside, the purchases put Pima County in the ranch management business, a responsibility that it was utterly unequipped to take on. Their solution was to lease the ranches back to the sellers on attractive terms provided they adhered to rules developed by desert ecologists. The one employee responsible for oversight of all the county's ranches showed up at a recent meeting with a stack of compact discs containing all the rules and regulations formulated by ecologists for their notions of "good" ranch management. These included reduced stocking rates. Whether those stipulations will work economically for the rancher-lessee remains to be seen.

But questions abound. Will the lessee maintain the improvements on property in which they have no ownership interest, such as housing, fences, water, and roads? Historically, short-term grazing leases on property owned by absentee landlords has resulted in some of the most abused rangeland. Had the county purchased conservation easements instead, the seller would have retained a sizable chunk of ownership and would be more likely to take better care of it. They would have retained equity positions that could grow in value and be passed down to their heirs.

Even so, the county's new land protects from housing development. This may force urban growth to cluster within its current boundaries, reducing the ugly, expensive urban sprawl that has infected Phoenix, Albuquerque, Denver, and other oasis cities of the American west. Pima County's ambitious plan is a work in progress and the outcome uncertain, as one of its framers, historian Thomas E. Sheridan, recently pointed out.

The Land Trust is doing a yeoman's job of promoting working ranches as the best means to hold the land together and prevent its conversion to exurban sprawl. In partnership with the University of Arizona's Range Program, they have sponsored rancher workshops on how conservation easements work, estate planning for keeping the ranch for the next generation, and finding grants to fund needed ranch improvements. This is an excellent example of collaborative conservation on the hoof.

Also, the range program offers a university credit course on conservation ranching. It begins with a discussion of Aldo Leopold's land ethic and how it applies to ranching. Then the students take to the field to find out how ranchers operate within the confines of ecological limits and the need to make a living from the land. Post-course assessment shows a greater understanding of how ranching and good grazing management contributes to land conservation, thus correcting decades of negative press from environmental activists.

Santa Cruz County is a blue-collar community and could not afford to go the Pima County route, even if inclined to do so. In the past twenty-five years, I've seen eleven ranches ranging in size from six hundred to six thousand acres, including the Rail X and the Lazy RR, ruined for cattle and damaged for wildlife. A few subdivisions have been thoughtfully done, with deed restrictions against lot splits, building envelopes, and underground utilities. But others are wildcat, snowball deals. Here, the land is divided into forty-acre parcels (the minimum size that requires few improvements) and allows multiple splits that attracts secondary speculation.

It works like this: The sub-dividers buy a ranch for one thousand dollars per acre, just as an example. They bulldoze in roads, and then split the ranch into forty-acre parcels for sale at three thousand dollars per acre. State law allows that buyer to split the forty acres four times. He or she then splits the forty into ten-acre parcels that sell for six thousand dollars per acre. Under Santa Cruz County zoning and Arizona's subdivision laws, the ten-acre buyer can split that parcel into two five-acre lots which might sell for ten thousand dollars per acre.

National Geographic recently published an analysis of the threats facing another beauty spot, the Greater Yellowstone Ecosystem. Development of vacation cottages to wilderness mansions are the most serious threat to the mostly unspoiled two-million-acre ecosystem. One embattled conservationist suggested that the best thing these newly minted, self-styled environmentalists could do for their watersheds would be to burn down their buildings and go home. That Edward Abbey–type solution would not work for southern Arizona either. In the Paradise Valley of the Yellowstone River, the minimum lot size is now twenty acres, a restriction that saved some of the natural beauty of one magnificent landscape.

Why conservation organizations like the Land Trust and Nature Conservancy don't push for a change in Arizona's subdivision laws remains a mystery. That would be cooperative conservation at its best. Some ranchers and farmers would join the push but others would be opposed. Perhaps they're biding their time until the land boom returns? The real estate lobby in Arizona is strong and maybe the nature organizations are fearful of their losing donor bases?

C6 ranch horse.

15

Cowboy Is a Verb

"Coyote Dun . . . I carried the Conquistador, Comanche, and Cowboy to glory."

—Lyrics by Ian Tyson, 1999

When I was a youngster, my mother gathered us up and boarded the train from Phoenix to Atlanta for the summer-long stay at my grandmother's farm in north Georgia. The farm was eighty acres of red clay and a few scattered pine woodlands with a creek running along one edge. She grew an acre-sized garden and kept a flock of hens to feed her outsized family. Around the homestead, a peach orchard made for plenty of pie fillings and preserves. A mean-spirited rooster kept me treed much of the time. Grandma had a chopping block in the back yard where on Saturday night she butchered a chicken for Sunday supper after church. One Saturday to my relief, she whacked the head off the rooster and dipped him into scalding water to loosen the feathers, his wings still flapping. Behind the barn, a pigsty had a couple of meat hogs fattening for slaughter and a separate stall for the farrowing sow. One of my jobs was to slop the hogs with dinner-table leftovers. My uncle milked a Jersey cow in the mornings, then turned her out to graze. In the evenings, we sat on the back porch taking turns cranking the ice cream maker for an unforgettably delicious peach ice cream.

On a downhill slope next to the cornfield, a weathered board shack sat tucked underneath the pines. A wizened-haired Negro man lived there on the edge of the farm. To a boy, he seemed immensely old, so old in fact that he could neither speak nor hear. Dummy, as my mother's people called him, helped out with the chores in exchange for a place to live and a little food. Once he had worked their corn ground with a team of mules and my uncle said that he plowed a straight furrow.

In the morning, I carried the old man his breakfast, Grandmother's day-old cornbread stuffed in a big glass of buttermilk so he could gum it down. On most days, our job was to drive the cattle down to the pasture alongside the creek where they could graze. Dummy carried a staff to poke them along while I took a gig in hopes of stabbing bullfrogs or crawdads for supper. As the afternoon sun dropped low, Dummy waved his staff at me and together we rounded up the cattle and drove them to the milk shed where my Uncle Wayne fed them a little corn and milked the Jersey again. The early American Cowboy no doubt arose from such humble beginnings.

From medieval times, the cowherd on the farm was often a child or mentally defective adult, good for little else except driving the cows to pasture and bringing them home to the barn before nightfall. But in the vast landscapes of the American west, cattle required a different sort of husbandry, wilder and less settled. To do his job in such wide-open, wild terrain, the cowherd acquired a horse, rope, spurs, and a gun. He had to learn to ride, throw a rope, and shoot. Such trappings and skills had long belonged exclusively to the privileged class (see Robinson, 1993).

For the heads-up farm hand who mastered horsemanship and got real handy with the rope, he became the aristocrat of wage earners. This may have been the only time in American labor history when a man (cowgirls came later) who sold his soul for thirty dollars a month was looked up to. The cowboy came into being out of the necessity of work, the job to be done, on a new kind of landscape far different and more exciting than the bucolic farm. That may be why his successor today has a hard time relating to the recreationist. We mistrust the play ethic as opposed to the work ethic.

The horse gave the cowboy his exalted status. As America spread westward in search of its Manifest Destiny, the early explorers ran into vast herds of feral horses, especially on the Southern Great Plains, estimated by historian Dan Flores to number one to two million head. These horses had escaped from the Spanish settlers or Native Americans to breed and multiply on the same fertile grasslands that supported twenty-five million bison. A lively trade sprang up with Native Americans and Anglo-Mexican horsemen capturing wild herds to sell to farmers, ranchers, wagoneers, and the military.

These horses carried the bloodlines of the Spanish Barb brought to the Mexican mainland by Spanish soldiers in the early 1500s. A compliant, loyal breed with tremendous stamina, the Spanish Barb was a cross between the Moorish horses of North Africa and the native Spanish Jennet. Compact and wide-bodied in conformation, with long mane, tail, and forelock, the Barb had a crested neck, large ears, and small-boned legs. Hernán Cortes landed near Veracruz, Mexico in 1519 with sixteen of these horses and con-quered the entire Aztec Empire in a matter of weeks. One soldier wrote that "Next to God, they [the horses] protected us the most." The conquistadors favored the coyote-colored dun horses trimmed in black.

R. B. Cunninghame-Graham, born a Scottish laird in 1852, immi-grated to Argentina in the 1870s and became a horseman, bronc rider, cowboy, cattle rancher, buffalo hunter, and soldier. Returning home in his declining years, he became a writer of renown and member of the British Parliament. Cunninghame-Graham eulogized the Spanish Barb in the books *Horses of the Conquest* and *Rodeo*. Two horses with similar bloodlines carried his friend, A. F. Tschiffely, on a three-year journey from Argentina to New York, 1925 to 1928. (See Tschiffely's Ride,1933).

One Christmas when our cows were tucked safely away on the mountain,

Spanish Barb horse, Lake District, Chile.

Diane and I escaped to Chile where the Spanish conquistadors had left behind a pure strain of the Spanish Barb. We rode a pair of geldings, bay and grulla-colored, into the Andes Mountains in search of the condor, the world's largest vulture. The horses carried us for miles through the heavy bog of temperate rain forest, crossing glacial-fed rivers belly deep, never missing a step as we climbed into the mountain strongholds. We did not see the bird, but the horses left an indelible imprint on me as a sure-footed, completely reliable breed.

The novelist and cutting horse rider, Thomas McGuane, penned biographies of cutting, roping, and ordinary ranch horses, essaying from his personal experience in the arena, and from his open-air Montana ranch. He suggested that the horse ought to replace the bald eagle as America's national symbol, given how much the horse did and still does for the West. This is a notion cowboys would whole-heartedly applaud.

Despite these and other exaltations, the horse is naturally a flighty creature, having come by its disposition honestly as a prey species of the open plains. That fact has forced on the cowboy's character a measure of patience, as well as caution. The making of a good cow horse requires starting with a good physical specimen, but after that, the outcome depends mostly on who gets the horse during the critical first years of its life. A high dollar pedigree can be sabotaged by the trainer trying to move too fast. Trust me, I know. I've seen it done. Measured, unhurried steps repeated day after day work the best. Many a promising youngster has been set back for months by the cowboy who ignores the horse for a week and then tries to play catch-up in a single day.

This need to go slow and steady before going fast has created persistence in the horseman's personality. The cowboy wakes at dawn and looks the day over with a skeptical eye knowing that he or she may have to make good with less than an ideal situation. Good cowboys and cowgirls are nothing if not resilient. They are observant, proud of what they do, resourceful and daring, but not foolhardy. Their work requires them to be constantly on alert and make quick decisions—the reader will remember how Bird made me pay when I got careless with the rope. As horsemen, cowboys have to remain calm through a storm to get to the other side. As Manuel Murrietta said one day after roping on the stubborn Windy Ryon gelding that I had brought back from the Reeves Ranch:

"I was getting so damn mad, I just put the horse up until tomorrow so I didn't do something I'd regret later."

In the end, that horse made a fair-to-middlin' cow pony and rodeo pick-up horse charging into bucking horses at top speed and dragging bulls out of the arena. A lesser horseman would have forced the issue and ruined a potentially good horse.

And yet when the rider finally "gets with" the finished horse—whether roping, cutting, dressage, or jumping—the two become a separate, third entity that adds up to something greater than the sum of each other. I've been that way with a couple of horses and the feeling was both thrilling and addictive, knowing that any time I rode into the arena we had a good chance to win. Most recently, a horse called Stormytiptop would always give his all, and on occasion make up for my mistakes. Several times on a pressure-packed roping run when I was a bit off balance reaching with the rope to catch a steer, I could feel him move back under me. Logically, I knew that was because he did not like the sensation of being off balance while running at top speed. But deep-down, I felt like we were blood brothers, joined together by the job to be done. Baldy, the little horse that got me through college was like that too. He just did everything right, every time.

"Cowboys have lots of try," is a common savvy saying. While persistence is an ingrained trait, sometimes it can be carried too far. Before I left the farm, I thought all I needed to be a cowboy was a strong right arm and an IQ above room temperature. So I decided to ride bulls. The second mistake I made was winning the first bull riding I entered. Unaware that I won only because I drew up on a dink instead of a bucker while everyone else was thrown off, I entered every bull riding I could get to without again making the whistle. Good bull riders are, like jockeys and gymnasts, small in stature, wiry, with a high ratio of strength to weight. I was over six feet tall and top-heavy, but I had lots of try. Fortunately, my brains kicked in before they got kicked out. The novice cowboy had tried to become a limited noun and failed.

Wallace Stegner, perhaps the dean of serious commentators on western culture claimed that the cowboy has persisted as a folk hero because he dressed in an irresistible costume: big hat, spurs, chaps, and boots. But the reality is that the cowboy dresses for work. The big hat is worn for the same reason a gardener wears a sun bonnet. Undershot-high-heeled boots keep the foot from getting hung up in the stirrups. Leather chaps and denim jeans protect from thorns and brush. Spurs make the horse more responsive. T. J. perks up when I wear them. Bird did not need them because he was All Go and No Whoa anyway. Another reason for the cowboy's persistence in Western culture may be nostalgia; there is a lack of reliable heroes in the twenty-first century.

Some city slickers claim that Westerners are by nature anti-social loners. The cowboys, cowgirls, and ranchers I know are not chatty, but will talk enthusiastically about their work and have a keen sense of humor of the self-deprecating bent, another trait that comes from working with livestock that can waylay their best laid plans. Except for a gravel mix of drifters and rodeo addicts they are family men and women who socialize with their own kind. They love their partners and children. They work hard and generously support their communities and schools. We may not be immediately welcoming to outsiders, but if someone wants to enter the community, they can earn the right.

The label "lonesome" may suggest a kind of pathology or maladjustment to societal norms. True, cowboys are less shaped and constrained by society, a freedom of thought and action we value highly. To the westerner the word has a strongly positive ring. This includes solitude away from the pathologies of the city, a time and place to think deeply and enjoy the watershed in its strength and beauty, to clear the cluttered mind and remember why we chose this life with its trade-off of the social safety net for independence and the big outside. For a balanced portrait of modern western ranching culture, writers Ivan Doig (*This House of Sky; The Montana Trilogy*), Sandra Day O'Conner and H. Alan Day (*Lazy B: Growing up on a Cattle Ranch in the American Southwest*), and Nathan F. Sayre (*Working Wilderness: The Malpai Borderlands Group and the Future of the Western Range*), are on the top shelf of my bookcase. And be sure to get *The Life and Times of Warner Glen*, compiled by Ed Ashurst. In the new millennium, things are changing out on the ranch, and for the better, I think.

And consider the common complaint that cowboys and westerners are closed-mouthed. We don't communicate well. This may be part of the individualism associated with the Western personality. To some degree this may be true, at least in my case, as Diane tells me now and then. Perhaps this trait comes from not wanting to spoil the trance of the untrammeled outside. I am reminded of the tale of the Buddhist monk walking up Japan's sacred Mount Fuji for the first time with his revered teacher. As they trudged silently up the mountain the monk suddenly woke up to the natural wonders all around them: birds, trees, clean air and blue sky, the mountain covered with snow.

As they neared the top, the monk cried out, "Teacher, I have been trying to tell you about all the beautiful things around us. Don't you agree?"

"Yes!" The old man sputtered. "But what a pity to say so!"

I feel that way when I ride out toward Mount Wrightson at the break of day on a good horse.

Moonset at sunrise over Mount Wrightson.

Selected Sources

Foreword
Sharp, Robert L. Sharp's *Cattle Country: Rawhide Ranching from Both Sides of the Border.* University of Arizona Press, Tucson, Arizona. 1985.

Chapter 1. Alamo Spring
Abbey, Edward. *Desert Solitaire.* University of Arizona Press, Tucson. 1968.
———. *The Monkey Wrench Gang.* Harper-Collins, New York. 1975.
Leopold, Aldo. *A Sand County Almanac.* Oxford University Press, New York. 1947.
McAuliffe, Joseph R. *Desert Soils.* pp 87–104.
Phillips, Stephen J. and Patricia Wentworth Comus, Eds. *A Natural History of the Sonoran Desert.* Arizona-Sonora Desert Museum Press, Tucson. 2000.
Scarborough, Robert. "The Geologic Origin of the Sonoran Desert." pp 71–85.
Van Devender, Thomas R. "Deep History of the Sonoran Desert." pp. 61–69.

Chapter 2. Fine Feathers.
Hadley, Drum. *The Voice of the Borderlands.* Rio Nuevo Publishers, Tucson. 2005.

Chapter 3. Tar Paper and Tin Shacks
McGuane, Thomas. *Some Horses.* Random House, Inc., New York. 1999.
Piper, Posie and Robert Bowman. "A History of the Santa Cruz County Fair and Rodeo Association, 1915–1990." Bowman Archive Room, Pioneer Hall, Santa Cruz County Fair and Rodeo Association Fairgrounds, Sonoita, Arizona. Their collection of local homesteader histories highlighted the Western spirit that is still alive today.
Sheridan, Thomas E. *Arizona: A History.* University of Arizona Press, Tucson. Revised Edition, 2012.
Ulph, Owen. *The Fiddleback: Lore of the Linecamp.* Brown Trout Publishers, Inc., San Francisco. 1995.

Chapter 4. What Goes Around
Montgomery, Sy. *Temple Grandin: How the Girl Who Loved Cows Embraced Autism and Changed the World.* Houghton Mifflin Harcourt, Boston. 2012.

Chapter 5. Living Close to Predicament
Hadley, Diana and Thomas E. Sheridan. "Land Use History of the San Rafael Valley, Arizona (1540–1960)." US Department of Agriculture, US Forest Service, Rocky Mountain Forest and Range Experiment Station, General Technical Report RM-GTR-269, Fort Collins, Colorado. 1995.

Iverson, Peter. *When Indians Become Cowboys. Native Peoples and Cattle Ranching in the American West.* University of Oklahoma Press. 1994.

McClaran, Mitchel P., Peter F. Folliott, and Carelton B. Edminster, technical coordinators. "Santa Rita Experimental Range: 100 years (1902–2003) of Accomplishments and Contributions." US Department of Agriculture, US Forest Service, Rocky Mountain Forest and Range Experiment Station, Proceedings, RMRS-P-30, Fort Collins, Colorado. 2003.

Sheridan, Thomas E. op cit.

Stegner, Wallace. *Beyond the Hundredth Meridian: John Wesley Powell and the Second Opening of the West.* Houghton Mifflin Company, New York. 1954.

Chapter 6. Rainfall, Cow Counts, and Climate Change

Cooperrider, C. K. and R. W. Hussey. "Range Appraisal Report for the Coronado National Forest." Book 8, Coronado National Forest, Tucson. 1924. In Hadley, Diana and Thomas E. Sheridan. Op. cit.

Leopold, Aldo. "A Plea for the Recognition of Artificial Works in Forest Erosion Control Policy." *Journal of Forestry* 19(3); 267–273. 1921. In Stauder, Jack. *The Blue and the Green: A Cultural History of an Arizona Ranching Community.* University of Nevada Press. 2016.

Sayre, Nathan F. The Politics of Scale: A History of Rangeland Science. Chapter 4. Fixing Stocking Rates. University of Chicago Press. 2017.

Chapter 7. The Seibold Ranch

Dietz, Harland E. Grass: *The Stockman's Crop.* Sunshine Unlimited, Inc., Lindsborg, Kansas. 1988.

Roach, M.E. "Estimating perennial grass utilization on semidesert cattle ranges by percentage of ungrazed plants." *Journal of Range Management* 3:182–185. 1950.

Smith, Lamar, George Ruyle, Judith Dyess, Walter Myer, and others. "Guide to Rangeland Monitoring and Assessment." Arizona Grazing Lands Conservation Association, January 2012. (A thorough presentation of all grass monitoring and assessment techniques and the interpretation of data as used in *Cowboy Is a Verb*.)

USDA, Forest Service, Coronado National Forest, Sierra Vista Ranger District. "Redrock Action Plan," July 21, 1991.

Chapter 8. Fences, Fires, and Drug Mules

Adams, Andy. *Log of a Cowboy: Narrative of the Old Trail Days.* University of Nebraska Press, Lincoln. 1964.

Collins, Richard. *Riding Behind the Padre: Horseback Views from Both Sides of the Border.* Wheatmark Press. 2014. (For more on immigrants crossing the C6 Ranch).

McMurtry, Larry. *Lonesome Dove.* Simon and Schuster, New York. 1985.

Wister, Owen. *The Virginian.* Macmillan Company, New York. 1902.

Chapter 10. Canelo Hills Coalition

Baier, Lowell E. *Inside the Equal Access to Justice Act: Environmental Litigation and the Crippling Battle over America's Lands, Endangered Species, and Critical Habitat.* Rowman and Littlefield, Lanham, MA. 2015. For compensation data for the Center for Biological Diversity see: Internal Revenue Service Form 990 (2013) online. Also see Center for Biological Diversity Annual Reports on line for legal fees returned.

Brown, J.P.S. *Chilton vs. The Center for Biological Diversity: Truth Rides a Cowhorse.* Make a Hand Publishing, LLC. 2016. (Includes complete transcript of the trial).

Grant, Richard. "El Jefe Was Here." *Smithsonian Magazine.* October, 2016, Vol. 47, No. 2, page 40.

Knight, Richard L. "Combat Biology." *Range Magazine.* Summer, 2015.

Sheridan, Thomas E. *Arizona: A History.* University of Arizona Press, Revised Edition, 2012, pages 324–328.

Chapter 11. Towards Practice of Limits

Charnley, Susan, Thomas E. Sheridan, and Gary P. Nabhan, eds. *Stitching the West Back Together: Conservation of Working Landscapes.* The University of Chicago Press, Chicago. 2014

Holochek, Jerry L., Terrell T. Baker, and Carlton H. Herbel. *Range Management; Principles and Practices*, 6th ed. Upper Saddle River, New Jersey. Prentice Hall. 2011.

Lien, Aaron M., et al. "The Land Ethic of Ranchers: A Core Value Despite Divergent Views of Government." *Rangeland Ecology and Management.* Vol 70:6, Nov 2017, pp 787–793.

Leopold, Aldo. Op cit.

Martin, Paul S. "Ghostly Grazers and Sky Islands." USDA Forest Service Proceedings RMRS-P-36, pp 26–34. 2005.

Sayre, Nathan F. *Ranching, Endangered Species, and Urbanization in the Southwest: Species of Capital.* The University of Arizona Press. 2005.

———. *Working Wilderness: The Malpai Borderlands Group and the Future of the Western Range.* Rio Nuevo Publishers, Tucson. 2005.

———. "Climax and 'Original Capacity;' The Science and Aesthetics of Ecological Restoration in the Southwestern USA." *In Ecological Restoration*, volume 28(2); 23–31. March, 2010.

———. The Politics of Scale: A History of Rangeland Science. University of Chicago Press. 2017.

Smith, Lamar, George Ruyle, Judith Dyess, and others. Guide to Rangeland Monitoring and Assessment. Arizona Grazing Lands Conservation Association. 2012.

USDA NRCS. "National Range and Pasture Handbook." 190-VI-NRPH. October, 2006.

USDA NRCS BLM. "Interpreting Indicators of Rangeland Health." Technical Reference 1734–6. 2000.

White, Courtney. "The Working Wilderness: A Call for a Land Health Movement. In: Berry, Wendell." *The Way of Ignorance*, pages 159-180. Shoemaker and Hoard, Berkley, CA. 2005.

Wood, Steven R., and George B. Ruyle. "Informal Rangeland Monitoring and Its Importance to Conservation in a US Ranching Community." *Rangeland Ecology and Management.* Volume 68:5, Sept 2015, pp 390–401.

Chapter 12. Taking Better Care
Smith, Burt. *Moving 'Em: A Guide to Low Stress Animal Handling.* The Grazers Hui, Kamuela, Hawaii. 1998.

Chapter 13. Habitat or Species
Collins, Richard, Bill Edwards, Dean Fish, Kim McReynolds, and George B. Ruyle. "Canelo Hills Coalition: A Watershed-based Partnership to Improve Rangeland Health and Ranch Economics in Redrock Canyon, Santa Cruz County." *Backyards and Beyond*, Spring, 2010.

Donaldson, MacFarland. Personal Communication. Sonoita, AZ. 2016.

Duncan, Douglas K. "Gila Topminnow Interactions With Western Mosquitofish: An Update." USDA US Forest Service Proceedings RMRS-P-67, pages 283–287. 2013.

Federal Register. "Interagency Cooperation-Endangered Species Act of 1973, as Amended; Final Rule on Incidental Take Statements." May 11, 2015.

Nabhan, G. P. "Plant Diversity Influenced by Indigenous Management of Freshwater Flora of Quitovac, Sonora, Mexico." *In Arid Springs in North America: Ecology and Conservation.* L.E. Stevens and V.J. Meretsky. University of Arizona Press. 2008.

Rea. A. M. "Historic and Prehistoric Ethnobiology of Desert Springs." Ibid.

Simms, Jeffery R. and Karen M. Simms. "Livestock Management and the Conservation of Imperiled Aquatic Species on the Las Cienegas Conservation Area, Arizona, 1990–2010." Arizona Rangelands.org. 2011.

US Department of the Interior, BLM. "Approved Las Cienegas Resource Management Plan and Record of Decision." July, 2003.

———. "Las Cienegas National Conservation Area, 2014 Annual Report," February 2015.

US Department of the Interior, Bureau of Reclamation; US Department of Agriculture, US Forest Service, Southwestern Region. "Native Fish Restoration in Redrock Canyon: Final Environmental Assessment," June 2008.

US Forest Service, US Fish and Wildlife Service. "Biological Assessments, Biological Opinions, Formal Consultation Documents." The Redrock Action Plan of 1991, and Recovery Plans for Gila topminnow can be found in US Forest Service files at: http://.fws.gov/southwest/es/arizona

Chapter 14. Why in Hell?

Arizona Land and Water Trust. "Annual Report-2015." Available online at www.alwt.org.

Augé, Marc. *Non-Places: An Introduction to an Anthropology of Supermodernity.* Versabooks.com. 2009.

Quammen, David. "Yellowstone: Wild Heart of a Continent." *National Geographic Magazine.* May, 2016.

Sheridan, Thomas E. "Cows, Condos, and the Contested Commons." *Human Organization,* Vol. 60, No. 2. 2001.

Wilkinson, Todd. *Last Stand: Ted Turner's Quest to Save a Troubled Planet.* Lyons Press. 2014.

Wilson, Edward O. *The Social Conquest of Earth.* W.W. Norton. New York. 2012.

Chapter 15. Cowboy Is a Verb

Ashurst, Ed. *The Life and Times of Warner Glenn.* Ed Ashurst Publishing Company, Douglas, AZ. 2017

Cunninghame-Graham, R.B. *Horses of the Conquest.* University of Oklahoma Press. 1949.

———. *Rodeo.* Doubleday, Doran, and Company, New York. 1936.

Diaz del Castillo, Bernal. *The Bernal Castillo Chronicles: The True Story of the Conquest of Mexico.* Translated by Albert Udell. Garden City, NY. Doubleday and Company. 1956.

Doig, Ivan. *This House of Sky* (with introduction). A Harvest Book-Harcourt, N.Y. 1999.

———. *English Creek: The Montana Trilogy.* Scribner, N.Y. 2005.

Flores, Dan. *American Serengeti: The Last Big Animals of the Great Plains.* University of Kansas Press, Lawrence, KS. 2016.

Matthiessen, Peter. *Nine-headed Dragon River.* Shambhala, Boston, MA. 1998. pp 251–252.

McGuane, Thomas. Op cit.

O'Conner, Sandra Day and H. Alan Day. *Lazy B: Growing Up on a Cattle Ranch In the American Southwest.* Random House 2002.

Robinson, Marilynne. *My Western Roots. In The Old West-New West: Centennial Essays.* Edited by Barbara Howard Meldrum. University of Idaho Press, Moscow, ID. 1993.

Sayre, Nathan F. *Working Wilderness: The Malpai Borderlands Group and the Future of the Western Range.* Rio Nuevo Publishers, Tucson, AZ. 2005

Stegner, Wallace. *The American West as Living Space.* University of Michigan Press, Ann Harbor, MI. 1987.

Acknowledgments

This book came in fits and starts, beginning with columns in the *Sonoita Bulletin* newspaper (now defunct), called "Commentary from Crittenden Pasture" and "Local History Matters." But it was not until I retired in 2015 that I had enough time and distance from all the plodding tasks of ranching to consider what the occupation had really meant to me and find the words and structure for this account. One learns very quickly that family is integral to ranching, so this history also belongs to my partner Diane, son Richard West, and to Jackie, Liam and Maelle Jennifer who joined up along the way. Good neighbors are second only to family. For this I am especially indebted to Tom Hunt and Ferdinand von Galen of the Rail X Ranch, not only for Tom's cheerful, acerbic advice, but also for Ferdinand's hospitality for lodging when we were building our home. Also, the neighbors who joined the Canelo Hills Coalition: Bob and Dusty Hudson of the Vaca Ranch, Chris and Larry Peterson of the Redrock (Kunde) Ranch, John McDonald of the Open Cross Ranch, and later Mac Donaldson. Mac and his father John (now deceased) were early examples of conservation-minded ranchers on the Empire Ranch before that became a stock phrase. Finally, I am indebted to historian Jim Turner, who read a late draft and made many valuable comments and additions, correcting me on points of history and calling out errors of grammar, spelling, and such.

Out in the country, "neighbors" means more than just those who live nearby. Mine included the Cooperative Extension folks from the University of Arizona's College of Agriculture: Dean Fish and Kim McReynolds, who were the first responders to pressures from the Endangered Species Act; later Dr. George B. Ruyle and his field crew of range evaluators and scientists, Katie Cline, John Hays, W. Walter Myer, and Jenny Cordrey. George's participation in our Canelo Hills Coalition provided scientific validity to our rangeland and riparian monitoring and grazing management. Others who contributed to monitoring included Dan Robinett, Jim Koweek, Jeff Simms, Phil Ogden, and Robert Lefevre. Coalition partners included active participation of staff from the Sierra

Vista Ranger District of the Coronado National Forest and the Coronado Resource Conservation and Development Area, Inc. Funding partners included Arizona Department of Environmental Quality, various programs in the US Department of Agriculture, Arizona State Livestock Crop Conservation Program, Arizona Game and Fish Department, US Forest Service, and the ranchers of the Canelo Hills Coalition.

This book is about ranching, cowboys, cow horses, cow dogs, and cows in the twenty-first century. Without them, there would be no book and little cultural value to write about. Among them, T. N. Wegner and Manuel Murrietta played essential and spirited roles on the C6 Ranch, as we called the outfit. Others included Tyler Basinger and the extended Basinger family, Abel Murrietta, Brent Cole, Guinella Partrick, Pete Partrick, Heather Bahti, Bud Bercich, Jim and Dawn Lewis, and others who helped, educated, and entertained me along the way. For the horses, cow dogs, and cows, the reader will find their stories in the book, but they are no less valued and remembered just because I do not list them here.

For photographic credits, opportunities, and editing, I am indebted to Lucas Zucker of the US Geological Service for the satellite image of the Canelo Hills; to Christine Peterson for the photo of Redrock Creek upstream from the dam site; Dean Knuth and the *Arizona Daily Star* for the Monument Fire photo; to Doug Ruppel for the airplane ride over the Canelo Hills; Ross Humphrey for topminnows; Jay Dusard for Manuel Murrietta schooling a three-year-old colt; Rebecca Graham and Richard McBain of Centric Photo for edits. All other photographs were taken by Diane Davis Collins and myself. The Similarity Index chart on page 144, the Ground Cover Trend graph on page 226, and the Redrock Canyon allotment map on page 182 were first produced by the University of Arizona Rangeland Monitoring Team using data from the Canelo Hills Coalition ranches through the courtesy of George B. Ruyle. Thanks to William Don Carlos and Marion Vendituoli for edits and manuscript preparation. Also, to Betty Barr for her excellent books on local history. Tom Jonas excellent maps added clarity and an important dimension to the story. Finally, I am deeply grateful for the expertise and patience of Alrica Goldstein of the University of Nevada Press for bringing the book through its final stages.

About the Author

Richard Collins was raised on a farm/ ranch near Phoenix, Arizona where he lived and worked until leaving for college. Educated at Arizona State University (BS) and the University of Arizona (MS and PhD), he competed on both rodeo teams winning regional championships. After graduation, he worked as a research biologist for the Centers for Disease Control on rural villages and farms in El Salvador and  Guatemala where he witnessed the environments of poverty, disease, and violence that are the root causes of much of the turmoil on today's borderlands. Since the 1980s, he has owned and operated farms and ranches in southern Arizona, including the thirteen-thousand-acre C6 Ranch located in eastern Santa Cruz County where he lives with Diane, his partner of fifty-six years. The Collins family received the 2005 Range Manager of the Year from the Society for Range Management, Arizona Section. His 2014 book, *Riding Behind the Padre: Horseback Views from Both Sides of the Border* was a Best Southwest Book of the Year selection by the Pima County Library and *Arizona Daily Star*; also winner of the best political book of 2015 by the New Mexico-Arizona Book Awards, as well as the runner-up for the best multicultural book.